A Ramble Round The Globe

Sir Thomas Robert Dewar (bart.)

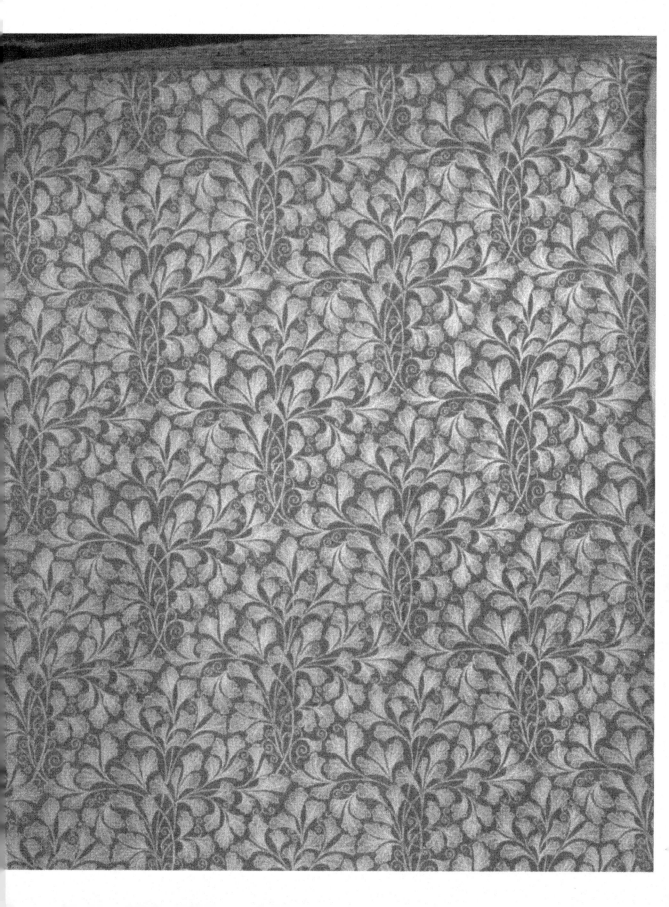

A RAMBLE
ROUND THE GLOBE

BY

THOMAS R. DEWAR

with 220 Illustrations by

W. L. WYLLIE, A.R.A. : SIDNEY COWELL

A. S. FORREST : JAMES GREIG : SEYMOUR NATION

STANLEY L. WOOD : ARCHIE MACGREGOR

AND THE AUTHOR

LONDON

CONTENTS

CHAPTER I

CHAPTER II

CHAPTER III

CHAPTER IX

CHAPTER X

CHAPTER XI

CHAPTER XII

PRINCIPAL ILLUSTRATIONS

A RAMBLE ROUND THE GLOBE

CHAPTER I

Why I went away—Leaving Liverpool—The *City of Paris*—The would-be Emigrant's Return—Moralising—An American Lady—A Modest Missionary—Wash-houses and Mosquitoes—'Stars and Stripes'—'Mister'—The Custom-house—Tender Scenes.

AS I do not lay claim to be anything very extraordinary as a literary man, no one will be surprised that I have not got the names of all the great authors at my tongue's end; or that, when I want to use a quotation, I can very seldom do it properly, as the difficulty arises where to look for it in order to work it up. There is a quotation somewhere that would come in most aptly at the beginning of this book, if I could only find it, so as to put it down correctly. As far as my memory serves me, it is something about great events springing up from little causes; and I should like to use it, as it was a very little cause

be the start of a book; still, such was the case in this instance.

It happened this way.   In March '92, when fighting for the Moderate' cause in West Marylebone for a seat in the London County Council, against representatives of the Church and the Bar, and amidst all the delights of blinding blizzards, east winds, and snow-storms, as well as my seat I caught a cold.   I could have done without the cold, had I been consulted on the matter; but I wasn't, so I had to put up with it.

That cold was evidently possessed of an inquisitive and exploring nature, for it was very restless. First it settled in one part, then went to another, then had a general tour round; till at last the grave and serious-looking medical gentleman who had been endeavouring for some time to 'fix' it looked graver and still more serious.

Warmer climes were ordered.   Now, it is not a very difficult matter to find a warmer climate than the one 'made for Great Britain'; but when a choice has to be

of my foreign travel and subsequent publication of this book.

The procuring of the necessary outfit for a journey through all parts of the globe is an awful bother; and then, when it has been got together, there is the packing. The plagues of Egypt may have been bad, but such an awful ordeal as superintending this packing, without doubt, eclipses the lot! It was done at last, though, and then a start was made.

Determining to travel with the sun, and begin with 'the West, to the West, the land of the free,' the actual starting-point was Euston Station; and this I left amidst farewells from friends. Liverpool was reached without incident, and August 17, '92, saw me located on board the *City of Paris*, ready to make a real start.

That starting is terrible business. The last tender arrives, passengers and friends come on board, the luggage and mails are transferred, out clangs the bell announcing that friends must leave the ship, as the tender is ready to depart; and then comes the affecting time. Good-bye has to be said, the time for parting has arrived; and many who have been talking

A MEDICAL GENTLEMAN

the tender moves one way, the *City of Paris* the other, and, with a sea of handkerchiefs waving from both, the one goes back to the wharf, while the other goes forward to face all the perils and dangers of the Atlantic.

The passage to Queenstown is spent in 'shaking down'; and here I must put in a word of praise for the admirable arrangements for sorting out luggage and putting it into the different cabins.

GOOD-BYE

is a grand ship. No care nor trouble was spared in her construction, the great idea being that, as far as human foresight could provide, she should be absolutely unsinkable, and the next, that she should be able to go at not less than 20 knots per hour throughout the voyage. She has a length of 560 feet, a beam of 63 feet, a depth of 43 feet, and has a 10,498 tonnage. Nearly 300 tons of coal are used every day while the vessel is at sea ; and as she has fifty-four furnaces to nine boilers, if any one likes to reckon out they will find that that is just about one ton every five minutes. I must say the arrangements on board are

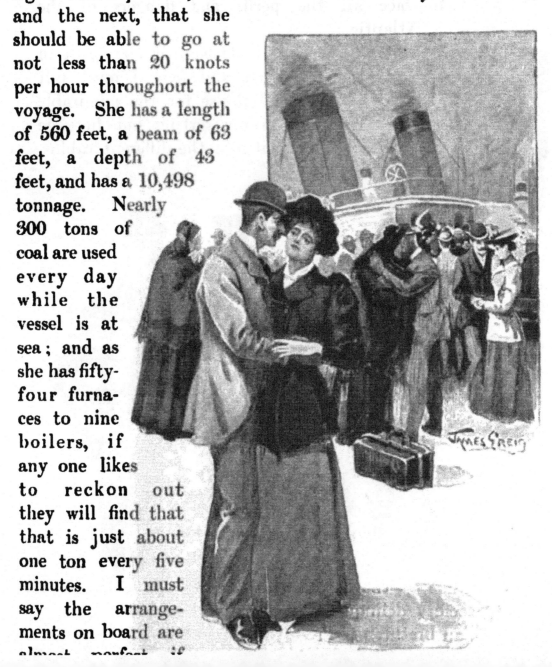

almost perfect, if

A very funny, and at the same time interesting, sight was seen at Queenstown. There were many more of the gentlemen about, whose regulation boots and big sticks so plainly betrayed their connection with the police, than there were at Liverpool; and they were far more observant of the passengers

THE TENDER MOVES ONE WAY, THE 'CITY OF PARIS' ANOTHER

coming on board, those wishing to make a new start in life

he did not at all wish it, was forced to return to attend
an interview with the powers that be. When a man's
modesty prompts him to forego the privilege of conversation
with those of higher estate than himself, it seems hard that
the ordeal should be forced upon him; but such is life, and
poor Paddy had to go. There was awful weeping and wailing
and gnashing of teeth here as the time for departure drew
nigh, and the noise was what I should imagine would be
raised provided some six or eight Irish 'wakes' were all rolled
into one.

It is after leaving Queenstown that one realises the fact
of leaving the Old Country. It is known then that, after
losing sight of 'Ould Oireland,' Sandy Hook is the next
land to be seen, and that that is some five or six days'
voyage ahead. The vessel steams on, the Emerald Isle
gets dimmer and dimmer in the distance, till at last the
little speck is lost to view—the Old Country has disappeared.

Here is a splendid chance for any one given to moralising,
for they can think for hours on the possibility of some of the
emigrants returning millionaires; of how many passengers will
die on the way out; of how many will ever see England again;
of how many lovers on board who, leaving their *fiancées* at
home, swore 'to be good and true' till their return, will be
married before twelve months. or engaged before the next land
is sighted; or of what the chances are that the ship and
every one in her won't go down to the bottom before she has
traversed a hundred miles. Oh! really there is beautiful

again for two whole days.   Poor young man ! he 'll know better next time.

The ship was crowded—every berth was occupied ; yet for the first two days there was plenty of room at table.   People soon began to appear, though, and get chummy.   There is one thing I must say for the American ladies : they do not mind asking for anything if they

1902.

want it, whether an 'introduction' has taken place or not. For instance, the morning after leaving Queenstown, as I was strolling down the deck, I was brought up by a most musical voice

SOME EMIGRANTS RETURN MILLIONAIRES

—even if it did possess a slight 'Ammurican twang'—saying,

her, around her feet. I am not much of a ladies' man, but I could not resist such a touching appeal, and the 'tucking in' was accomplished in no time. That young lady and I were friends for the rest of the voyage.

There were only about three per cent. English amongst the passengers, the rest being made up of Americans and others returning home after travelling in their usual go-ahead manner—'round the world in six weeks' —more or less. Why is it, I wonder, that so many Americans, after doing Europe thoroughly, or as thoroughly as their incessant gallop will permit, will go back with the idea, 'Yes, all very good, very

THE 'TUCKING-IN' WAS ACCOMPLISHED

running some forty feet high. At least, that was what I was told—I didn't measure it. We had a service on board on Sunday, when an American missionary of the Moody and Sankey type delivered a very long oration about civilising the whole world, speaking very modestly of his own countrymen, and contenting himself with saying that Americans were improved Englishmen once removed. Modesty is always beautiful, but in a clerical gentleman especially so. The steward told me before landing that the sale of Irish whisky had been double that of any voyage during the past twelve months, and said he accounted for it from the fact of there being six Irish priests on board! I don't think stewards are very great respecters of religion.

On the Wednesday following the one on which we left Liverpool there was great excitement on board, for we were close in to New York; and to those who, like myself, were going to get their first sight of that wonderful place, the

time was particularly interesting.   The young lady whom I had
befriended early in the voyage repaid my gallantry by pointing

wash-houses, but on mentioning this was most indignantly told that those were the Forts! My fair young guide pointed out New Jersey. I timidly inquired what it might be famous for, and got the reply, 'Mosquitoes.' I found out afterwards that the young lady was right. Certainly the approach to New York is a very fine view; the great statue of Liberty, standing well out as it does, seems to give a welcome to all who are approaching that great and marvellous country — America. As we gradually drew near land, the enthusiasm of the American portion of the passengers grew more intense, and almost wild excitement glared from every eye. Suddenly, without seemingly any warning, there burst out from the shore and on board a waving of miniature 'Stars and Stripes.' Almost everybody

FLAG-WAVING ON NEARING NEW YORK

the Queen'; and now, much to my surprise, it was sung again
with redoubled vigour.   I liked this feeling very much, and
remarked on it to my fair guide; but to my astonishment she
stared at me.   'What, can't you tell the difference between
your own National Anthem and "Land of Freedom"?   Tune's
the same, but the words are altogether different.   Guess you
want to say we don't speak plain!'   I was in a state; but, 'pon
my word, the nasal twang stopped me from hearing the
difference.

Well, friends came on board, and sought out those they
wished to meet in the enormous crowd; and the greetings, and
kissings, and handshakings made one feel how nice it must be
to get home again after being away.   Then there was a
scramble for the shore, and the many hundreds who had been
safely borne across the Atlantic through storms and gales in
the old *City of Paris* soon found themselves on land once
more, and on the shores of what is called the 'land of the
free'!

They were not free, however, all at once, or indeed for some
little time.   The ordeal of the Custom-house had to be gone
through, and this was very trying indeed.   It was terrible
trouble getting through, and in my impatience while waiting
I said to some one, 'Why on earth can't they have Free Trade
here, and save all this bother?'   'Say, mister,' said the gentleman, 'you'd think different to that, I guess, if you made
$40,000 a year through Protection like I do!'

What struck me as very strange in all this crowd was the
general use of 'mister'; there was no 'sir.'   It was peculiar at
first, especially from the men who kept coming up saying,
'Telegraph to Europe, mister? telegraph to Europe?'   It was

But I really do think that that Custom-house business could be done much quicker. However, it does not do to say anything, as Custom-house officers have an awkward knack of making things disagreeable, as I saw in one case. An American girl next to me, who was having her baggage examined, cheeked the officer more than he cared for; so, opening a huge trunk, he carefully slid his hands down the sides to the bottom, and in bringing them up turned the whole

THE POOR GIRL HAD TO REPACK THE WHOLE LOT

of the contents topsy-turvy. My! I never saw such a lot of

whole lot.   I felt very sorry for her, and would have helped, but thought I had better not, as, not being used to such garments, I might fold them up wrongly.

The American ladies certainly do look after themselves well on landing, and won't stand any nonsense; they know what has to be done, and they see they are not imposed upon.

At last the inquisitorial business is over, and the release from incarceration is hailed with delight; there is a regular thanksgiving all round, and a general farewell amongst those who have formed friendships on the voyage.   Addresses are given, and invitations to call; and here and there a tender little scene is witnessed between a couple who, strangers at the start, have developed a friendship, and then said, with Moore,

> ' Oh, call it by some better name,
> For Friendship sounds too cold.'

Ah! an ocean voyage has a lot to answer for!   My baggage is passed, and I am free, and, released from the Custom-house and outside its walls, I really feel I am in New York.

CHAPTER II

New York—An Inquisitive Crowd—Cabs and Road-cars—Discovery of the North Pole—Baggage—The 'Blue Line'—Washington—Philosophy from a Nigger—'Scotch' in the White House—Baltimore and Steam-whistles—Philadelphia—Hell Gate—Newport—A Bathroom Episode —An Altercation—Boston—Culture and Pants.

YES, I am really in New York, and, released from the Custom-house, go direct to the Hoffman House: a grand hotel, run on the English and American system, and everything is remarkably good.

Now I am hardly vain enough to think that this book will

a wonderful place; but I had not been there long before I came
to the conclusion that the streets were about the worst I had
ever seen, and I am still of this opinion. I suppose the reason
is that it is such an awfully busy place, and everybody is so
much on the rush striving to make money, they have not time
to look after such matters as cleaning the streets or keeping
them in good order. It is a busy place, a very busy place
indeed; and really everybody seems wild on the one idea—
make money. I asked an American, soon after I got there,
what was the use of all this rush and bustle and excitement?
What came of it? Was there anything attached to it?
What did men do after they had made their 'pile'? He
simply replied, 'I guess they die.'

Everybody knows the style in which New York is built—long
streets running north and south called avenues, and then other
streets running crossways from east to west. In the older part
of the city streets are found of the irregular style we Europeans
are used to; but the area covered by these is not large.
The square style seems strange to a European at first, and
hardly takes his fancy; but afterwards, when the utility of it is
seen, he alters his mind. It is certainly easier to find one's
way about when told one's destination is, say, Fifth Avenue,
Twenty-fourth Street, than it would be to a stranger here if
told, say, Duke Street, St. James's.

Broadway is the principal street—in fact, *the* street—of New
York. Every one promenades here, and the promenaders are
just as inquisitive as are people in the City of London. The

opened a drain, and the whole crowd were peering into it most ardently. Whether they expected to see anything or not I don't know; all I know is, the odour was thick enough to be seen, and I passed on as rapidly as I could.

New York abounds with Irish people, and the Irish vote is a very strong one at elections. It strikes any one on their first arrival here that the Irishman's sole idea is to become either a policeman or a politician, and certainly they succeed in both quarters, for it would appear they are the only foreigners in Congress or the ' force.'

New Yorkers are very hospitable people, and I was treated right royally wherever I went, and was made an honorary member of most of the best clubs. These clubs are very elaborate affairs, and far more gorgeous than those we are accustomed to on our side.

The commercial buildings of New York are enormous, running from twelve to sixteen stories high; but, luckily, it is not necessary to tramp upstairs if you want the top floor,

A POLICEMAN

me; for although I only went a short distance, the fare was a dollar.　After that I gave up cabs, and threw in my lot with the millionaires and niggers by always using the 'street-car.' Every one uses the car, and I am not surprised at it, for the horrible streets make you think of 'the rocky road to Dublin'; and then the fare is very moderate, for five cents will take one anywhere.　Cabs are very dear, and very bad.　The elevated railroad is by no means a bad way of getting about, and it is used very extensively.　The chief business places seem to be railway booking - offices, safe - deposit companies, insurance offices — Americans are awfully keen on insurance —and real estate and house agencies.　Yes, yes; but I must not forget the barber - shops, with their coloured sugar-stick poles sticking out, for they are very numerous, and all do a good trade.　An American is not content unless he enters a barber-shop twice a day, and gets his boots brushed three times.

A POLITICIAN

with the result. On getting near the Pole these worthies distinctly saw something sticking out of the ground with colours upon it, and something by the side. Getting closer,

they made out that what *must* be the Pole was painted in red and white, sugar-stick fashion, and that the other thing looked very suspiciously like a small tent. They got close up, and were surprised to see the form of a man come from the tent, and to be accosted in an undoubted American manner with: 'Want a shave this morning, gents?' An enterprising Yankee had been before them, and, painting the Pole in the orthodox manner, had erected a tent at the side of it and started a barber-shop, knowing very well that before long some intrepid explorer would be following in his footsteps. The nature of the American is decidedly of the enter-

York—in fact, about three times the price of what it would be in London. Taking the place all round, I was very pleased with it, and came to the conclusion that there were one or two things that could advantageously be copied on this side ; but I think what pleased me most was the ' check-baggage system ' of the railway companies. We are far behind in this matter— in fact, I think, altogether in railway travelling—as compared with our American cousins. Baggage is no bother on the other side ; all you carry is a brass check for each package you have handed in, and, arriving at your destination, you find everything sorted out ready to be claimed. You can then ' express ' it to your hotel on the same system. This is simply luxury after being used to the worry and bother of pushing and struggling occasioned in ' claiming your luggage ' at any of our railway stations.

Knowing who I am, and what I am, some readers may expect me to go into certain business questions connected with the various places I visited ; but as these wouldn't be of interest to every one, I intend to refrain from doing so, and instead, would refer any one to the letters I contributed to the *Morning Advertiser* and other papers, and also the interview which appeared in the first-named paper after my return.

Leaving New York, I went by the ' Blue Line ' to Washington, and had my first experience of dining on the American cars. It was not at all a bad experience either. To be sure, the crust of the claret got stirred up a bit ; but what did that matter ? We were travelling about fifty miles an hour.

York is entirely absent. An aristocratic quiet pervades the place, and to talk of dollars and cents, dry goods and business, seems to be sacrilege of the lowest order. Just before I arrived, the electric cable-cars had been started, and everybody was very pleased with them. They run along smoothly and quietly at from twelve to fifteen miles an hour. The streets in Washington are all well asphalted and wood-paved; they can hardly be called streets, though, for they are wide avenues, with plenty of trees, and are more like Parisian boulevards. Beautiful is really the only word by which the capital of the States can be fitly described. A kind of shudder goes through one when the place where President Garfield was shot is pointed out, for the idea of such a good man being shot in such a beautiful place is very repugnant. My nigger cabdriver (a different type of man to our cabby) was a bit of a philosopher; for when I asked what possible reason the murderer could have had for committing such a crime, he said : ' Ah, boss, dar is in most countries people what am dissatisfied wid eberyting.'

The Capitol is a magnificent erection. This building covers about $3\frac{1}{2}$ acres, and is a kind of central building with two wings. It is surmounted by a great white dome made of iron. The wings are white marble, and the main building is built of freestone. But most people are now familiar with the photographs of the place, which are about everywhere, so I need not describe it. Marble is predominant in the interior. It is the headquarters of the country, and the Hall of Representatives in the south wing is an enormous room containing space for 300 members and 1500 spectators. The mention

contained.   He was expatiating proudly on the fact that everything, or nearly everything, was American-made, when I mentioned that he must not forget there was something from Scotland in the cellar.   At first he looked hurt; but when I gave him my card, and he saw who I was, his countenance relaxed, and the meaning smile which beamed over it proved that he was as well aware as I of what had

MY NIGGER CABDRIVER

for Baltimore. This is not a place I would recommend to any one suffering from weak nerves, for there seems to be an almost ceaseless screeching of steam-whistles from morning till night, and the noise and bustle are equal to anything in the States. Chimney-stacks—and of no mean dimensions—are very plentiful; in fact, if asked for what Baltimore was famous, I should unhesitatingly say, 'Chimneys and steam-whistles.' It is a very good city, no doubt, but decidedly not the place to

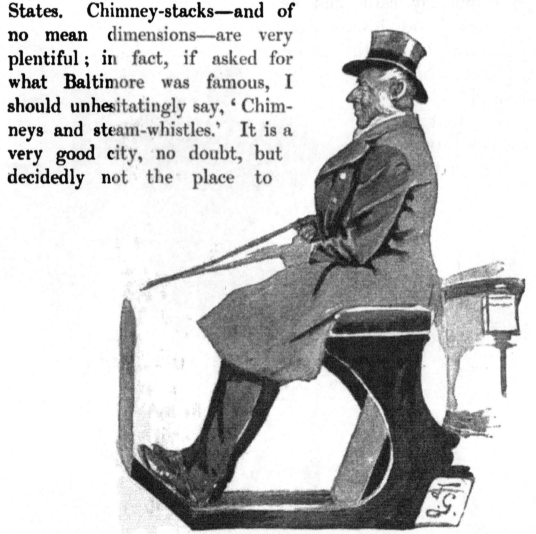

OUR CABBY

rusticate in; so I wasn't long before I was 'off to Philadelphia.'

pleased with the food provided; and, considering the kitchen is only about five feet square, it is wonderful how such a good six-course dinner can be prepared.

After another look round New York, I took a boat and sailed for Newport, the fashionable watering-place. This is a very nice journey, and there is a lot to be seen by the way. The boat goes under Brooklyn Bridge, so one gets a very good view of this from all points; and it is not surprising that Americans are so proud of this picture of refined engineering skill, for it is really, as they say, a 'most elegant' structure. Then one gets almost a better view of the great Statue of Liberty than when arriving on a liner; and the statue is certainly worthy of all the praise bestowed upon it, although in describing it the well-known modesty of the American comes to the fore. Again, on the Brooklyn side is one of the Standard Oil Co.'s large factories. This oil business is one of the greatest monopolies of the States, and the Company can turn out any amount of it. An idea of the business really done, and the quantity obtained, may be gathered from the fact that whereas, not many years ago, the oil was sold at 3s. and 4s. per gallon, it can now be obtained at less than so many pence. It is a most lucrative business in more ways than one, for there is hardly any expense connected with it, and it would appear that nearly the whole of the trouble consisted of 'turning on the tap.'

But the most important and interesting item on this short

survey of the place previous to its destruction. About 1851, attempts were made to remove the reefs, but without much success. However, with that pertinacity so innate in our American friends, proceedings were continued, and it was decided to do the thing on a big scale, as they usually do. The minor rocks had been got rid of, but the largest, Flood Rock, about nine acres in extent, remained to be disposed of. Operations were commenced, and the rock was honey-combed below low-water mark with tunnels. Twenty-four galleries were made running in one direction, and these were intersected by forty-six others running at right angles; then the walls were pierced with drill-holes in every direction, close upon 13,000 holes being made, 9 feet deep and about 3 inches in diameter— in all, there being over 20 miles of these holes. Then came the filling-up process; each hole was charged, first with a cartridge of rackarock, an explosive consisting of 79 parts of chlorate of potash and 21 parts of dinitrobenzole, and secondly with a cartridge of dynamite, and the whole were connected by wires, so that they could be discharged simultaneously by electricity. The amount of explosives used was enormous, being 240,399 lbs. of rackarock and 42,331 lbs. of dynamite.

At last, after several years of working, everything was ready; and on 10th October 1885, by placing her finger on a small button, a little child started the current and blew the whole rock to pieces. A dull thud was heard, the earth shook a little, a huge volume of water, some 1400 feet long and 800 feet wide, rose about 200 feet in the air, and all was over—the only damage done on land consisting of a few panes of glass

is looked upon—by the members—as the *crème de la crème* of an exalted aristocracy. Yet, after all, what is it? The only qualification is the almighty dollar; and so long as this is possessed to an inordinate extent, and the ladies are enabled to smother themselves in diamonds, the end is attained; the greater the amount of dollars and diamonds, the greater is the respect shown to the possessor. But are the natives of Newport alone in this particular? I think not. Still, the affair is carried to such an extreme there, it is impossible not to view it from its ludicrous side. For instance, the mansions, or almost castles, of which the place chiefly consists, are called cottages; and the cottage which Mr. Vanderbilt has erected, from what we read in the Bible, completely puts in the shade that elaborate building called 'Solomon's Temple.' This cottage, it is said, has cost several millions of dollars, and it certainly looks like it. It is built of pure white marble, and I was informed every stone was obtained from Europe.

Bathing is a very favourite amusement here. I stayed at the Ocean

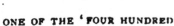

ONE OF THE 'FOUR HUNDRED'

two doors in my room.   I opened the one I thought I came in
at ; but, as the poet says,

> 'Confusion thrilled me then, and secret joy
> Fast throbbing stole its treasures from my heart,
> And mantling upward turned my face to crimson.'

This door led into a bathroom, and the room was occupied

BATHING-TIME AT NEWPORT

by a lady was ... the same costume as Eve before the fall !

Another lively little episode happened here during my stay, but I was not involved this time. A dandified young gentle-

when another gentleman arrived and saw what was going on. Gentleman No. 2 recognised Gentleman No. 1, and thereupon sought out the lady's father, and told him he thought it

was his duty to inform him that the gentleman who was paying such attention to his daughter was not only a noted forger of Government bonds, but that he had 'done time' for various periods on three different occasions! Then the noise began. The father interviewed Gentleman No. 1, and afterwards Gentleman

Sydney Cowell

living.　Mr. Ex-convict suddenly terminated his stay at the hotel; and the next day a leading New York paper contained a detailed account of the whole affair, and also gave a

A MOST CHARMING YOUNG LADY

Now, it may not be generally known in this country, but it is well known in Boston, that there is one place in the world, and that is Boston. Everything here is extremely proper—in fact, almost ultra-English. There are heaps of people in this headquarters of 'cult' who would much rather be found dead on Boston Common than live for ever in a double-barrelled mansion in Michigan! In fact, I have heard that when the first real Bostonian died, and went aloft, St. Peter hesitated to

let him through the gate; and upon the defunct one expostu- lating, and saying he came from Boston, St. Peter remarked that that was just the difficulty. 'However,' said he, 'come in; but *please don't be disap- pointed!*' I fancy there must be a bit of satire intended somewhere in that.

It is certainly an important place, and the remarkable in- terest taken by natives in litera- ture, science, and art is well known. This interest, too, is real in a way, for the place contains an enormous number of literary and kindred societies.

It is one of the old places, and was founded in 1630, so that naturally it has a

the inhabitants get more and more important—in their own
estimation—and think they are more than ever entitled

to dub their city 'the Hub of the Universe.'   Well, their
doing so pleases them, and
doesn't hurt any-
body else; so what
does it matter?
Names don't hurt
a bit.

A stranger might
almost imagine that
Boston was owned

should be any one left to buy them. Some people think that Boston must have been founded by some patriotic Highlanders, and that, when the highly cultured era set in, the more advanced of the inhabitants began to look askance at the national costume of 'bonnie Scotland'; therefore some enterprising Yankee immediately seized the opportunity to start a 'pant' business, and, prospering so much, rapidly brought around him a whole crowd of competitors. This is not my idea, though. Still, however the thing originated, there is no getting away from the fact that Boston is famous for culture and 'pants.' I went to the theatre here to see that regular American play, 'The Old Homestead,' and was very pleased with it. By the way, one night at a theatre here—the occasion of a new play, I think it was—the front row of the dress circle was occupied by some young gentlemen, supposed to be students, in evening dress; and when the *prima donna* appeared they all threw back their overcoats and showed expansive shirt-fronts, bearing the words boldly displayed: 'Do you wear pants? If not, go to So-and-so's Pant Co.!'

DO YOU WEAR PANTS?

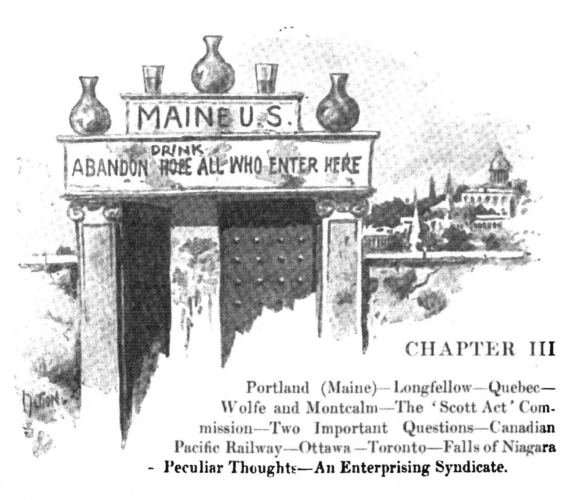

CHAPTER III

Portland (Maine)—Longfellow—Quebec—
Wolfe and Montcalm—The 'Scott Act' Com-
mission—Two Important Questions—Canadian
Pacific Railway—Ottawa—Toronto—Falls of Niagara
- Peculiar Thoughts—An Enterprising Syndicate.

FEELING that Boston was just a 'wee bittie' too cultured,
and getting tired of seeing 'pants' staring me in the face
all day and haunting my dreams at night, I made another
move, and started off for the prohibition State of Maine, and
its capital, Portland, in particular. Any one who wants
to know my views on prohibition can have it in one word,
and that word is 'bosh.' Portland in itself is a most uninteresting place, and hardly has a single redeeming feature
in it

he was a great and grand poet, and one whose memory will be for ever green.

From here I toured up into Canada, and made my first stop at Quebec. This was a splendid journey, and the scenery through the White Mountains in the bright moonlight was simply grand. At every turn, look wherever one would, the picturesque grandeur of the thickly wooded mountains and valleys was enough to almost turn the brain of any landscape painter. It was a magnificent, a noble sight, and I was really sorry when sleep compelled me to 'turn in.' By this time I was getting used to travelling *à l'Américain*, and felt perfectly at home on board the Grand Trunk Railway, by which I travelled.

I don't care who the man may be: coming from our country, his first sight of Quebec must bring up thoughts of long ago, and recall to him the many stirring pages of history he has read referring to this ancient and famous city. It can hardly be called remarkably ancient, for it has not been founded quite three hundred years. It was founded in 1608, and was taken possession of by the English in 1629. It was restored again, however, in 1632. Then the English attacked it again in 1690, but without success; but in 1759, under General Wolfe, the English again returned to the attack.

Who, that has ever read it, has forgotten that page of English history when, after several weeks of desultory manœuvring and occasional fighting, with an army of some 3600 men, on the morning of September 13, 1759, General Wolfe made a bold and successful attack upon the French, and again added Quebec to the British Empire? The name of Wolfe stands bright in the annals of British glory, and his

THE WHITE MOUNTAINS

French, the Marquis de Montcalm ; for his name will for ever be associated with that of Wolfe and of Quebec. He made a gallant struggle during the weeks Wolfe was oppressing him, and in the fight itself was struck down while courageously endeavouring to rally his men. Carried back to the city, and told his end was fast approaching, he, like Wolfe, expired with a true soldier's spirit, and with the words, 'So much the better ; I shall not live to see the surrender of Quebec.' A noble tribute to the memory of both these brave men now stands in the midst of the Government Gardens of Quebec in the shape of an obelisk sixty feet in height ; and inscribed upon the front, facing the direction along which the French general moved, is the word 'MONTCALM,' while upon the other side, facing the way from which the British advanced, is the word 'WOLFE.' In 1775 the Americans had a hard struggle to capture the place, but were unsuccessful, losing their leader, Montgomery, and having their second in command, Arnold, severely and seriously wounded.

I am not going to describe British battles all the way through this book, or 'trim its pages round with gore'; but that little digression was, I think, excusable, for it wants a very heavy brick indeed upon the top of patriotism to keep it down on special occasions. While I am on the warlike strain, I could, if I wished, launch boldly forth upon the strategic position of Quebec ; but I won't, because I'm not a soldier, or even a volunteer. It is a grand-looking place, though ; and, standing as it does upon a huge cliff, towering high above the water's

When I arrived in the city, a Commission was sitting to consider the advisability of applying 'prohibition' to the whole of Canada; but the witnesses examined were very much opposed to it in every way. Some of the wild teetotal papers took me rather severely to task because I had the temerity to send in to the Commissioners some statistics showing the average life of various classes of drinkers; amongst them being the total abstainers, who had the shortest average, and the habitual drunkard, whose average was two years *longer*! Prohibitionists have a very peculiar idea of a 'brandy-and-sodaist,' but the remarks of these teetotal literary gentlemen did me no harm; I wasn't mobbed, neither was there any attempt to lynch me. Prohibition has been tried in several parts of Canada, but has not found much favour. By the way, before I forget it, I may mention a rather amusing experience here. I was going through a 'prohibition' State, and tried to get some whisky from the conductor of the train, but without success. 'Can't do it, boss; we're in a prohibition State, and I can't do it.' However, he eventually advised me to try at a store at the next stopping-place, and this I did. 'Do you sell whisky?' 'Are you sick, mister, or got a medical certificate?' 'No.' 'Then I can't do it. See, this is a prohibition State, so I can't sell it; but I reckon our cholera mixture'll about fix you. Try a bottle of that.' I did, but to my great astonishment received a very familiar bottle, which, although it was labelled on one side 'Cholera Mixture: a wine-glassful to be taken every two hours, or oftener as required,' had upon the other side the well-known label of a firm of Scotch whisky distillers, whose name modesty requires me to suppress!

Just about this time the whole of the State was excited by

between Corbett and Sullivan.   The fight was everything, and the papers were full of it; even the niggers, when not singing

of that marvellous achievement of railway engineering and skill, which is rightly numbered amongst the wonders of the world— the Canadian Pacific Railway. There are railways and there are railways; but, go where you will, there is not at present any railway which for system, management, comfort in travelling, and downright general excellence comes within miles of the

THE CHOLERA MIXTURE

recall the old days of the French settlements around here. Montreal is not only very picturesque, but is also imposing in appearance, especially when looked at from the river front, for then the full effect is got of the gently rising terraces of which the city is built, and the grand background to the whole of the wooded heights of Mount Royal—a mountain standing over 700 feet above the level of the river. The city is well built, and the streets are good. The population is a mixture of English and French; and, although the latter are in the major-ity, the trade is controlled by the for-mer, as they are wealthier and far more energetic and industrious. In fact, the French have kept the place

CANADIAN PACIFIC RAILWAY

back very considerably. Still, Montreal is the commercial and financial centre of the Dominion. There is plenty of money in the place, and there is more continually being made. The cold about here is very intense in the winter, and the frost at times is so great that goods trains have been run across the St

Jack is very much marked here; but really throughout the whole of Canada a strong loyal feeling towards the Empire is most observable on every side.   Possibly I may have noticed this the more after hearing the Old Country slanged so much in the States, for the lower-class American considers it the right thing to 'go for' everything British.   I may say that this is not the case with the more reasoning and common-sense American, though; and I was pleased to find it so.

PARLIAMENT HOUSE, OTTAWA

ance of the place—in fact, to the contrary, for the city gives one a splendid impression of industry and government. Its imposing public buildings and Parliament House give it an air of public and national importance, and the numerous and enormous mills and places of business stamp it as a great commercial centre.

Well, when one gets on the great American continent, whether it be the States, or whether it be in Canada, a spirit of restlessness and anxiety to keep moving arises, and there is no help for it. The very atmosphere seems to be laden with a 'go-ahead' idea, and go ahead one must. I 'cavorted' round the place, here, there, and everywhere, and eventually found myself on board the Canadian Pacific again, bound for Toronto. This is a very fine place, and, as in the other Canadian cities, the streets are good. So far, nothing has come up—no, down —to the level of New York in the matter of streets. Yes, Toronto is a very fine place, and I should like to have stayed there longer, especially as I met some friends of my late relative, the Hon. Alexander Mackenzie, a late Premier of Canada —I believe a much-respected man, and who, as the story goes, started there as a bricklayer; but the spirit of travel was upon me, and, as I could almost hear the mighty roar of Niagara, there was no staying still, so off I went to view that greatest of Nature's wonders—the Falls of Niagara.

And when I arrived there—what a sight!

I will not attempt to become eulogistic upon the subject, for it is one that has puzzled the heads of far wiser folks than I can ever hope to be. To do ample justice in words to the awe-

does further down.   However, it gradually gains impetus, its velocity becomes greater and greater, it breaks into furious rapids, when, Goat Island dividing it, one part of the river rushes madly on to the American fall, while the other part is impelled with terrific force round the other side of the island, and, arrived at the brink of the awful precipice, the huge volume of water hurls itself over into the depths below with a thundering roar that stays in one's ears for days, and which has been heard at a distance of fifty miles. The fall on the American side of the river is about 1000 feet broad, and the descent is between 160 and 170 feet.   The fall on the Canadian side is in the shape of a horseshoe, and the outline is about 2600 feet, with a descent of some 160 feet.   It is estimated that about 15,000,000 cubic feet of water sweeps over this huge precipice every minute.   Below the Falls, again, is another scene most awful in its grandeur. It is possible to take a walk underneath the Falls, but I should hardly recommend this kind of stroll to persons suffering from nerves.   You go down a lift for about 60 feet to get to the edge of the river below, and then take your stroll.   I went.   I 'wasn't a bit frightened,' but somehow I began

'WHAT A SIGHT!'

to wonder how many wicked things I had done in my life, and whether I had been guilty of a very egregious crime in my juvenile days when, in order to lessen a plague of rats, my

slip of the foot here is quite sufficient to bring the whole of one's past life before one with a rush.

The deafening rush and roar was such, any one would hardly think it possible to hear oneself think; but you can, and I thought the place was one where any one would feel much more comfortable after saying a hymn than 'saying a swear.' I hope no one will think I was nervous, because I am only recording my impressions, and one of these, I remember, was that I was not nervous.

Familiarity, however, breeds a certain contempt in time, and the natives and residents have found that, becoming used to the surroundings, the 'fine feeling' at first produced will soon wear off, and enable them to work upon the feelings of others. And they do. I said natives, but I think thieves would be the more appropriate word, for the souvenirs of the place purchased by visitors before the terrestrial thoughts have quite returned, are charged just about five times the price for which they can be obtained

SUFFERING FROM NERVES

elsewhere. Then again, wicked men are supposed to take portraits of visitors against the Falls; but the visitors are participators in this fraud, for they are really taken in a studio and then

for a morning dip ; neither would I like to emulate the intrepid Blondin and cross the Falls in mid-air on a rope.

Falls for the purpose of utilising the water-power of the Falls for electric lighting and tramways. It is calculated that about 200,000 horse-power will be obtained, and that the cost will be only $5 per horse-power per annum. New York is only 450 miles from here, but the syndicate contend that the power will be quite sufficient to work a line as far as there.

CHAPTER IV

Oil City and Pittsburg—Natural Gas—
Protection and Millionaire Philanthropists—'Billy Pinkerton'—Riots
at Homestead—Andrew Carnegie—'Pistol Practice'—A Suicide—
A Morning Walk—Voyage to Detroit—'New Corn'—Detroit—The
'Empress' Train—George.

AFTER being 'rooked,' like every other visitor to the marvellous
Falls, and taking a final look at the wonderful place, I took
train again and moved off to Pittsburg, going by way of
Buffalo and Oil City. It would almost seem that some of the
American towns are named after whatever they are famous for.
I don't mean to say that Buffalo is so called because the animal
of that name is to be found roaming at will all over the place,
asleep on doorsteps or kept in families as a domestic pet; but
no more appropriate name than Oil City could be found for

This gas has been almost universally used here for over ten years both for manufacturing and domestic purposes ; and, as it is very pure, very clean, and possesses great heating power, it is a remarkably good substitute for coal. It is obtained from various districts within a radius of about twenty miles from Pittsburg, and is supplied by different companies. The earth is drilled to perhaps nearly 1500 feet, and then out rushes the gas with a pressure of about 500 lbs. to the square inch, which is amply sufficient to force it through the pipes. I was told that the estimated daily consumption was as near as possible 8,000,000 feet, and that the length of piping used in bringing it to the city and delivering it to the houses, mills, etc., exceeded 1200 miles.

The chief industries in Pittsburg are those connected with iron and steel, and some of the factories—or mills, as they call them—might almost be called miniature Black Countries. Downright hard work is the rule here, and it is well carried out. Still, it seemed to me a pity that such monopolies should exist as do now in the iron and oil trades. Protection may be all very well in some things, but as carried out in America it makes the rich man richer and the poor man poorer. It would be well for those monopolists who visit our shores, give away money, decry our country, and pose as philanthropists of the first water, if they would remember the source from which they obtain their wealth, and, instead of preaching against a country to which they are so closely allied, they would go back to their own land, and look into matters connected with their

over the States, and is really a kind of cross between a detective and police agency and a 'Scotland Yard,' farmed out by the authorities to be worked by private enterprise. It will be remembered, in connection with the Homestead riots in 1892, that Pinkerton's men played a very active part at the outset, meeting with a decidedly hostile reception from the strikers, and not coming off altogether best in the sanguinary fight which ensued.

Being so close to Homestead, it was only natural I should run over and have a look at the place; and a rare collection of chimney-stacks I found it, while the smoke about the place would have done justice to some of the smokiest parts of our own midland counties. On the hill-side, overlooking the valley, was the encampment of the Pennsylvania Militia, who had been called out to subdue the rioters and keep order. This certainly had a very picturesque effect; but it was very sad to think such things should have to be, especially when at this particular time the strike was being carried on for the advantage of a few agitators, who here, as in every other country, live on the working-men by preaching to them of imaginary wrongs and suchlike. The mills at and around Pittsburg are simply enormous. Natural gas is used all over the place for smelting, etc., and everything seems to be carried on with such ease, dexterity, and precision, one would think the handling and smelting of iron were the easiest thing imaginable. It is poured about like so much treacle, and it almost seems that the iron bars and rails are made ready for use before the molten mass has had time to lose the hot, red glow it possessed when poured from the furnace. And it's all done

the industrial place it now is. Starting life in Pittsburg in connection with the railway, he gradually improved his position until he became an important official at the depôt there; then, going into the iron trade, his prosperous career continued, until, at the present day, he stands in the foremost rank of American millionaires.

On board the train going from Pittsburg to Cleveland I fell in with a downright jolly party, some genuine Americans and some partly acclimatised Englishmen; and, to their shame, I must say that the acclimatised Englishmen were far worse against the Old Country than the Americans. It was in the smoking-car, and everybody was very chummy. A little way out from Pittsburg, when we were not going very fast, we heard several pistol-shots and some screaming, which seemed to come from a passing train. Naturally I was curious, and wondered what was the matter. I had heard about 'holding-up' trains, and had a faint idea that something of the kind might be going to happen now; but one of the Yankees explained that he guessed it was only a little 'pistol practice' going on. But I called attention to the screams. 'Guess some one got hit,' said he. 'You know, mister, this is a free country, and in some parts, if one man wants to shoot another man, why, he just does it before the other man gets a chance of shooting him!' I said, 'Yes, you call it a free country; but it seems to me, to use one of your country's expressions, it's a "darned sight" too free!' This brought a rather funny tale from one of the party, and one which showed how an American will put such a lot into a few words. This man told us that some years ago he knew another man who came out from England to try and find his brother, from whom he had not heard for about four years.

the sudden deluge came from. The gentleman had a rough and ferocious aspect, and the sight of a sheath-knife stuck in one side of his belt and a 'six-shooter' in the other did not make things look more attractive. Overcoming his awe for this terrible person, the somewhat timid Englishman approached, and ventured to ask the gentleman if he had been in those parts long.

'Guess it's five-and-twenty year.'

'Five-and-twenty years! Then perhaps you can give me the information I require. I am trying to find my brother; he was in this neighbourhood about four or five years ago. His name was Williamson.'

'Williamson—kinder boss-eyed chap?'

Sidney Cowell

WE HEARD SEVERAL PISTOL-SHOTS

'What! my brother committed suicide? Why, he was the last man in the world I should have thought would have done such a thing. **Was** he ill, or in trouble, or what?'

where the wet came from! And so the time went on; but I must admit that at times I somewhat doubted the truth of some of the narratives I heard.

Cleveland is also a great oil centre, and, as well, it boasts of large iron-foundries, lumber-yards, and shipbuilding-yards. It is at the mouth of a river rejoicing in the pretty name of Cuzahoga, on the south shore of Lake Erie; and about half a mile from the shore, opposite the mouth of the river, an immense breakwater has been constructed about two miles long, thus forming a safe and commodious harbour for a large number of vessels. A good harbour is necessary here, for what is called *Lake* Erie covers an area of over 9000 square miles; and when the wind blows, such things as storms are by no means unknown.

At first sight, people would think there was only one street in Cleveland; but of course there are others. Still, Superior Street, which is the business centre of the place, is getting on for a mile long, and is over 130 feet wide, so there is plenty of it. I found in many American towns that there was really plenty of street, and room for a couple of omnibuses to drive down without damaging the paint on each other's wheels. More than once, in different places, I thought that if I crossed to the other side of the street I should be going as far as the whole length of an ordinary street (say Lime Street) in the City of London. Still, if you did want to get on to the other side, you were obliged to walk; cable-cars don't run from pavement to pavement, and a cab would cost a dollar, so to get over that way

somewhere about £30,000,000 sterling! It seems hardly possible to believe that such fabulous wealth could be obtained by one man starting at zero; but it is generally supposed that that is his 'pile.' He is one of the Standard Oil kings; and, although so enormously rich, perhaps his greatest pride consists in exhibiting his books showing his expenditure when he had to live on fifty dollars a month. There is rather a difference between half a hundred and half a million dollars as a monthly stipend!

Leaving Cleveland, I went to Detroit, and for a change took a boat across the 'Lake.' Of course, I don't mean that I hired a kind of Thames skiff and sculled across. That would have been a little too much. No, it was almost a young ocean-steamer, and going across the 'Lake' was almost a voyage.

I was always ready for a new experience, and, as I had heard a lot about 'new corn,' determined to try some, while on board, when feeding-time came. It was brought to me on a plate, and certainly looked and smelt very nice; but the difficulty was how to eat it. The whole cob—about six or eight inches long—was on the plate, and there was evidently a science in getting off the corn. First I got a fork and tried to pick it off, pea by pea; but the thing wouldn't keep still—it kept twirling over and over, and nearly came into my lap twice. Then I thought if I cut it into two I might get it to stand steady, as well as preserve the two halves to make 'corn-cob' pipes with. I nearly lost it altogether in attempting to do this. It was so hard the knife would make no impression, and, getting blunted,

nibbled the corn off like rabbits ; as they started, one of them said, ' Say, mister, this is how you must do it !' Then I was all right, and got on famously, both with the ' new corn ' and the new young ladies.

The boat was not wrecked on the voyage—I was glad of it, for the ' Lake ' is quite 200 feet deep—and eventually we dropped anchor at Detroit. I didn't find this place particularly interesting, although it is a good commercial centre, and there are plenty of smelting-works about, as well as flour-mills, places where railroad cars are made, boot and shoe factories, and a whole host of other industries. It is one

TWO PRETTY AMERICAN GIRLS

Consequently, I collected once more my various belongings, and got on the move again.

The train I went by was a remarkably good one, and ran from New York to Chicago, a distance of 980 miles, in twenty-five hours. It is really a splendid train, and its name, the 'Empress,' shows that, Republican as the Americans are, they like to have something about them to remind them of royalty. There is no mistaking the fact that Americans do know how to travel. In this train there were dining-, drawing-, and smoke-

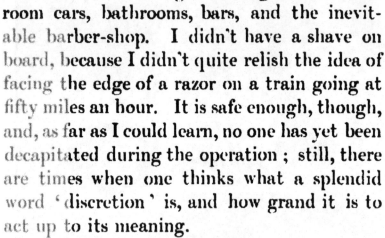

room cars, bathrooms, bars, and the inevitable barber-shop. I didn't have a shave on board, because I didn't quite relish the idea of facing the edge of a razor on a train going at fifty miles an hour. It is safe enough, though, and, as far as I could learn, no one has yet been decapitated during the operation ; still, there are times when one thinks what a splendid word 'discretion' is, and how grand it is to act up to its meaning.

The feeding arrangements on board the 'Empress' are first-class, and all the passengers seem to have large appetites. I wasn't very far behind in this respect, and soon made away with my eight- or ten-course dinner—I forget whether it was eight or ten courses. By this time I was getting thoroughly acclimatised and used to the customs of the country, and did the same as the most american American, and took fifty miles for my dinner and the next five miles for my toothpick. Toothpicks are quite

niggers—I beg their pardon, men of colour; and they all seem to have one name, George. If you wish a little extra attention, call a waiter George Washington; this has a wonderful effect, and causes his face to beam with a smile that looks as though it had been put on hot and run all over. Every one reveres the name of the first President of the United States, and nigger mothers do homage to his memory by christening their male offspring George. Some people say these attendants, as well as in hotels, don't take tips; but when George comes up to you with a grin on his face and a clothes-brush in his hand, to inquire if you would like a 'brush down, boss,' it would be a more than ordinarily obtuse individual who didn't divine that this was a hint for a small gift. Some little time after dinner and the exercise of the toothpick, the 'Empress' gradually slowed up, and when she stopped I found we had reached Chicago.

CHAPTER V

The Chicago Fire—Jealousy of New Yorkers—Gum-chewing—Expectoration—The 'Quid'—Onions or Indians—Wonderful Prosperity—Sunday—World's Fair—The Stock-yards—Killing a Steer—A Hospital Job—'Piggie's' Executioner—The End of the Porker.

It is really almost difficult to know how to start upon this chapter, for Chicago is certainly a most wonderful place, and one can hardly realise that it is little more than twenty years since it was practically a heap of cinders. The terrible conflagration which occurred in October 1871 will never be forgotten. Starting in a small barn on the south-western outskirts of the city, and not being attended to with the usual alacrity, the fire rapidly spread amongst the wooden buildings, and the

beyond human control, and swept at its own sweet will in one
vast wave of flame over acres and acres of ground, leaving
behind it black ruin, desolation, and death. Seeing the direction in which the flames were travelling, the authorities commenced blowing up houses, so as, if possible, to make a kind of
boundary; and luckily this and some rain had good effect, and
eventually the fire was stopped about three and a half miles
from where it commenced, and after raging upwards of twenty-
six hours. Thousands of people were rendered homeless, and
property worth millions was destroyed.

And now, what do we see? Not only a well-built city with
handsome public buildings, lofty and substantial places of
business, good streets, and indeed everything civilisation and
science can suggest, but the most flourishing and rapidly
increasing city in the States.

The way in which Chicago is so rapidly coming to the front is
a very sore point with New Yorkers; and if you want to have a
few minutes' rest from talking and spend that time in listening
to Yankee eloquence, all you have to do is to ask a New Yorker
how long he thinks it will be before Chicago becomes the first
city in the States? The language used by the gentlemen of
New York is decidedly impressive while stating how utterly
impossible it is for Chicago ever to be anything but a second-
class city, even if it be not convincing; and it is often embellished with those flowery flashes of rhetoric which are so
peculiarly 'America's own.' This jealousy is not confined to
the male natives, though, for the ladies are equally vehement
against any place daring to even think of passing their own
beloved New York; and when, after a long tirade, they pause

I imagined, than anywhere else, although the average American is never without his 'quid.' When I first went out in Chicago I really thought that the ladies were indulging in the same habit, for almost every one I met had her little mouth working away most industriously at something or other; but luckily it turned out to be nothing more harmful than 'gum.' The retailing of 'chewing gum' is a very profitable affair in the States. This gum is pretty well guaranteed to cure 'the

THE SPRIGHTLY STALL-KEEPER

for about a minute, and then the confounded stuff began to get into shape, and would stick about wherever there was a tooth to lay hold of. At last, with a smothered blessing—which I need not repeat here—that gum was dismissed, and I registered a vow never to try the game on again.

I was pleased to see one thing, and that was, that although the ladies chew so much, they have not yet acquired—at least, in public—that other habit of the male sex—expectorating! Spittoons are quite an essential piece of furniture—well, not alone in Chicago, but all over the States; and they are to be seen in every room, store, hall—in fact, everywhere. About the only place I did not see one was on the ferry-boat going to New Jersey, and here was placarded up pretty plentifully: 'Through respect for the presence of ladies, you are requested not to spit over the floor.' By the way, I remember seeing in an office a notice saying: 'Gentlemen do not, and others *must not*, spit over the floor.' This sort of thing is anything but nice; but what can you expect when it is encouraged so, and advertisements are so prevalent: 'For a nice chew, use So-and-so's tobacco'? Liquorice is used tremendously in 'chewing-tobacco,' and is sold to tobacconists almost as largely as it is in our country to brewers of stout. Some people might take an interest in the contrast that, while in England men drink the liquorice, in America they spit it out.

A good thing about the Americans is that they are very

It's a funny name, and some people think that it was so christened from an Indian word for 'wild onion,' as a very long time ago wild onions were most prolific about the neighbourhood of the river. But the majority don't like to associate onions with the name of their city; so, although I don't think they are quite correct, they prefer going to a different source, and say that it is derived from *checaqua*, an Indian word meaning 'strong,' and a term which was applied to the Indian chiefs of the Illini tribe when that fraternity located themselves in the neighbourhood. Both derivations are good, and whether the place really gets its name from an onion or a defunct Indian chief doesn't much matter; it's 'going ahead,' and that is the main question.

The Jesuit missionaries were the first white men known to visit the place, about 1662. They were Frenchmen, and the French claimed all that part in those days; but the British couldn't keep their hands off, and they accordingly took possession in 1759, but, as every one knows, eventually relinquished it.

Originally an Indian trading station, it has gradually developed, until now its area is somewhere about 405 square miles, and its population bordering upon 1,000,000. The reason of its commercial success is that it possesses such unrivalled facilities for transportation, both by water and by rail. Vessels direct from England can go direct up to the city, and it is entered by some sixty railways. The industries of the place comprise just every conceivable thing on earth, and the manufacture is good. It doesn't matter what you want in Chicago, you can get it; and if the people have never heard of it or seen it before, they'll make it while you sit down and have a quiet 'chew.'

the thing is 'discharged,' up it shoots—you fancy the moon at least is going to be your destination, especially if you get 'expressed' up to the eighteenth or nineteenth floor; but really, before you have got over the sensation of starting you have got to your stopping-place. The ordinary doesn't go beyond the eighth floor, and doesn't go quite so fast, but still there is not much difference. All these big buildings are fire-proof, or as near as science can render them so. This applies also to the hotels, which, by the way, are not at all badly managed; but I am sorry to think that the hotel-keepers are going on a very bad principle. Each wants to be first, and there is not that amicable feeling existing between proprietors which might be. It is all very well to encourage a feeling which prompts one to success, but 'the devil take the hindermost' is not altogether a sentiment to be fostered and cherished. I asked a man one day whether it wasn't dangerous to build houses so high for fear of their falling and causing loss of life; but he coolly replied that if they did fall, and people got killed, it would give others a chance, and they would start clearing and building again next day.

HE COOLLY REPLIED

Oh, wouldn't some of our goody-goody people be shocked if

for it hot and strong. The folks who in our country would try and make out a decent weekly salary by denouncing such things are either bundled on one side in the frantic rush, or lose the power of speech; or else they get excited, and join themselves in the mad helter-skelter race after the 'almighty dollar.' But it is only fair to say that there is another side to Chicago, and that the city contains a large number of churches.

The 'World's Fair' has been so much discussed in almost every publication extant, that I shall not say anything about it here, especially as I only saw the buildings, etc., in the state of perfection they had reached in October '92, when I was one of about 20,000 to pay my 25 cents to have a look round. There is only one thing, how

was the first in the contest to show, not only the site, but also the guarantee of **10,000,000** dollars.

Any description of Chicago, however slight, without mention of its gigantic stock-yards would be no description at all; for I don't think I am wrong in saying that, occupying nearly 350 acres of land, they make the largest live-stock market in the universe. I thought I had seen a lot of remarkable sights in America one way or another; but when I went to have a look over these yards, and the slaughter- and packing-houses, I was fairly bewildered. Let me say, to start, that the places are simply enormous, and that a regular network of railway seems spread all around. The first establishment I was taken to I entered the refrigerator warehouses. Not very sultry here, I will admit, but hundreds of carcases were hanging around; and another department just here was simply for cutting up. Seemingly various joints of beef were flying all over the place, the different joints falling in front of a man; and they all seemed to know the man they had to go to, for each operator carves away at a similar joint all day. All they have to do is to clear the bone of meat. The man appears to give the joint three or four slashes with a big knife (just like I used to do with a sword, when in the yeomanry, doing 'heads-and-posts') to clear the bone; then the beef tumbles into one receiver to be trundled off to be tinned, or preserved, or made sausages of, or something like that, while the bone is thrown into another receiver, from whence some of it goes to be converted into knife-handles, etc., but the majority to be boiled up for soup.

while. Two men are continually filling these loose-boxes with oxen (or steers, as they are called on the other side); and as soon as both animals arrive, one is greeted by the gentleman on the platform, who, swinging his huge

sledge - hammer round, allows it to alight on the animal's forehead; the other undergoes a similar welcome, and, both falling in a heap, the floor tilting up, they are shot through into the skinning department, and in almost less time than it takes to write the steer is hanging up from a sort of suspended tramway or trolley arrangement and starts on his journey.

The first man skins the head and cuts it off, then passes the animal on to four men, who just jump on it and skin it with about the same ease and celerity with which a street ruffian whips off his coat when he wishes to engage in the ' noble art.' Then there are other cutting and slicing operations ; but everything is done with such clockwork regularity that the time taken up between the entrance of the steer into the box and the final operation is comparatively little more than it has taken to write it.

From this it will be seen that, should the animal be only stunned by the sledge-hammers, the rapidity of the subsequent operations entirely prevents any return to consciousness. At the same time there is a story that a man once had six weeks in the infirmary suffering from a broken leg, caused by a kick from the hind leg of a steer soon after it had been decapitated, skinned, and disembowelled. I was introduced to a gentleman who confirmed this story : it seems hardly probable, but then it must not be forgotten that America is a wonderful country. Nothing whatever belonging to the animal is wasted ; everything is utilised and turned into money. The horns go to Paris and other parts to be made into knife-handles, combs, etc. ; the bones, as I have already described, are first boiled, and after being ground down are mixed with the stomach and blood, compressed into cakes, and sold as a highly useful fertiliser. Not only a fertiliser, though ; for a lot of this hard compressed mixture is made into buttons, and eventually finds itself displayed in this form upon the smart

this item alone, one firm netts $100,000 per annum, or about £20,000. At the slaughter-house I inspected the daily average 'kill' is 3000 head of cattle.

The *modus operandi* of ending the troubles of the homely porker (or hog, to give him his correct name) is somewhat similar, and equally expeditious.

But what a picture is the executioner! He stands in a commanding position, a small knife in his hand and an enormous chew of tobacco in his mouth, knee-deep in blood, and bespattered with the same from the crown of his head downwards.

The hog arrives, a chain is passed round his hind leg, and up he goes, hind leg foremost, to the trolley, which starts immediately. Of course, there is a terrific squeal, but it has hardly commenced before he is silenced by the sanguinary gentleman's knife. One stab does it as piggy is passing on the inclined trolley; and as the knife is withdrawn, the carcase, which, fixed to the trolley, is always on the move, is plunged into scalding water, and so on through the other operations. 'Now, look you here, mister,' said my Yankee guide, 'just you watch that 'ere hog there, the one just swung up, and you see if he isn't killed, scraped, and real finished just before you have time to say your prayers.' This was a very 'fine' way of putting it, to say the least; still, however, I must say that if the time taken by matutinal or evening devotions by an individual were only as long as that occupied from the swing-ing up to the finishing of that hog, I think those devotions would be the same as those of a gentleman who had his prayers

this, and finished by saying, ' The only thing we can't catch is the squeal of the hog, but I reckon we'll fix that before long and make something out of it !'

The wonderful thing is, it is only the men who are insured who ever get their fingers cut. A premium of $20 a year insures a man $15 a week during disablement and $1500 at death. Now I must be on the move again.

CHAPTER VI

Leaving Chicago—Real Estate—Jumping a Claim—The Mississippi—
Exhibitions, Teetotalers, Concrete Men, and Mud-Niggers—Rival
Towns—Dakota District—Pioneers and Indians—An Intolerable
Tongue-wagger—An Unnatural Scottie—Winnipeg—How to Light
Gas—Shooting and Winter Sports—Down a Well—The Hudson's
Bay Co.

I SAID good-bye to Chicago, with all its worry and bustle and
skurry and rush after the almighty dollar, and sought 'fresh
fields and pastures new.' There didn't seem much of any very
great importance between Chicago and 'Frisco, so I thought I
would go back to Canada and have a look at some of the
places there. Accordingly, I boarded a train for Winnipeg,
but made up my mind to have a look at St. Paul and Minnea-

sections, with roads marked, and quite ready for building to commence. Boards were up everywhere announcing 'Real estate—so many acres for sale; apply, etc. etc.' The Americans are big on real estate, and some of them make a nice little 'pile' dabbling in it.

When I saw this land staked out I couldn't help thinking of a little tale I once heard connected with the opening up of new land. When a new territory is to be opened up, no one is allowed over the border until a given time, and the large crowd that gathers weeks before the time is kept back by soldiers and police; then, at a given signal, away goes everybody to select the best spot he has time to do, and stake it out.

On one of these occasions, during the night before the grand charge was to be made, a man managed to evade the guards and get over the boundary. Then, having everything to himself, he selected and staked out a very nice piece that could hardly help becoming valuable in time. Having done this, he wrapped himself in his blanket and went to sleep on his newly acquired property.

When the signal was given, and the grand rush started, one man in a cart, which contained all his belongings, got well ahead of the crowd, and soon came up with the slumbering owner of the new claim. Seeing the spot was a good one, he quietly took a tent from his cart, erected it as quietly over the sleeping man, then entered it himself, rolled himself in his blanket, and lay down to wait events. First man wakes up,

It's marvellous how quickly a new town arises in America. One would think they kept houses, stores, saloons, and churches ready-made, and just went and planted them about when a new town was wanted. I wouldn't mind saying that in about a year's time all the land I saw marked out will be built over, the electric cars be running, and the place be well inhabited.

At St. Paul I got my first sight of that wonderful river that 'licks creation'—the Mississipi. There are a lot of tales to be told about this gigantic river, but Mark Twain has used them all up, and I won't poach on the ground of a brother author.

At Minneapolis I saw the Convention Hall, where for these parts the President is nominated, but was not

'LOOK YOU HERE, SONNY'

he was a regular Uncle Sam, and spoke the 'Amurican language' beautifully—'guessed' and 'calc'lated' all over the place.   This Exhibition was a marvellous collection of peculiarities.   There was one stand presided over by ladies who were professional teetotalers.   They looked it.   I felt I could talk with them without any amorous feelings arising, so consulted them as to the advisability of turning teetotaler. Two elderly maidens began to harangue Uncle Sam and myself in vigorous tones, and crammed tracts and all manner of cold-water literature into our hands the while. After about a quarter of an hour of this sort of thing, it began to get a bit monotonous, especially as by this time we had several pounds weight of tracts, etc., between us ; so Uncle Sam put a stop to it with, ' Well, look you here, ladies, if you ain't a bit tired, I reckon we are.   My friend and I will just go and have a cocktail, and then come straight away back for the wind-up !' There were phonographs which, after you put a nickel in the slot, buzzed out wobbly versions of Irish songs ; in fact, there were all manner of funny things.   But the one that interested me most was

A COLONEL

for thousands of years back, this clearly proved that he (the showman) was the first to enter the cave from incalculable time. In foraging around he came upon many curiosities, but the most curious one was the one he was now showing. A large piece of rock took his fancy, from some unaccountable reason ; and, giving one end of it a gigantic blow with his botanist's hammer, about a foot of the rock fell in two pieces at his feet— the two pieces were shown, and they fitted together beautifully — leaving protruding from the other piece the skull of a man. Fearing lest he should damage this, he had carefully brought the whole away without venturing to seek

TWO ELDERLY MAIDENS BEGAN TO HARANGUE

runnin'.' Sold again! In my guilelessness I had believed the attendant's yarn, but Uncle Sam told me afterwards, the thing was very common. It was only a skull stuck on the top of a lump of concrete! Then he told me that he was once consulted about a rather peculiar case. A showman was exhibiting a ' mud-nigger '—that was, a nigger who, since his childhood, had simply lived in a bed of mud, his head only protruding. During three-and-thirty years that nigger had never been known to leave that mud! 'But,' he added, 'that experiment didn't answer; ten days in the mud killed that nigger!' 'Well,' said I, 'how did things turn out? What was said at the inquest?' 'Said? why, nothing—what could be said? Guess you don't take on he was only a nigger!'

Minneapolis is famous for its saw-mills, and contains a large number of factories where furniture of all kinds is made; but neither of these industries comes up to the flour-mills, for these are everywhere. Water being so very plentiful here, water-power is used in almost all the factories; and yet, only some comparatively few years ago, there was nothing but prairie here, and buffaloes and other prairie pets used to regularly spend their Saturday half-holiday in disporting themselves on the site now occupied by this town.

I went from here to St. Paul in an electric trolley-car. The distance is ten miles, but the ground is soon got over, for the cars travel at a good speed. Along the way on both sides are to be seen signs of disappearing prairie-land, for almost every-where are boards giving the address of ' Real Estate Agents '

more on board the lugger—I mean train—off we go for Winnipeg.

This is a very interesting ride indeed, for it goes through the finest wheat-growing land in the States—Dakota district. It is a wonderfully fertile part, and it has been known where wheat has been grown on the same land for forty years consecutively. The wheat-fields vary in size from 1000 to 20,000 acres; and although the average yield is about twenty bushels to the acre, in some parts it goes as high as forty bushels! One can imagine what a sight it must be at harvesting time, when armies of workers and hundreds of the most scientifically constructed 'harvesters' are to be seen at work as far as the eye can travel in every direction! The grain finds its way to St. Paul and Minneapolis, and is there ground into flour; and immense quantities of this eventually find their way to our own country. As far as the straw is concerned, it would never pay to cart this away, so it is simply 'fired,' *i.e.* burned, and the ashes blown to the winds.

Here and there large tracts of country have been bought up by speculators, who have simply let the grass grow instead of cultivating it; and this is such a height that it is scarcely possible to see more than about the top half of the heads of any horses that might be meandering around in it. At some of the stations—or depots, to be more correct—that we stop at, some very homely sights are seen. The stations are little more than wooden sheds, but outside some of these a buggy is seen waiting to meet the husband or son on his return, to take him home; and right away in the distance, close upon the

and merciless death at the hands of the savage and pitiless Indians.

Now, I'm not generally supposed to be a vindictive man, or one who is in the habit of wishing harm to anyone, but there was one man on board our train whom it would have given me the greatest pleasure to hand over to the tender mercies of one of the ancient and gentle Choctaws, Cherokees, Arapahoes, Pawnees, or Sioux, for he was a perfect nuisance. We all wanted to go to sleep; but as this man was going to get off the train about four in the morning, he didn't, and

only have got one of Buffalo Bill's Indians with a tomahawk to illustrate scalping upon this intolerable tongue-wagger, we would have returned most devout thanks for such a deliverance; but this was not to be, and we had to put up with it.

THE TONGUE-WAGGER

'Union Jack' to the 'Stars and Stripes.' He still, however, re-
tained a little sympathy for Scotland and the Scotch, but everything English, and England itself, was bad, and existed only
to be slanged. Even an American pulled him up for his
vituperation, and told him he must have left England for
England's good, and that it would
not be well for him to return, or
else that he had an Irishman for
a neighbour, to talk such rubbish.
Trust a Yankee for hitting the
right nail. It came out afterwards that the friendly neighbour was not only an Irishman,
but one who had bolted
from the country to
escape arrest for be-
ing a very ener-
getic member of a
Fenian Society!
   The first thing
to be seen on
crossing the
Canadian border
is a church steeple,
and this looks well,
which however, is more than

W, for it *is* a wide street. A double line of cars runs down the middle of it, and they are hardly seen ; while it would be next to an impossibility to recognise even one's most intimate friend if he were on the other side of the way. I cannot understand why, where there are such wide streets, some enterprising person doesn't start

HALFPENNY 'BUSES

halfpenny 'buses to run from one side of the road to the other.

winter, when it is a very common thing to light a gas-jet by causing a friction with your feet by rubbing them on the carpet, and then placing your finger on the burner! At least, so I was told.

Although this is such an 'on the distant prairie' sort of place, it musn't be thought it is not worth visiting, for it is really a very charming place, especially by the river Winnipeg, which is a thickly wooded place, and where many houses are now being built. Bears are made a lot of here, and are kept for household pets and watch-dogs. Very nice for those that like them—but give me a good fox-terrier.

There is some rare good sport to be had all round; and if a man has an hour or two to spare he just takes his gun and goes shooting prairie-hens. One afternoon I went out and bagged over ten brace of birds. All round this district is a perfect paradise for sportsmen. The winters are long and severe, but there is plenty of skating and other amusement going on, so times are not so bad; and the old Scotch spirit rises on these occasions, for 'curling' is played most extensively.

Almost every second man you meet is said to be a university man, or the son of some high and mighty family at home, and is now either 'hustling lumber' or farming at four or five dollars a week. Of course, the value of a farm is increased enormously if water can be found on it; and it is said that two Cambridge men who owned a farm went to work hard at digging a well, hoping to reach fresh cold water. They took turn and turn

The one in charge of the windlass did as he was desired, and bolted home, while the one down below waited patiently to be drawn up. He waited all the afternoon, occupying his time in shouting, and also all night. Next morning a half-breed Indian passing near the place was very much surprised to hear stifled groans coming from the well, and after a deal of trouble succeeded in rescuing the man from below. He

HE FOUND HIS COMPANION STRETCHED ON THE FLOOR

then went home to his log-cabin, and found his companion stretched on the floor in a most profound sleep, with the

and both men and horses are smartly drilled, a 'turn-out' being accomplished in about seven seconds. But one thing must not be forgotten in connection with Winnipeg, and that is, that it has for some years been the chief post of the Hudson's Bay Company. This wonderful trading Company is deserving of comment, for it is, in a way, greatly responsible for a lot of the trade in the Dominion. I expect it is pretty generally known that the Company came into existence in 1670, when Charles II. granted a charter to Prince Rupert and seventeen noblemen, giving them exclusive powers of trading over an almost unlimited territory in North America. But for some long time they confined themselves chiefly to trading in the coast districts.

The affair was not a remarkably prosperous one at first, for great losses were made, principally on account of the fights with the French, who endeavoured to take possession of the Company's forts, and caused them considerable annoyance and loss. Then again, when all Canada came into the possession of the British in 1783, a tremendous lot of fur-traders spread all over the country, and didn't altogether hold the lands of the Company sacred. These adventurers eventually formed themselves into the North-West Fur Company of Montreal, and soon proved themselves very powerful rivals of the Hudson's Bay Company. Competition was carried to an enormous pitch, and neither side stuck at anything. Fur-bearing animals were slaughtered indiscriminately, without regard to age or sex; and by each Company endeavouring to gain over the Indians to their side, these worthies became utterly demoralised, and many deadly fights took place between the rival parties,

which all their rights lapsed, and trading was thrown open to all.

The Company, however, still claimed large territories as their own, and it was not until 1869 that this matter was definitely settled up.   The territorial rights they claimed were then made over to the British Government, on payment of an indemnity of £300,000 by the Dominion of Canada, and it was also agreed that the Company should retain possession of their forts and a considerable area of their original grant of land. This has placed the Company in a splendid position, and it is now perhaps one of the best managed and most prosperous trading companies in the world.

CHAPTER VII

Prairies and Indians—An Intoxicated Cook—Peculiar Names—' Regular
Gorge, 50 cents '—Cockneys and Crofters—The Rocky Mountains—
Banff—Magnificent Scenery—Salmon in the River Fraser—Vancouver
—' Labour with Capital '—John Chinaman—A Five-dollar Hurry—
Schoolboy Books—Going to 'Frisco—Marvellous Vegetation—' No
pullee, no pushee, go like hellee ! '—Poor Polly—Buying a Kodak.

I now commenced the longest and most pleasant railway
journey it has yet been my lot to experience, and that was
from Winnipeg to Vancouver. Of course, we didn't get on the
train and go straight ahead to Vancouver without stopping ; we
made one or two short stays at different places, but for no
great length of time ; so it was in reality a continuous journey,
and part of it the most magnificent scenery conceivable. I
should imagine this journey was always one of interest to any
traveller ; but to any one making it for the first time it is
wonderfully so. The first part of the time the train goes

or other.   These Indians were very much like those I had seen at Buffalo Bill's show at Earl's Court; but I noticed that they hardly had such a decidedly Cockney accent as some of the showman's had.   The atmosphere and climate may have some-

BARGAINING WITH INDIANS

evidence of his importance, for he won't take less than he asks for an article; when a smaller sum is offered, he stalks away with an air of offended dignity, and throws his blanket around him with a gesture which might have been learned from the Romans of old when the wind got blowing their togas about.

Buffaloes used to be very plentiful some time ago, but now they are almost extinct, apart from the specimens which are kept in the various parts. I am sorry for this, because buffalo tongue is very good, and when all the animals are dead I expect there will be no more of it. I don't know, though; for the whole continent of America is a wonderful country, and, as there are parts where I have heard six hams are got from one hog, I daresay that somehow or other the luxury of buffalo tongue will be provided for all time, whether there are any of the animals left or not.

The stations and bits of villages passed are very primitive, and all built of wood. There was a bit of a disturbance on board our train the second night after dinner. The chief cook was so indiscreet as to get intoxicated, very much so—indeed, I think drunk would be the more correct word—and, while he was in this state, got particularly argumentative with those around him. Well, that didn't matter much; but when he attempted to enforce an argument with a large carving-knife, the conductor thought it time to interfere. Mr. Chief Cook was taken to the end of the train and quietly dropped overboard, the conductor remarking, 'I believe he'll sober up soon now, for there's no place of any sort within a dozen miles of here, go which way you will.' Moral—If you get drunk on board a train in a prairie, don't try to stab anybody, unless you're prepared for a long walk.

ment station, by the way; there are several of them along the track, and the train generally stops about half an hour at these to allow any one who wishes it to regale himself. I remember seeing a notice stuck up in a restaurant in the States, 'Good meal, 25 cents; regular gorge, 50 cents'; and it is

A MEAL

something of the kind at these stations, for one can have a 'regular gorge' for 50 cents,

habit, though, and that is a very bad one.   They *will* distil
their own whisky.

The Cockneys, who are sent out by some East End London
Mission, are anything but a success, according to my friend.
Still, as he was a solicitor, he said he didn't mind telling me
that they had put some money into his pocket, for he was
frequently engaged by the authorities in prosecuting them.   It
appears that after they have got located in the place, and begin
to know their way about, they show their gratitude, at times, to
their employer, by 'making tracks' with a watch, money, horse,
or whatever they can most conveniently get away with.

Getting towards a place called Langevin, a little excitement
springs up, for it is here that one gets a first sight of that
wonderful range of mountains, the Rockies.   It is just the
higher peaks of them that can be seen, provided the day be
clear, and from here prairies, ranches, and seas of waving grass
begin to disappear, and a great change comes over the face of
the earth.   While travelling on the American route, one might
well have put in his diary, 'This was a wheat day,' 'All corn
again to-day,' etc. ; but here things are different, and the acres
and acres of prairie give place to the wild and magnificent
grandeur of the Rockies.   During the whole trip on this train
we had been gradually ascending above the level of the sea,
till, at a place called the Gap, an altitude of 4200 feet was
reached, as against the 700 feet at Winnipeg.

But the Gap!   This is the entrance to the Rockies, and is
a fine foretaste of the scenery that is to come.   Just before
reaching this place, the Kananaskis river is crossed by a high
iron bridge, and the sensation going over is peculiar in the extreme, to say the least of it ; especially when, as I experienced
it, the sun is just rising and shedding a warm, ruddy glow all

Mountains seem to come abruptly forward, and almost before one is aware of the change the train goes round a curve, and is

ENTERING THE ROCKIES

magnificent scenery. But how to describe this rugged, weird, and awe-inspiring view is beyond me. There is too much to describe in a few lines, or even a few pages; it is simply a series

showing their strata as plainly and distinctly as before any disturbance, and looking as though they would every moment press forward and demolish the contrivance which the ingenuity of man has devised by which to enter their sacred presence; now through the gorge, a vast space opens up to view, almost

CANADIAN PACIFIC RAILWAY

A stoppage is made at Banff (at an altitude of 4500 feet), which is the station for the hot springs and the National Park. This park was formed at the suggestion of the Marquis of Lorne when he was Governor-General, and is a fairly good-sized one, rather different from Hyde Park ; but then it covers about twenty-five square miles, so there is plenty of room to make a good show of mountains, waterfalls, and suchlike. At Banff I had a hot sulphur bath, the water coming straight from the rocks, and the heat being about 80 degrees. There is a very good hotel at Banff, that is kept open during the summer months, when the place is well patronised both as a health and pleasure resort. Not far from the hotel was a lady who, being so entranced with the scenery, was 'camping out' for the purpose of sketching and painting ; the various kinds of insects that fly and crawl about this district had evidently been trying what they could do in this way on her, for she looked as though she had been thoroughly tattooed ! They had certainly given her a most hearty welcome.

Not long after leaving Banff, which is really a most charming spot, the line reaches its highest point, a place called Stephen, at an altitude of 5296 feet, and called by this name in honour of the first President of the Canadian Pacific Railway. Still running through scenery increasing in grandeur at almost every yard, the train gradually gets on, until a perfectly lovely spot is reached called Glacier. Here I joined a very

ance of the wooded parts, they cover such an enormous area. Some people who are more anxious to get the land ready for cultivation than make money on the timber, simply set fire to the trees and burn them down.

This sometimes happens accidentally, however, and now and then some terrible fires occur. The river is well stocked with fish, salmon beingvery freely caught, especially by the Indians, who spear them. According to the inhabitants, the Fraser presents a wonderful appearance just about the spawning season, for then the salmon go up from the sea in such crowds that for some

A LADY WAS 'CAMPING OUT'

A story is told that when the boundary line between Canada and the States was being arranged, some big authority (an enthusiastic angler) was appealed to about a part of the disputed ground; and the reply he sent back was, 'Country not worth consideration; fish won't take a fly.'

Just before getting into Vancouver, at a station—for some reason or other, goodness only knows what—I shouted to the engine-driver of the train in Gaelic, and to my astonishment, and also that of the shooting party I was with, he replied in the same terms; not only replied, but rattled out such a lot— he was a Scotchman—and was so pleased to hear the language again, he almost forgot all his duties connected with the train. Vancouver is a very nice place, and very pleasantly situated at the mouth of the Fraser River, on a large bay in which a quantity of shipping is always lying, including one or other of the magnificent steamships recently built by the Canadian Pacific Railway Company to connect Vancouver with Japan. The harbour here is classed amongst the finest in the world, and there can be no possible doubt but what the city has a very good future in store. Times were good, and the place is prospering wonderfully; it only wants time to develop into perhaps the most important city in British North America. A peculiar thing is that it is the only place which has not been thoroughly boomed and worked up, as it were, artificially. It has grown rapidly, but genuinely; and no one can quite realise that in 1885 the site was a dense forest. Yet such is the case, and it was May 1886 when wooden houses first began to spring

credit to any city that could be mentioned. It is a wonderfully English place, and there are only a very few Americans and Canadians included in the 20,000 inhabitants which it now boasts of—not nearly so many as one would expect to find in a rising place occupying such a commanding position. There is plenty of room for another 20,000 people, or even treble that number; in fact, the cry all over the place is, 'Labour with Capital.' The two must go together; and for any one with a small capital, and able to work, Vancouver would be by no means an undesirable place. This must not be confounded with Vancouver Island, of which Victoria is the capital, for that is some little distance away. Small-pox was on the rampage on this island when I was at Vancouver (in fact, the 'yellow flag' was out at various houses in Vancouver); so I didn't ferry across to it, but satisfied myself with reading and hearing about it, and looking at photographs.

John Chinaman is very much in evidence here, and, as everywhere else he goes, is reducing the price of labour. He is all very well as a washerwoman—that hardly sounds correct, but what I mean is, he is good at laundry work—in fact, he will give any European 'chalks and a beating' at it; but he is not admired much beyond this.

Now I started for San Francisco, and had a good overland journey. Baggage was examined on the American frontier; and although one of my travelling companions had been talking rather loudly about getting his trunks 'chalked' without their being examined, he seemed to forget all about it when he was 'bailed up.' He told me that a few years ago he landed in New York with a lot of dutiable stuff amongst his things, but didn't

declared this was true, but I had my doubts, as it was dis-
paraging to the character of the American custom-house
officers, and these worthies ought to be looked upon as the
soul of honour. The dollar can work many wonders, but bribe
an American custom-house officer! Well, of course, there's
no knowing what *may* happen.

We passed through some most wonderful country, forest suc-
ceeding forest, and huge mountainous parts lending a fascinating
grandeur to the whole scene, while the log-huts completed a
picture which for its *extremeness* might almost be called
domesticity and barbarity. The lumber-men all about this
region are really young giants; scarce a man amongst them
under about six feet, and broad and well made in proportion.
It is true their appearance has not that innocent and gentle
air so peculiar to childhood—in fact, in many cases it approaches
the roughness of a horror seen in a nightmare; but they are by
no means a bad set of fellows. The northern part of Washington Territory is developing wonderfully just now, but some
of the places are rather what may be termed primitive.
Seattle, for instance, is a very rustic-looking settlement. The
whole country round brings one back to those schoolboy books
so wild and exciting, and whose pages teem with thrilling
adventures with Indians, burning forests, and feats of pro-
digious valour performed by some apparently insignificant
youth, who, after slaying about a hundred Indians with his own
strong arm and carving-knife, or putting out an acre or two of

of wooden hut, and over the door was painted the word 'Bank'!

The journey by boat from Seattle to Tacona is past islands and land covered with timber, growing and cut down. On the waterside are immense piles waiting to be sawn up, and dotted here and there are huge saw-mills hard at work, and constantly on the go; yet, for all this, and despite the large army of men always 'at it,' it is calculated that several centuries will elapse before the land is clear. Settlers in this district, unlike those in the

'OH! IT'S NOTHING'

prairies, get 160 acres free if they clear the timber; and in heaps of cases they adopt the quickest method of doing this, and burn it down.

Portland (Oregon) is the next place of interest, and the

every description, not forgetting the indispensable 'barber.' These shops in the basement save a visitor a wonderful lot of trouble.

Now I get on board the train again, and make a real start for 'Frisco, the Golden City, stopping on the way at Mount Shasta to sample the water of the Shasta natural mineral spring, which is really very good indeed, and the sight of the water coming jumping up is very strange.   The entrance to

SAN FRANCISCO : THE GOLDEN GATES

'Frisco by this railway is not calculated to make one go into ecstasies over the place, for bogland and prairie have to be

ordinary luck, after the third year, he should be making $5000 a year nett profit. There is a sort of blackberry-bush that grows to an immense size if properly cultivated. I didn't see it, but I was told that it was nothing for one of these *bushes* to cover one or two hundred yards of ground ; in fact, if a man had room enough to grow a couple of them he could make a good living ! Wonderful place, America ! Everything so large about it ! At least, not exactly *everything*; minute, and at the same time objectionable, things might be mentioned.

Well, we're in the wonderful city of 'Frisco, and the Palace Hotel, where I stayed, is always popularly supposed to be the largest in the world ; the manager says he isn't quite sure how many people he can accommodate, but he thinks he can put up almost 1000 people ! The Presidential election excitement wasn't quite over during my visit ; and, I presume in order to stimulate the voters, a band of musicians — well, that's what they called themselves —dressed as volunteers, discoursed a terrible row every evening in the courtyard of the hotel. It would really be a libel on a noble art to

of London, the German bands or hurdy-gurdies, are refinement compared with that conglomeration of hideous noises.

The streets in 'Frisco are very good, and the cable-car system is just A1. When the cable-car system was first introduced, it was altogether too much for John Chinaman; his celestial mind couldn't grasp the idea at all, and he looked upon it as something almost supernatural. 'No pullee, no pushee, go like hellee,' John would say, and then jump over the lines. Nothing would induce him to *walk* across. He is getting to understand it now, though. Theatres, public-houses or 'saloons,' and churches

it is just as well for the visitor to prepare his nerves, and make up his mind not to be too squeamish, for during the whole tour he will be surrounded by dirt, stench, and immorality. I don't think I will go into details. There are a lot of French here, and the Irish muster very strongly too in different parts, but perhaps more especially at Golden Gate Park, and they are all 'patriots.' While touring round there one day, I heard a story of a green parrot whistling 'Boyne Water,' much to the annoyance of a Paddy. 'Och, ye divil,' said Pat, 'shure, it's only your colour that saves ye! If ye were a canary, begorra, I'd wring your neck!' Poor Polly!

A long time can be very profitably spent in 'Frisco, for there is plenty to see, and the inhabitants are without doubt 'all sorts and conditions of men.' One day I was very much amused. I had just been to a Republican meeting, the principal part of the speeches at which seemed to be 'Fellow-citizens'; and outside the hall some man was suddenly inspired, and, jumping on a barrow, commenced to harangue the crowd on the evils of intemperance. He hadn't got far when he was ignominiously pitched from his barrow, and the little attentions he received from his erstwhile hearers were such that the police had to interfere and protect him. Just before leaving 'Frisco,

Dour'—(he couldn't fix *Dewar*)—'for I guess that's who it is.
Shake hands! I'm going the same trip. What's your
stateroom?' To our astonishment we found we were to share
the same stateroom. A friend had given him an introduction
to me; but, making a bold shot for it, he had anticipated events,
and not waited till he got on board. He may possibly have
the temerity to read through these pages, otherwise I should
say that a nicer American, a more genuine man, or a livelier or
jollier travelling companion I never met. But there are times
when it is not advisable to say all one thinks, so I will pass
over the gentleman's good qualities in silence; but as he kept
me company for some months, he will have to be mentioned
more than once again.

CHAPTER VIII

ALTHOUGH I really believe that, if a traveller wishes to go everywhere and see as much as he can, the best thing is for him to
go by himself, I must say I was not sorry to fall in with such
a genial and jovial companion as the one I met buying a
kodak.

There are times when one meets unexpectedly a congenial
spirit, and this happened to be one of those times. We seemed
to have the same ideas and tastes in everything, and there
seemed to be only about one trait in which we differed : he was
extremely susceptible to the charms of the fair sex : I preserved

time to enjoy the glorious view presented on leaving 'Frisco
harbour.

We left in the evening just before sunset, and dropped gently
down the waterway which connects San Francisco Bay with
the Pacific, the rays of the setting sun lending a glowing colour
to the magnificent scenery we were leaving behind; but as the
steamer glided on, and eventually steamed into the great
Pacific Ocean, a more than beautiful sight burst upon us.   Far
away ahead were sparkling, dancing, blue rippling waves, beneath
which the monarch of the day was just dipping; while astern
was the coast of that gigantic country across which I had
travelled, the huge rocks on each side of the entrance to the
bay we had left looking indeed the 'Golden Gates' they were
called, for they were bathed in the glorious rays of that golden
sun which was fast disappearing below the horizon.   I'm a bit
of an artist in a way, and must confess I was fairly carried away
by this sight.

I said to my Yankee friend, who was by:

'This is magnificent!'

'Well, yes,' said he, 'I reckon it's fairly good; but would
you believe it, not long ago some storekeepers tried to use
those rocks for advertising. Right in front there, where everybody can see coming in, a coon got painted up big, " Buy
Brown's Boots"; and two days later another coon painted
underneath, and bigger, "If you can't get Smith's!" Smart
man. Smith!' Smith may have been smart, but both he and

to be perfectly and entirely lost in one of the opposite sex, and feel that the world exists only for two people, the other part of the inhabitants being thrown in just to do anything that those two require; but, all the same, it's rare fun for those not interested.

Ah, well, the ocean is a mighty leveller.   It seemed to wake up a bit during the first night out, and in the morning was dancing to a very lively tune.   The romantic and amorous thoughts of the honey- mooners were rudely dispersed, and they fell suddenly from the heights of bliss to the depths of indescrib- able misery.

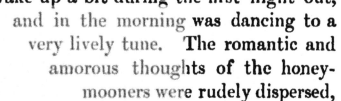

There were a very few people on deck—luckily, I am a very good sailor— but at quiet intervals a sad and despond- ing pair would ascend the steps. The newly made husband would

deathlike faces they would anxiously 'seek the seclusion that a cabin grants.'

One or two lady passengers courageously braved the elements, and thoroughly enjoyed the breeze, also the breakfast after their blow. There were not many people at breakfast the

first morning, or indeed at any of the meals the first day. As for the missionaries, I think only the steward knew where they really were. They were quite *non est.* There were a rare lot of missionaries on board, and two or three Scotch ministers. Folks began to turn up on the second day, when the weather cleared a bit, and then we could see who was who. The fourth day out was a very sad one, and we witnessed one of those solemn and distressing scenes, a burial at sea; and this reminded me of the first I saw some years ago, on a voyage to Natal, when a man who was leaving his country for his country's good, shot him-

self.

near the side of the ship and placed on a plank, which
balanced over the side of the vessel.   Every one stood around,
and a most unusual quiet reigned over all.   The sea was
calm, the light was fading away, and the gentle splash of the
waves on the side of the vessel seemed to keep time with the
words of the burial service as it was being read.   Then, at a
signal, the screw of the steamer stopped, one
end of the plank was gently raised, the
body slid off, and with a quiet splash disappeared beneath the waves.   Perhaps the
most trying part of the whole scene was
that minute when, in order to get clear of
the body, the screw was stopped, and the
almost deathlike silence was broken by the
gentle splash which told that the body of one
who a few days ago had been amongst us
had been committed to the deep.   However,
not to appear irreverent, it was something
like a soldier's funeral, where on the march
to the grave the band plays funeral marches,
but on the way back to the barracks in-
dulges in 'The girl I left behind me, and
similar tunes of a non-funereal character;
for I am sadly afraid that a very short
time after all was over, the whole matter
was looked upon merely as an 'incident.'

A RARE LOT

It evidently, though, awoke the missionary
crowd to a sense of their duties, and to the
fact that they had 'played at Sunday' in their
cabins on the first day out instead of trying to improvise
a service; for in the evening one of them, a Scottish teetotal

of ark, and all that sort of thing, he drew comparisons of the people on board, and amongst others was: 'We have missionaries on board going to convert the heathen, and we have a heathen grog-seller on board going to convert the civilised to the evils of whisky-drinking, and encourage those who are already wallowing in that degrading and pernicious vice!' Good old missionary! I didn't pay him anything for the advertisement, although at the time I wondered whether he would expect anything. I must say, however, that my feelings were very considerably hurt by being called a 'heathen'! I, who had been brought up most strictly in the tenets of the Shorter Catechism, the Scottish Kirk, and porridge, to be called a heathen! It was too bad of the gentleman—altogether too bad. He could not have believed in—I believe it was Byron, who says:

' There 's nothing cheers the heart so much
As rum and true religion.'

Very possibly he had tried the rum, but I am quite sure it isn't true religion to call members of the Free Kirk of Scotland heathens.

Well, on the seventh day from 'Frisco we landed at Honolulu, and I had my first sight

called the Paradise of the Pacific, and no better term could be applied to them. Palm-trees, cocoa-nut trees, bananas, oranges, flowers, ferns—in fact, every conceivable kind of tropical vegetation, and all in profusion—a perfect climate, swept by ocean breezes,—what can one wish for more? It is fairyland in reality.

One afternoon I was lying on an almost velvet kind of bank, under palms and banana-trees, admiring the grandeur and beauty of everything around, and wondering whether I could really be in the world, or only dreaming. I had perfectly lost myself in the magnificence of the whole scene, and quite expected every minute to see fairies come tripping from between the trees and behind the gigantic ferns, when I was rudely awakened from my sweet *dolce far niente* by a dirty, dark coppercoloured native youngster who, carrying a huge bundle of cocoanuts, burst suddenly and unceremoniously through some beautiful foliage, and started at the top of his vile young voice that awful refrain, ' Ta-ra-ra-boom-deay!' Ye gods! if I could have caught that youngster, or pulled up a cocoanut-tree and dropped it on him! or if the author, or even

perfect fairyland, to have it screeched at me by a copper-coloured youngster! It was too much. I went for that youngster; but either my sudden spring from a recumbent to an upright position, or the tremendous yell of rage I gave vent to, scared him, for he made tracks, and with a howl of fright disappeared about as suddenly and mysteriously as he had come upon the scene.

Honolulu, the capital of the group of islands, is a well-built and good business place. Like 'Frisco, it has a big Chinese and Japanese population, and Chinese labour is pretty general in the coffee, sugar, and rice industries. John Chinaman has his own part of the town, and imports from the Celestial Empire nearly everything he wants. I got a fine prescription made up here at a Chinese chemist's. It consisted of powdered glass, dried black-beetles, dried snails, dried worms, and a variety of other peculiar things. This had to be mixed in boiling water, stewed for a short time, and thinned down until liquid enough to drink, then taken off in one draught! I sadly wanted my American friend to try it, but he 'guessed he wasn't sick,' and would not be prevailed upon. Some people are obstinate.

The mosquitoes here were remarkably chummy—in fact, quite embarrassingly so; and they bit me within about an inch of my life. By the way, the Chinese gods in John's temple are most attractive-looking atrocities, but I won't attempt to describe them. My friend and I were told we ought to attend a service at the temple; but as we knew it took about a week to get

at the time of writing this there appears very little prospect of the young lady ever attaining her rights ; but even revolutions sometimes get revolutionised, so the time may come when the daughter of a pushing Scotchman will rule over Paradise— I mean the Paradise of the Pacific.

The population of Honolulu is chiefly European and American (not forgetting the Chinese and Japanese) ; but the natives are plentiful, and in some of the islands very much so. They are quiet and inoffensive people, and anything but objectionable, while the dresses of the ladies—Mother Hubbard costumes—put one in mind of the good old days of the nursery. Before leaving Honolulu, I must mention the 'Hawaiian Band,' for it is one which is well known in the western hemisphere. It is maintained by the Government, and consists of thirty native performers, with a German conductor. I am quite sure that if it ever came over to this country it would make even some of our military bands ' sit up.'

There are twelve islands in the group, but four of them are barren ; and a tour in a steamer round the lot will soon show any one how it is that, as well as Paradise, etc., the ' Inferno of the world ' is also so justly applicable ; for here is found, if not the largest, the most remarkable volcano in the world. I cannot really say all I want to about these islands here, for it would make a book of itself, and I almost think I shall some day write one specially devoted to their wonders and their beauties. One island which no one can visit without feelings of the greatest sorrow is that of Molokai, the home of the lepers, of whom there are some 1100 or 1200. Apart however from the

I needn't say anything about Captain Cook, who discovered the islands, and was eventually killed at Kealakekua Bay, in the island of Hawaii, for everybody knows all about that; but at the same time I should like to say that I saw here, at several places, the *identical spear* with which he was killed. I had seen several in London; but of course that goes for nothing, for one can see anything and everything in London, and no doubt the one in our Metropolis is the most authentic. After spending a most jolly time in these delightful islands, we went for another sea voyage, and shipped to Samoa. This voyage was eventful chiefly for the length of time we lay on our backs each day, for it was right through the tropics and across the equator, or 'line,' as sailors call it. Any one can imagine that rest was far cooler than exercise. Pheugh, it was hot! It was a perfect luxury in the early morning, in place of a bath, to have the hose turned on to you on deck; but even then the water was anything but cold. There was no 'bump' as we crossed the line, as some people had imagined; and when the officers said, 'Now we are across,' I looked astern, but couldn't see anything but water of mill-pond smoothness.

There was something left of us when we got to Apia, although we had undergone such a roasting for a week; and as we approached the place from the sea, I thought it was not at all strange that Robert Louis Stevenson should have taken such a fancy to the place, for it was really lovely.

Very few people in England, perhaps, know very much about

A SAMOAN CANOE IN A GALE

harbour and got to sea, while every other vessel in the harbour was lost and several hundreds of persons were drowned. The terrible disaster is still fresh in the minds of all the inhabitants, and is talked about now almost as much as it was at the time. Some of the natives speak fairly good English ; and one of these, a boatman who took us a sail round the coral reefs, warmed up immensely when telling us the horrors of the scene. He drew a most graphic picture of the whole, and we could almost see the *Calliope*, with the brave captain and his equally brave crew, battling with the storm to get free of the reefs, and hear the crews of the fast-sinking American and German vessels cheering that plucky handful of men, as, going about one mile an hour, inch by inch they neared the open sea. He described how terrible it was for those on land, who were powerless to render assistance although men were drowning within twenty yards of the shore, and wound up with, ' But English ships too strong, English sailors too good to sink.' Although he never even hinted at it, I heard afterwards that this man was one of the most energetic in rendering assistance during that awful time, and was instrumental in saving a great number of lives.

Although at present Samoa is under the triple protectorate of England, America, and Germany, from what I could see and what I heard, things seemed tending to the floating of the Union Jack alone. One native told me that they would never have the Germans alone, as they didn't like them ; but that they didn't mind either of the others, although they would

short and raised my hat. He touched his, and said ' 'Morning.'
It was not a lengthy conversation, certainly, but quite sufficient
to enable me to say that I had been in close personal contact
with Royalty. Possibly closer than that Royalty cared for—
but that is a detail! But now, here, thousands of miles away
from home, I visited a King! Not only visited him, but had a
long and friendly chat with him; also some bananas. It was
King Malietoa; and although he couldn't speak English very
well, his Majesty and I got on very well indeed together. His
surroundings may not have been equal to those of European
Courts, or even royal in the strict sense of the word, neither
was his residence to be compared with Buckingham Palace; but,
nevertheless, he was a king, and I visited him. Nay, more, I
pointed out to his Majesty that his clock was wrong, and put
it right and wound it up for him. This pleased him so much
that he wanted to create me a Knight of the Order of the
Cocoanut on the spot; but I explained that our Queen always
liked her subjects to consult her before they accepted any distinguished foreign orders, so he allowed me to decline the
honour. He is a nice, quiet old man, and the clock that I
manipulated was a gorgeous piece of furniture; it was of
American make, and would, I should imagine, cost at least a
dollar! But then, Royalty spares no expense.

The same as in Canada with the Indians, any one selling or
giving alcoholic liquors to the natives is fined or imprisoned,
and any native found drunk or drinking is punished severely.
The reason for this is that, when they reach a certain stage

royal, method.   My American friend and I went one day to see it made.   The 'distillery' was a very large hut in the woods, and the working staff consisted of about five-and-twenty natives; but an admiring crowd had followed us to the place, so that there was quite an audience.   The operation consists of grind-

THE SPIRIT OF THEIR FOREFATHERS RISES

ing the root of the *kava* between stones, then putting it into a

English said the cause of the excitement was that they all declared I made it as though I had always been in the business.

We tasted it—oh, yes! we tasted it; and then, to show the generosity of the white man, we distributed the remainder amongst the crowd. They liked it: we were very glad they did. Reader, would you like to taste this native drink? If so, boil a cabbage, when it gets cold squeeze all the moisture out of it that you can, flavour with soft-soap, and drink it— you then get a very fair idea of what *kava* is like. But the royal method of making it is different, and this is only adopted by persons of high degree, and when they wish to pay more than ordinary honour to some distinguished personage. It is made by young girls of from twelve to twenty years of age, having very good teeth; and the operation is very simple, for these girls simply chew the root and spit it into a bowl, instead of crushing it between stones! Several individuals, including my friend King Malietoa, were most anxious to extend this high honour to us; but we explained that we were modest in nature, and, although we might be princes in our own country, we were travelling strictly *incognito*, and that, while we appreciated the proffered honour at its very highest, we begged to be allowed to decline it. The guide who took us all over the island to see the different sights was about the most perfectly modelled young fellow I have ever seen; and although he was but fourteen years old, he stood just over six feet high. He gave me three sittings for my kodak, and this honour nearly made him another inch higher. The natives are very

Mother Hubbard costume, which is by no means unbecoming; but I never cared to get too close to any of them, because of the amount of cocoa-nut oil about, which they considered

necessary to enhance their beauty. Even my susceptible American friend 'guessed they would look more kissable to a Christian if they 'd hold on a bit with the oil.'

They are, taken as a whole, a harmless, simple set of people, rather more inclined to laziness than energy; but they are thorough sportsmen, and so long as they can hunt and fish just when they want to, they are perfectly happy. The

way of amusement. This pretty game is no child's play, and in this instance three of the players got clubbed a bit too much, and retired to other worlds 'where all is peace and happiness, and "clubbing" is unknown.' This little matter didn't trouble the natives, though.

We attended a native service on Sunday in Apia, and, although we couldn't understand, we were struck by the attention paid by the congregation. The ladies, dressed *à la* Mother Hubbard in Manchester prints of various and alarming colours, occupied one side; the gentlemen, dressed—well, slightly, occupied the other; while the white people were on a platform. Round the interior of the place several pictures were nailed up, such as Gladstone, Parnell, Irving, etc. One could hardly call them religious subjects; but still they were pictures. Most of them were from Christmas numbers of the *Graphic, Illustrated London News*, etc.; but one which particularly took my fancy was the large plate from the *Graphic* containing all the portraits of the members of the London County Council elected in March 1892, my own being amongst the number!

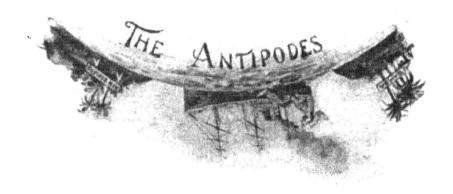

CHAPTER IX

THERE is nothing like variety to keep the mind well occupied and prevent one from getting dull; and here was another change.

The poetic and romantic Samoa, with its hundred and one attractions, had to be left; for although I would gladly have followed the example of Robert Louis Stevenson and made the islands my home, to fulfil my mission I had other climates to sample. So with a good-bye sad and sorrowful, I once more packed up my nail-brush, sponge, slippers, and other *impedimenta*, and went on board a boat bound for New Zealand. I was sorry we could not look in at the New Hebrides, as the name was so familiar to me. I remembered I had often seen my mother writing to people about these islands, and I knew

would suggest the transparency of the globe, and the possibility in such a case of my seeing the soles of the feet of my dear old friends in London. But it never got as far as that;

On this voyage the boat behaved herself very well. By the way, I wonder why a boat is called *her*. It has always struck me as being peculiar; and perhaps, as, amongst other Companies of the City of London, I am a liveryman of that Worshipful

WRITING TO PEOPLE ABOUT THESE ISLANDS

Between Samoa and New Zealand, both the wind and the sea have plenty to do to attend to their business, for they are very busy, although not boisterously so. Trade winds, etc., and currents are all about the place. I can't imagine how it is they don't get mixed up, but they don't.

The different winds about kept the air delightfully cool; and now and then, when a current would take charge of the boat, we went along at a much increased speed. One day we ran for over forty miles with a current; and then in the morning we had about four hours' very nasty rolling about, caused, as I was told, from going with a current that ran between two mountains under the sea. It would be better if those mountains were taken away; the motion of the vessel is not pleasant when in their neighbourhood. Then we crossed the meridian, and had to skip a day in the almanac, so as to make matters right on the other side, and not be a day behind. They manage all these things very well at sea: there is no arguing about it—they just do it, and there you are. The sailors don't get docked or credited a day's pay, so they don't mind a bit.

New Zealand is sighted, and before very long our anchor is dropped in Auckland harbour, and we are once more on dry land. I say 'dry land,' because I believe that is the proper phrase; but in reality the land was anything but dry—in fact, it was very wet, for it was raining very hard, and had been for some time. We were told that Auckland had more rain than any other town in Australasia; and we could almost believe it, for it was wet during by far the greater part of our stay there. And when I say wet I mean it, for the rain seems to be different from English rain. It is more like a heavy Scotch mist, and seems to come from everywhere—not in drops, as ours does; and it is pretty continual. However, we did see

Auckland is a funny place, and a typical Scotch town. After the carefully and squarely arranged towns and cities of the States it looked a little 'straggly,' but at the same time it certainly looked 'homely.' The 'fire-bell' arrangement is peculiar; these bells are all over the place, and, when a fire occurs, first one bell goes, then the other, and the engine turns out. The inhabitants also are very homely, although they look a bit rough.

Ah, if we could only get oysters in London at the same price as in Auckland! The best are 3d. per dozen, and by the sack even less than that! They lie in thousands on the north shore, and the only expense is gathering them. In hotels 6d. per dozen is charged; but even at that advanced figure one's lordly feelings arise, and oysters and stout are indulged in without giving even one thought to the expense. How different from the Whitstable native in London, which is really no better! I was exceedingly lucky one day. My friend and I had bought some oysters, and were having a jolly *al fresco* banquet; at the finish one oyster was left. Politeness forbade either of us taking it, so we 'matched' for it. We call it tossing, or, as I believe it is vulgarly called, 'Tommy Dodd,' but my Yankee friend would have it the proper term was 'matching.'

Well, I won, and the oyster was opened, and I found I was the possessor of two pearls as well, for these were in one shell. One was as big as a small pea, and, mounted for a scarf-pin, looked remarkably well. The other one, inferior in every

One day at the hotel my friend came up to me with a big curiosity; it was a Maori penny, for which he had given a shilling! Yes, yes, I must have one of those coins, and was taking note where to get one, when the barmaid said, 'Why can't you buy some of ours? We've got a whole drawerful here, and I'll let you have a dozen for a shilling if you want as many as that!' I bought my penny at the hotel.

The great wonder of New Zealand is the hot-lakes district, and we decided to go right through this and see whether the region was really as marvellous as it was described, so started off for Okoroire, the commencement of the district.

Upon reaching this place, a drive of about two or three miles brought us to the hot-springs hotel—a wooden-built house with an iron roof, and situated in the midst of a perfect wilderness, although the grounds close round have been made very attractive, and the fare provided by the landlord was very good. Rain was in full swing here, and of another different kind. No mist. It reminded me of the way sailors put the hose on to us in the mornings when we were going through the tropics; but we were determined that we would lose no time in trying the open-air hot-bath, so under the guidance of the land-lord, who had a big lantern—for it was very dark, and nearly 10 P.M.—we started, enveloped in macintoshes, for the spring and bath. When we got there—or, to be more correct, as we gradually got near—thoughts seemed to arise of what a foolish expedition it was—going to have an open-air hot-bath while it

by the aid of the lantern, we could just see a bubbling pool.
We were soon inside this, and thoroughly enjoyed it. The
temperature of the water was about 75 degrees, and the depth
a good five feet; the sand at the bottom was quite hot, and
the tingling sensation in the lower limbs as a bather sinks to
his knees in it is very strange. We got rather wet over the
head and shoulders from the rain while swimming about, but
that was rather jolly, for it seemed to act as a sort of shower-
bath. After arranging our toilet again in the 'dressing-
room,' the procession re-formed, and we returned to the hotel
feeling much refreshed, but anything but at home with the
surroundings, which seemed to be nothing but 'gurgling
darkness'!

Had to be up very early next morning, as the coach started
at eight o'clock, and, being of the 'mail' kind, was bound to
be punctual. Our destination was perhaps the headquarters of
the geyser and hot-spring arrangement, Rotorua, and Whakarewarewa, and well into Maoriland. The musical sound of
the Maori language as applied to towns and districts is all very
well, but the thing is how to pronounce the names, and remember them after they have been pronounced. We used to
bet on them as we came across a good one; but as a rule we
were both wrong, and eventually gave it up, for it was tiring
work walking round a Maori word three or four times before
you could fix it. For instance, in one of the Maori legends
there is a chief called Tamatepokaiwhenua, and a pool we
passed in our travels went by the name of Te Mimiahomai-
terangi! These come fairly easy when you 've been in training a

At some parts the mud was so bad the coach sank in up to the axles; but the horses worked with a will, and we were landed at the end at registered time. There was not much to see on the way, barring the mud and 'bush'; here and there a squatter's sheep-farm could be seen, and now and then a *whare*, or Maori's hut, as well as occasionally a Maori pig; while to me a strange item was the peculiar chattering of strange birds.

One very peculiar tree grows on the road, though. The Maoris call it the *rata*, whatever that might mean; but, 'pon my word, I don't know what I should call it unless it were a 'serpentine.' It grows up to a fairly good height, then a branch sprouting out from the top grows downward, twining round the trunk on its way, as though it wanted to see how the bark was getting on. Then when it reaches the bottom it goes into the ground to see if the original roots are all right, then turns round, and starts an upward journey once more to see how affairs are up at the top, twining round again as before, eventually swallowing up the whole of the original trunk.

My American friend, who always carried a loaded revolver, was firing at everything we came across, just to keep his hand in, as he said. Judging from the number of times he hit his mark, notwithstanding the jolting of the coach, I didn't think his hand wanted much keeping in, and should not like to have played at being the target with him. I chaffed him about carrying the thing, but he said, 'My dear Dour, I reckon if you'd travelled in some of the Southern States that I have, where you almost want an umbrella to keep off the bullets, you'd carry a revolver pretty slick!' Well, perhaps I might—

the world, seen any place where revolvers were required—with the exception perhaps of the West-end of London, which part I considered was really dangerous; but that even there I thought there were better ways of relieving oneself of the attentions of 'prowlers' than by shooting.

We arrived at the Geyser Hotel, Whakarewarewa, just in time for dinner, and quite ready for it, but also very much inclined to walk as lightly as possible, for fear our weight should break through the crust of the earth and send us to explore the hot springs at their base. The 'gurgling' was going on all around, and here and there geysers were shooting up scalding water high into the air, steam was blowing about like smoke from a prairie fire, and altogether we could but think we were treading on 'delicate ground.'

This is such a wonderful place, and visited by so many tourists, it is hardly to be wondered at that the Maoris have settled around in the quantities they have; for, like all other tribes, they prefer to get their living as easily as possible, and do not care to do more work than they are absolutely obliged. Still, they are a fine race, and it is sad to think they are dying out; but no doubt they are disappearing, slowly but surely. They are very different now from the original Maori, and the attempts at civilisation have by no means improved them. Of course, it has put a stop to cannibalism; but that is a detail. What poet is it that says something about 'first comes civilisation, then industry, then wealth, luxury, vice, and last again barbarism'? Whoever it may be, this seems to be the case with the noble Maori, and it makes one think that those who take the civilising business in hand go about it in

he do anything egregiously wrong; but, once taught to believe there is an all-forgiving Power, his natural instinct for doing wrong strongly develops, and no dependence can be placed upon him. This is their experience, and it would appear that things are very similar in Maoriland ; for, the same as all savage races when they get Christianised or civilised, they also get thoroughly demoralised by acquiring all the evil habits of the low whites, without attaining to any of the better qualities of the good ones. It is an altogether mistaken idea that putting a nigger into a pair of trousers and a tall hat makes a Christian of him.

Many instances can be quoted in any *kainga* (Maori village) of full- or half-bred Maoris who have been educated, and have lived for some time amongst white people, going back to the *whare* and living Maori lives as before—but *plus* the failings and vicious accomplishments of their recent associates. This seems hardly possible to those who have not realised it: but none the less it is than anything else; and although in days gone by they were good at carving, mat-making, and many useful occupations such as these, about the only thing they really do now is to plant and cultivate potatoes—their staple article of food. Occasionally, when the Government buys up some of their land, the money is divided equally throughout the tribe; and then, until this is exhausted, better living than potatoes is resorted to—in fact, to use a common expression, the whole lot have a 'high old time.' They just start in and spend the money in a most reckless manner; nothing is really good enough for them; and, like thorough sportsmen, they are always ready to try some other experiment whereby they may either win or lose more money.

SOPHIA

Everybody who has been to Whakarewarewa during the last —well, number of years, knows of Sophia, the Maori lady-guide, who takes the money at the entrance to the large area of geysers, and shows you round, explaining how hot this is, how high this water shoots up, etc. etc. Sophia is a very shrewd, intelligent, and interesting individual; she has very good

I would often leave the hotel, and go and sit by her *whare*
and discuss Maori subjects over a smoke. The lady generally
used to smoke a pipe, but she would always discard this for
a cigarette. The real way to win a Maori's heart is through
a packet of cigarettes.

Once I touched upon politics, and then Sophia waxed very
eloquent. 'White man no *capi* (good) coming and take land
for beads, tobacco, rum, knives, pistols from Maori. Now you
boss what Maori should boss—Maori outcast, slave!'

'But,' I said, 'Maoris all right; you do better now than
before.'

'Yes, but Maoris dress now; white man clothes get wet,
got no change to put on, get damp, catch cold and die, else
undress and sit in hot spring till clothes dry! Maori now
get sugar, tea, beer, rum, and all that, and not want Maoris'
right food. No, no; white man no *capi*. Maoris better never
saw white man. Maoris not be alive soon!' I am bound to
say that in a measure I was obliged to acquiesce, inwardly,
with a lot that Sophia had said. She has one great grievance,
and I think a just one; and that is, she did not get a medal
for all the work she did during the night of the great
eruption.

In a way this lady rules over the whole lot of Maoris in this
district, and she is a person of great importance, living almost
in luxury. Her *whare* is the aristocratic meeting-place, and
at times a kind of levee is held there, and cards are indulged
in. The stakes played for are not enormous: matches are
very popular, but cigarettes are looked upon as very 'swagger'
play. The *élite* of the tribe occasionally play for real money,
Sophia attending to the financial business and keeping accounts.

MAORIS CARD-PLAYING

selected for conversation. I was sorry for this, as I wanted to hear from her whether it were really true that when the Maoris first began to dress, when the rain came on they would take off their clothes, fold them up, and sit upon them until the rain had finished, to keep them dry; but, expecting such a query would in all probability raise the lady's ire once more, I refrained.

Another story I wanted verified, but which I thought it advisable to 'ease off' on, also related to the earlier days of the noble Maori and some of his manners and customs. I had heard that among their other national games and sports an entertainment called 'clubbing' was very popular, and frequently indulged in. It was a somewhat rough game, and at its conclusion many corpses strewed the ground; but what did that matter? The natives were very fond of it, and saw no harm in it; but for all that the authorities determined to put a stop to it and make an example of the chief 'clubbist.' The tribes were summoned, and the chief secured; then in a harangue of the best Maori language at their command the authorities explained to the multitude what they were going to do, and why; then, dressing the victim in white, they concluded the proceedings by hanging him on the branch of a tree. Long, silently, and gravely the assembled Maoris looked on, then quietly and thoughtfully departed to their own quarters. A week's quiet assured the white men of the success of their experiment, and they were pleased; but in the midst of their congratulations came a rude awakening. Seeing and hearing signs of

One day I persuaded Sophia to have her photograph taken with me, as I wished to patronise the local photographer. Being a bit of an amateur photographer, when we had been finished I went into the gentleman's dark room to see him develop the negative, and while there experienced a new fri—, no, sensation. Just as he was beginning operations, the wooden floor, which was about a foot from the ground, seemed to get rather unsteady, and there was a very ominous bump, bump, bump, directly underneath, that was the reverse of pleasant or reassuring. The photographer explained matters.

'That's only a small geyser beginning to work,' said he. 'I have three below here that work at regular intervals—the one just starting, another one there'—pointing to a corner—'and the other one just underneath where you are standing.'

Geysers!—starting! I could see it better outside, so outside I went.

I don't quite remember now whether I opened the door, or whether it opened of its own accord, or whether it fell down; but I know in my anxiety to see the marvellous sight I didn't take long in getting out of that dark room. The photographer went on with his work coolly and calmly, and let the baby geyser bubble and gurgle under his floor just in its own sweet way, whilst I, watching it from a position of advantage, expected every minute to see the 'dark apartment' lifted high into the air on the summit of a boiling column. But no; the building stood firm, the photographer developed the plate, and the infantile geyser gurgled and fizzed itself out. Of course, being an F.R.G.S., I ought to know everything about these things; but, somehow or other, I

by various tribes with the sole purpose of getting plenty of dead men in order to celebrate a birthday or some such important anniversary. I don't wish to impugn the veracity of these gentlemen; but while they were talking, the wonderful tales that had often been told to me by sailors came to my mind

I WAS INTRODUCED TO TWO OLD MAORI GENTLEMEN

more than once. They said, however, that they had never cared to eat white men; as they eat salt, and such a lot of

but after being 'down below' for a couple of years or so the corpse is dug up again, and all the bones, after being well

Sydney Cowell

OLD BONE-SCRAPER

having forsworn such habits, if the scraping were a first operation, I am sadly afraid that, being in the midst of it so much,
the temptation to have a chop or steak as in the days of yore
would be a little too strong for the old gentleman. I hinted
at this to Sophia, but she wouldn't say anything about it.
Civilisation has even extended so far as to the scraping performance, for the old man is armed with a large and most un-
mistakable Sheffield knife! This he is always ready to lay
aside for a time, and 'rest from his labours,' when he sees
there is a chance of a chat, with a cigarette or two thrown in.
He is not nearly the dull or morose individual one would
imagine his occupation would cause him to be; but, on the
contrary, he is an agreeable, chatty old fellow.

The Maori ladies find that ' to err is human,' and, as others
of their sex in different countries, they occasionally show their
humanity. It is a serious matter, though, for the family and
relations of a wife who becomes untrue; for the husband
and his friends take all the father's cattle, and in addition to this her brothers, cousins, etc. etc., have to give up
something by way of compensation. After this the whole
tribe hold humiliation meetings over the delinquent, and
then, as a rule, she is received back by her husband. Before I left this quarter I witnessed one of these meetings,
and a more gloomy, dismal affair I cannot imagine. The
wailing and doleful chanting over the unfaithful wife were most
miserable.

This idea does not seem at all a bad one, although perhaps
it would hardly work in such a crowded place as London.
It would be a remarkable sight to see, after the delivery of a
verdict in a ' society ' case in our court, a grand stampede of

in Hyde Park (if it were large enough), and await the result there.

Using her influence amongst the Maoris, Sophia got up a *haka-haka*, or native dance, for our benefit. This resembles the Moorish and Egyptian dances, and is very similar to the *hula-hula* of Honolulu, or the *meke-meke* of Fiji, etc. Twenty women and twenty men took part in this performance, and kept it up most vigorously for over two hours, only stopping occasionally for cigarettes and beer. They did not have much beer, though, although some of their number were told off to superintend the drawing of what they did have; for they had found out that landlords had a trick of drawing *some* beer, and filling the gallon measure up from 'the cow with the iron tail'! Excisemen were not plentiful, so this didn't matter.

But to the dance. All engaged worked very hard, but the chief performer put them all in the shade by his exertions. His bloodvessels must have been tin-lined, otherwise I am sure they would have burst. He began the business with a weird and dismal kind of chant, which was afterwards taken up by the native orchestra, and eventually the forty performers commenced their part, which consisted of yelling and shrieking at the top of their voices, and putting themselves into almost indescribable positions. As the dance proceeds, both men and women work themselves up into a perfect frenzy of excitement,

whole thing stops dead, and the performers squat tailor-fashion all over the place, and indulge in a smoke or a chew. Before leaving this chapter I must really mention the proprietor of the Geyser Hotel, for he was the most extraordinary philosopher I ever met. The son of a Swedish professor, he ran away to sea when a boy, and went through a whole heap of experiences in every corner of the globe, until now, at over sixty years of age, he 'bosses' the Geyser. He is a perfect master of fifteen languages, and his occupation previous to hotel proprietorship was that of interpreter and land-purchase agent to the New Zealand Government. He is looked up to as an authority on all Maori

PROPRIETOR OF THE GEYSER HOTEL

matters; and as he has lived amongst them, and almost as one of themselves for fifteen years, his experience is un-

pelago, landed at Java and other islands; then, going through the Torres Straits, they got into the Pacific, and amongst the islands there—for, as he points out, they are of the Polynesian race (Shemites). There seems to be a lot in his theory; but, as is known, recognised authorities contradict it, and, as he himself points out, the strange part is how they came to miss Australia. However, this is almost too deep a subject for me to go into here.

CHAPTER X

Digging a Bath—'Here is Hades'—Early Rising—Across Country in a Coach—A 'Spill'—'Tipping' Proprietors—Sights around Taupo—Tarawera—The Landlord's Niece—Shattered Hopes—Dairy Work —Poetry—Magnificent Scenery—Maori Socialism—Return to Civilisation—Napier—Luxuriant Grazing-land—My Friend in Love again—Wellington—Humane New Zealand Little Boys.

THERE does not seem much doubt about the fact that sooner or later the land all round the Geyser Hotel will subside and make a big extension of the lake close to. According to all accounts, there is already one village at the bottom of this lake; and I am really not at all surprised at it, for the earth seems to be simply a kind of thin and dilapidated lid made of hot cinders and lava, partially covering a huge caldron of boiling water, and through the worn-away parts of which the scalding water and steam are continually escaping. While we were at the hotel, the proprietor thought he would try and get

little time, sending up water which was far too hot to touch. My Yankee friend very irreverently suggested to the landlord that he should hang some beef and potatoes down the hole, and get them cooked on the cheap. Some people really seem to have no soul.

Now, I don't wish to be thought conceited, but when I found that scalding water was spouting through the kitchen floor, my thoughts tended more towards the wonderful formation of the earth, and I contemplated how terrible were the dangers with which every human being is surrounded. In London, one might get knocked down by a hansom; in a train, one might get pulped into an unrecognisable mass through a collision; on board a vessel, one might suddenly descend to the depths of the ocean through too close contact of the vessel with a snag of rock; and here, in New Zealand, one might find himself, or herself, suddenly squirted from below by a stream of scalding water!

It needs a Dante to at all adequately describe this hot-spring district; for, setting apart the wonderful sights on every side, of steam and hot water bubbling up a few inches from the earth or shooting high into the air, or the little lakes and fountains of mud, there is that weird and haunting bubbling and gurgling which cannot be seen, and a rumbling as well, which would almost convince one there was a thunderstorm going on deep down in the bowels of the earth. The whole business is so different from anything that is seen in other parts;

Rotorua and Whakarewarewa, we took coach again and set out for Taupo. This is a drive of about sixty miles through

A GENTLEMAN IN RED

uncultivated land, little else but wild ferns and bush, with, of

There is one thing I must say about New Zealanders, and that is, they do get up early in the morning. Why, these coaches leave at seven o'clock in the morning as a rule! Considering what has to be done in the morning, one way or another, it seems hardly worth while going to bed at all to get up so early; but then the weather is nice first thing in the morning, provided always—as lawyers say—that Jupiter Pluvius locks the hose up and doesn't let any of his assistants play at squirting the people down below.

At parts, during this drive, the scenery was very like the Highlands of Scotland. Larks, hawks, and other birds were flying about, and now and then we saw herds of wild horses, wild cattle, and also wild pigs; but it must not be thought that these are really naturally wild, for that is hardly the case. Horses and cattle often escape from stations, and, roaming about, come across a herd of their kin, join lots, and so become wild and uncivilised. Then, again, mares in foal often get away; and there are many instances on record of their being caught some years after their escape, but then being blessed with a family.

About the only part showing signs of human life between Rotorua and Taupo is a place called Ateamuri, and here we stayed for lunch. The house of call was not a bad one, and the owner was very jolly indeed. Referring to what I said a little while back about cattle straying, he told us that, some time before, a bull of his strayed from his paddock (paddocks vary from one to several thousand acres) and four months

took us clean across country for about a dozen miles at a gallop! It seemed more like fifty miles from what we could think between the times of holding on and saying our prayers. Conversation wasn't very brisk during that bit of the ride. Now and then one or other of us would summon up courage enough to yell at him to stop, but he only answered the yell with a 'Whoop!' that made the horses put on an additional spurt. I verily believe that if my Yankee friend hadn't wanted both his hands to hold on by, one would have gone in search of his 'six-shooter,' and then the genial driver would suddenly have felt a pain somewhere. However, at last he pulled up, with his good-temper restored, and said, as he thought he had given us a good doing and shown us what his horses *could* do, he hoped we were satisfied. Satisfied! We'd be anything, so as to be on a fairly decent road again, and know that our Jehu was really sane.

The road that we got on to was not quite like an English highway, though, as I soon found out. It was a downhill part with plenty of mud and boulders about, and the way was not smooth. During an extra lurch I parted company with the coach rather suddenly; in fact, I was hardly aware of it until I found myself in the mud. This was great amusement to the driver and *other* passenger; in fact, the latter laughed so, he nearly came off as well. As it was, I only strained my wrist a little, beyond leaving a pretty good 'mould' of my figure in the mud. After these two experiences we not only made a point of advising others always to be polite to their drivers, but we never lost an opportunity of impressing upon drivers the ridiculousness of being reckless, and the importance of the people's lives who might entrust themselves to their care. When I had been cleaned down a little, and taken my seat again, I took the ribbons, and drove up hill and down dale for

stayed at was a very good one, carried on by a limited company consisting of three people, all of whom worked hard in their different departments, one being waiter, the other boots, and the third coachdriver, while all three were Scotchmen. It was not until just before we were leaving that we discovered that we had been giving 'tips' to the proprietors!

The population here is not very extensive; but what is missing in numbers is made up by loyalty, for this is most openly demonstrated, and pictures of the Queen and

I PARTED COMPANY WITH THE COACH

he could hang it out somewhere; but this was an article not kept by any one. There are many little excursions to be made from Taupo; and it is a pity that the majority of tourists only stop at the place one day, for a week can be put in very easily.

The trip to Alum Cave is a peculiar one: driving part of the way, riding part of the way, a bit of boating thrown in, and lastly a walk up a gentle slope—like the side of a house that had been knocked about a bit by a gas explosion, and had got the washing-day steam fizzing out of the cracks. It was actually fine when we got there, and the sun, shining right into the cave, lighted it up beautifully. The opening is about thirty feet wide and high; and just through this is another slope, but this descending, and at an angle of about forty-five degrees for nearly fifty yards. Then comes a very nice, clear pool. On the way down are some very fine tree-ferns, which lend a singular and beautiful aspect to the scene, especially when taken with the delightful colours of the roof. Large blocks of rock are strewn all over the floor, and these are coated with a very fine deposit of alum, almost marvellous in its whiteness. This is all very beautiful and very nice to look upon; but, at the same time, one cannot get rid of the 'inferno' idea, for by the pool is a large cavity in the rock, and from this the most unearthly noises, rumblings, bumps, and thuds proceed, as well as a stifling heat, flavoured with sulphur, though all the time nothing can be seen.

Within a few miles of this region is a whole forest of geysers and hot springs, but it is not considered safe to get too much amongst them. From here a good view is obtained of those enormous volcanoes, Ruapehu and Tongariro, the latter of which still emits large clouds of steam and smoke. Then

flighty geyser, or dislocating our jaws in trying to pronounce the names of the various places we visited, we got on the move again, and took the coach to Tarawera.

The road was very much similar to the ones we had already been doing, rather different from the Row or Piccadilly; but we were very careful this time not to keep the coachman waiting, or to make remarks other than complimentary upon his teams, while, as an extra precaution, I again 'took the ribbons.' There was a *whare* to be seen here and there, and now and then a herd of horses on the loose; they had gigantic manes, but still more prolific tails, and they added a life to the wild scenery which made it still more attractive. Getting to Tarawera in the evening, we found it a very nice little place in a valley; and the sight of the mountains on the side from which we had to get out made us think it would be almost a week's journey to get to the top, but we dared not speculate on what was to happen going down on the other side. The Tarawera Hotel was our stopping-place, and our first business a swim. After nearly seventy miles' driving, this was very refreshing, and we were then both of us ready to show the landlord what an American and a Scotchman could do in the way of eating.

Ah, me! That stay at the Tarawera Hotel nearly altered the whole course of my future existence. My friend said the same about himself; and I am sure, had it not been for a little incident, I should have had to buy a revolver, practise shooting, and then play at making targets of each other with him! There would have been no help for it! That landlord had a niece, and she was really a lovely girl. Never before had I

my hand, my heart, my luggage, and myself at the feet of my fair enchantress, and ask her to be mine.

I went out, and, going to the part of the hotel where I thought she would be, I suddenly came upon her—kissing our coachman! I coughed demurely, but they both burst out laughing, then told me they were sweethearts, and were going to be married very shortly! Alas, for the hopes of man!

With my one great (though sudden) thought of happiness so rudely dashed to the ground, I returned once more to my adamantine shell, and the dining-room. With a liveliness born of despair, I chaffed my friend upon his susceptibility, and worked him up to such a frenzy of excitement that, avowing his determination then and there to risk his future, he left

THE LANDLORD'S NIECE

a fervent 'hand-shake' we buried our sorrow and—had a smoke.

Next day, in order not to be too near the house and temptation, we took a wonderful interest in gardening, and while our coachman 'spooned' we assisted the landlord in planting potatoes and doing dairy work. Having learned to milk cows in my juvenile days, I was soon busy, and going at it like a veteran.

KISSING THE COACHMAN

'Say, Dour, that looks easy,' said my friend. 'Guess I'll have a try.' 'Do,' I said, and put him on to a cow whose tail I had observed twitching rather uneasily.

He started, and in a second, pail, stool, and Yank were all flying in different directions, and a sound as of language filled the air. It is wonderful how the misfortunes of some administer to the pleasure and welfare of others. My woe was all forgotten, and I felt that there was something to laugh at in life after all. My friend re-

little island would have been burnt down!' And then he
retired.

We had made a point of always putting poetry in the

PAIL, STOOL, AND YANK WERE FLYING IN ALL DIRECTIONS

so before leaving here we composed and inserted the following :—

> ' Tarawera hotel is all very well,
> If you don't milk cows or fall in love,
> Do either of these, and then, if you please,
> You 'll come off your perch with a shove.'

The lines seem simple, but to the initiated there is a great amount of pathos in them.

Leaving the place that had nearly turned the tide of our existence, we entered upon the last stage of our coach-drive, and started at eight o'clock in the morning for Napier, the capital of Hawkes Bay.

A strange change seemed to have come over our coachman, and, instead of his fidgeting about as usual a quarter of an hour or more before the time we had settled to start, we had to worry him up. I believe he would like to have stayed there another day. When we did get away, we found very soon that we were fixed for the grandest scenery on the whole route, and my friend afterwards admitted that it beat anything that he had ever seen. This from an American means a lot, for it takes a great deal to move one of our transatlantic cousins to admit there are finer sights outside the land of Stars and Stripes than there are within it.

None the less, he was quite right; and although when we started we commenced to while away the time by playing

is made. The highest point is 3000 feet above the sea-level, and here we found that the beauty of the scene reached a climax, for we could turn and review the whole. And a magnificent panorama it was.

Away in the distance was the village of Tarawera that we had left in the morning, looking little larger than an ordinary white speck; and now and again parts of a white line, looking like a huge serpent twisting itself through the fern, showed us the road up which we had climbed. Blue-peaked mountains, backed by a bright purple sky, seemed to extend for miles and miles; cliffs and glens gave charm to the scene; shaded valleys surrounded by verdure-clad hills; and the majestic native trees added to it, the indescribably beautiful ferns which were to be seen on every side studding hill and dale, and the soft, delicate-hued haze which seemed to form the vanishing point for the whole, made up a picture of unrivalled and enchanting beauty—a picture that must be seen to be realised—a picture that, for majesty and magnificence, nature alone can produce.

By the way, it was about here that I found Socialism had entered even into Maori life, for we heard one of the tribe 'going for' a chief, and saying: 'I do not care for you. We are all equal. I am the same as you. I got hair, fingers, feet the same. You look no different; and if people not say, no one know you are a chief!' Here was insubordination! The maligned chief arose in all the majesty of offended dignity, and stalked away, saying: 'I treat you as mud on my feet, you are not better!'

doing well. Some very large hawks, almost like ravens, were
hovering about; and our driver told us they were very destruc-
tive amongst the lambs. They fly down and kill them, but
only eat the fat from around the heart.

All this part out of the volcanic belt is being cultivated now
fairly rapidly; the ferns are cut down and grass-seed sown,
and the sheep being turned on to it trample the seed well in.
While going up and down these almost precipices, we remarked
to our driver what a pity it was such good land wasn't on the
flat. He said it was; but if we looked at the survey-map
where this was marked out for sale, we should see it described
as 'slightly undulating ground'! If a gradient of about one
in two is slightly undulating, the description is perfectly
correct.

On the last stage of our journey we got thoroughly into
cultivated parts, and seemed to be almost suddenly shot into
a world of luxuriant crops. Fields of corn and hay were all
around; sheep stations, looking like young mansions, after
what we had been used to for some time, were dotted about;
but the greatest sign of return to civilisation was a school that
we passed just at 'coming out' time. Fine specimens of
young New Zealanders these youngsters were. Strong, healthy-
looking lads and girls, freckled and bronzed by being so much
in the sun and fresh air, and with a free and happy look
upon their faces that was quite enjoyable to see. There were
a dozen or more ponies about the school door, and these we
were told belonged to those who came from a distance, some

in the evening we drove into Napier, and ended one of the most interesting coach-drives it has ever been or will be my lot to experience.

It took us some little time, after getting into civilised

A VERY SMART DOGCART

Napier, was something we could not all at once understand. It is a quiet, peaceful town, with a natural sea-frontage of about four miles; and the people claim that the bay there is second only to Naples. It is one of the principal ports of North Island; but really everything was so quiet, I couldn't help likening it to London on a Sunday, or say about three or four A.M. when returning from a dance, etc., which are about the only times in the London streets one can hear the chirp of the cheeky Cockney sparrow, or the ponderous footfall of Robert on his beat.

We naturally went to see the works where mutton is frozen for transit to England and elsewhere. This freezing process was a perfect godsend to, if not the salvation of, New Zealand; and the stations are now having far better times than previously. In fact, as farming generally goes, I soon made up my mind that New Zealand was the place of the future. I am not a farmer; but at the same time, if I were, I really think I should give up engagements, etc., in this country, and make a start in New Zealand, where the climate and everything seems to be so much more in favour of prosperity than here. Now, we made up our minds to go to Wellington, and do this journey by rail. We nearly lost the train, for my friend was late; but just through this fact we had a rare good example of New Zealand courtesy and good-nature, for the station-master actually kept the train back for him when I explained, 'Very sorry, wanted to go, etc. etc.—friend saying good-bye to sweetheart,' and all that sort of thing. Good Mr. Station-master, thank you for your kindness! But, all the same, I believe you were in love, and that it was that sweetheart tale that fetched you.

cultivation. Land was selling at from £30 to £40 per acre in some districts, and at this price yields sufficient to pay well. Round about Hawkes Bay district hundreds and hundreds of acres of grass are seen, almost burying the fine large sheep for whose benefit it is grown, and who simply eat just as much as they like without having to move a yard unless they wish it.

'Say, Dour,' said my friend, 'I guess some of our Californian sheep 'ud like to be over here. Those poor beggars have to go into training if they want to walk far enough to get a decent feed!'

I always live on the product of the country I am in, and I must praise the mutton I had, for it was certainly the finest I ever tasted; and yet they say, as we say in Scotland about the salmon, that all the best goes to London.

A New Zealander can form no idea of what London can be like; to him it is the mainspring and heart of the world, the place where everything goes to and everything comes from, and that is about as far as he can go. There being no cable from the Pacific side of Canada or the States, all telegrams from these countries have to go to Australia and New Zealand *viâ* London; and this increases the importance of the metropolis most wonderfully in the minds of the people in those territories. We got to Wellington about 11 P.M.; and as it was then too late to do anything, we went to bed.

Next day—alas! alas! that I should have to say it!—my susceptible friend, forgetting all about his experience in Tarawera, was in love again. He was in love twice, and the second day we were there he had three divinities amongst whom to divide

Houses of Parliament and Government House seem to be the only places of any interest, though the harbour is very good. The town is said to be the society centre, but I presume this is owing to its being the capital. However, it is growing rapidly in importance, and now-adays many steamers leave the harbour direct for England, *viâ* Rio de Janeiro; in fact, a great part of the frozen meat goes this way.

One morning, while rambling about outside the town enjoying the beautiful air, which reminded me so much of an English summer's day, I saw some boys with a bird-nest, and my heart went out to them at once.

SOME BOYS WITH A BIRD'S-NEST

Then the little chorus began about the eggs being quite cold, and the mother having deserted the nest before they took it; how much they liked thrushes, and how they wouldn't for worlds take a thrush's nest, unless forsaken, etc. These boys puzzled me; they were rather more humane than boys were when I was a boy, and I rather liked them for it. I certainly never took a nest with the mother in it, because she always flew away when I got up to it; but these boys, carefully waiting to see whether she would come back—well, it was new to me. Not for long, however; for later in the day, when I was mentioning the matter to some one, I was informed that, as thrushes had only been introduced into the district during recent years, it was a crime to kill them or rob their nests, and that every such offence found out was rewarded with ten days' imprisonment. Then I saw through the professed humanity of the little boys.

CHAPTER XI

An Antidote to Love-making—'Juicy' Fresh Air—Pulpy Baggage—
Christchurch—A Dinner-party and Result—Dunedin—The 'Whisky
Steeple'—A 'Washing Name'—Stewart Island Oysters—'Dirty'
Weather—Professionals—Hobart and the Olden Days—Hobart in
the Present Day—Off to Melbourne.

BEGINNING to feel nervous lest my friend should so far forget
himself as to propose to one of his charmers, I made arrangements for leaving; and, having heard that a sea-blow was a
really good antidote to love-making, I persuaded him to tear
himself away and leave by boat for Lyttleton, in South Island,
and the port for Christchurch, where I had some friends. The
parting was rather affecting, but it was soon over, and on a
lovely evening we steamed away and left Wellington behind.
We soon 'turned in,' and found that the steward had carefully
fastened our porthole, so that we didn't get the fresh air we

like, for a wave came right through the porthole and landed in the lower berth, which was mine. A second dose of sea-water brought me to my senses, and I struggled to close up the hole, but was met by a third sea which nearly floored me. I can't be exactly sure of the amount of pressure to the square inch, but the effect seemed to me to be about the same as though a dozen or two fire-engine hoses had joined into one and delivered themselves in one big squirt. The idea can be arrived at by trying to imagine a good-sized wave coming

THE PARTING WAS AFFECTING

swish through a hole as big as a soup-plate, and concentrating all its energy in the reduced volume. I believe this is ex-pressed somewhat nautically but am not quite sure. Soon

and small luggage were holding a gay regatta on it.   A pretty
state of things, seeing all one's belongings turned into a nice
pulp !   It was rather an upsetting piece of business, and spoilt
our night's rest; but by the time we reached Lyttleton in the
morning we were able to laugh at the whole business, although
it was aggravating on opening portmanteaus to find gloves,
ties, and other things that had been carefully stored away in

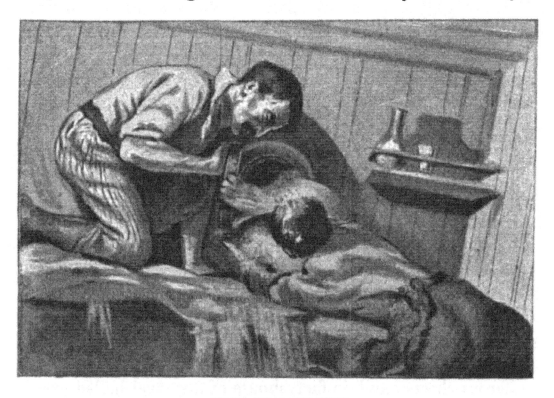

FRESH AIR A BIT JUICY

England for use in Australia all one mass of pulp, and showing

of the Thames district at home, about Maidenhead or Goring; for there was a very pretty river running through it, with some remarkably good weeping-willows growing on the banks. This tree was imported from England, and has turned out most successfully, for the climate suits it wonderfully, and it really grows far more luxuriantly than in England. I soon felt thoroughly at home in Christchurch, and my friends were quite determined that I should have a rollicking time, for I seemed to be going somewhere or other every minute of the day—or night, even to shooting black swans at most unearthly hours in the morning. Ah, that shooting business was all very well when it was once started, but the preliminaries—such as 'turning out' in the very early morning, etc.—were anything but pleasant. Still, when you were at it, it was really downright good sport; and I can now almost hear the splash as the birds came down into the water after they had been hit.

To wind up everything I gave a dinner-party, and I really thought this was never coming to an end. Everybody had a toast to propose, not only connected with those present, but of whatever they could think. Loyal and patriotic toasts were uproariously received; frozen mutton was greeted with vociferous cheers , and, in fact, shouts of approval hailed everything. Early in the morning this jovial party broke up, but the last was not heard of it. I had one or two pressmen amongst the party, and the morning papers contained a long account of the whole proceedings, embellished with many flowery additions.

This was too much for the teetotal faddists of the place, and

he besought the young ladies of the place never to think of marrying any but total abstainers, and strenuously exhorted every one to join him and his brethren in their work of trying to 'sweep away the mischief caused by those who sold whisky.'

Gentle, kind-hearted man, to trouble himself so much on my behalf! I didn't want to marry anybody, and yet this tender-hearted Christian gentleman warned all the young ladies against me! He hammered at me and all whisky-sellers during the whole of the address, and yet he said he was addressing the crowd on 'Mind your own business'! This sort of thing may be showing a Christian spirit, but to me it seemed remarkably like either boycotting or intimidation. Whichever it may be, it was certainly rather hard on a timid young bachelor like myself to be howled at in such a manner, especially as some day I may alter my views on bachelorism.

Well, festivities couldn't last for ever, and we had to 'make tracks' at last, this time shaping our course for Dunedin. Arrived there, I at once began to exclaim that my foot was on my native heath, for the place is thorough, downright Scotch, even down to the number of kirks about. The spire of one of the kirks reminded me very strongly of that of one of the

HE HAMMERED AT ME

much like being in the land of my birth that I didn't stay very long. In fact, it is said the place is so very Scotch, the Chinese laundrymen won't leave the washing unless the owner has a 'Mac' before his name, so that every one who uses a Chinese laundry has a 'washing name'—Mac-So-and-So.

However, it is the most important city in New Zealand, and has been going well ahead ever since it was founded by some members of the Free Church of Scotland in 1848. The population is not enormous yet, but it is steadily increasing; and the place possesses several good schools, as well as public buildings, etc.

Here came my first 'indisposition' since leaving home, for my friend and I both caught hay-fever, influenza, or something of the kind, and had to 'lay up' for a few days. It was very touching, the way in which we endeavoured to nurse each other; but it was really owing to the good treatment we received from the proprietor of the Grand Hotel, where we were staying, that we pulled through so quickly. He was a rare good fellow, and we were sorry, when the time arrived, that we had to leave him.

Not far from Dunedin is a place called the Bluff, and thither we repaired in order to take a boat for Tasmania.

Amongst other things, when we arrived here, we went a tour to try some of the famous Stewart Island oysters. These were really excellent, and after we had sampled a dozen we 'matched' for nine dozen to take on board. Proudly, carefully, and expectantly did we carry our purchase on board; and soon after we put to sea we started on our feast. Oyster No. 1 had not a very appetising look, so it went overboard. No. 2 having a decided tortoise-shell appearance, speedily went to look after No. 1: while the scent from No. 3 as the shell was being opened

done,' said he, 'like a lot more people before you. Those thieves keep two sacks of oysters. You would taste some out of the good sack; then, when it came to buying any for fetching away, you would get the "wrongers."' Acting upon the captain's advice, we did not waste more time, but dropped the whole lot overboard. We had been done—there was no mistake about it; and it was lucky we only paid 3d. per dozen for them. However, it was consoling to know we were not the only folks who had been 'sold' so. The captain told us he had fifteen dozen once, and there wasn't a single good one amongst the lot!

We settled down for this voyage to Hobart, and expected a good trip, for we had on board a concert company, a nigger troupe, and a theatrical company; so we were right as far as entertainments went. It was beautifully fine when we started, but before evening things began to look a bit 'dirty' —that, I believe, is the correct nautical expression—and before morning things began to look extremely 'dirty.' About an hour after we had gone to our cabin— we were careful to keep the porthole

THE CAPTAIN GREETED US WITH
A MIGHTY ROAR

closed this time—we heard the wind whistling through everything on deck, and howling round the vessel; then the rain came down in torrents: and, what with the thunder and

our state-room, so continually and rapidly did they all keep changing places. There was not much sleep about with all these noises; especially, the tremendous 'swish' of the waves as they dashed over the deck didn't exactly make one feel drowsy, although being 'rocked in the cradle of the deep.' About 2 A.M. a tremendous sea struck the bow of the boat with a thundering noise that almost deafened us; there was a terrific crash of glass, a terrible rush of water down the stairs, and for a moment the ship seemed perfectly still. 'Dour,' said my friend, 'guess this means foundering!' Those were just my thoughts, and I imagined I had finished my mission of sampling climates on this side the Styx; but we were not in doubt long, for we were rolling about and pitching and tossing in no time, and during one good lurch we saw daylight through the glass of our porthole. Once through stress of weather I was in the Bay of Biscay for two days longer than was usual, but even that storm fell short of this one. It was two days before things cooled down sufficiently to allow of the deck being made a promenade again, but at the end of that time we began making appearances by detachments. There was a lot of talk about, for everybody seemed anxious to relate his or her feelings during the storm. The women said that when not ill they were at their devotions.

The captain, of course, like all skippers, said, 'Oh, that was only a squall; you should be in a gale if you want to see what weather is!' The majority thought that, having experienced a 'squall,' they would prefer leaving the gale alone.

Squall or not, the vessel had been very much knocked about;

like hoar-frost.   This was caused by the heat of the iron con-
densing the salt as the waves dashed over it.

The remainder of the voyage was very good, and the time
passed most pleasantly.   Deck-quoits and all manner of games
went on during the day ; and in the evening we would turn on
some of the professional talent which abounded on board, and
have concerts and other entertainments.   Of course, it goes
without saying that flirting was also indulged in.   In fact, this
was a very important item in both the day and evening pro-
grammes.   My poor friend was again hopelessly gone, but this

ANXIOUS TO RELATE HIS FEELINGS

time he found he had to ' play careful,' for the young lady got
very spoony as well.

We arrived at Hobart about 7.30 in the morning, and very
nice it looked in the early morning sun. Far different from what
it looked some fifty or sixty years ago, when it was almost the
headquarters of our convict system.   It is forty years now
since transportation to the island was abolished, and since then

quarie Harbour, which some sixty years ago was far more appropriately called 'Hell Gates'—not only because of the bad entrance to the harbour, but of the fearful atrocities committed there, both by the convicts themselves and, I am afraid, in only too many cases by those placed in authority over them. Suicides of most appalling character took place here, and death was freely courted except by those hardened ruffians whose death would have been a blessing to the community.   Escape, although almost impossible, was attempted time and again, with the nearly certain fate of starvation or recapture taking place ere long, because of the 'hell' of the surroundings. Men have been known to escape in parties of small numbers, and evade recapture for some weeks, and then one, or perhaps two, to give themselves up half dead and half crazy, with the tale that the others were dead. True enough, they were dead; but it was their very death which had enabled the others to keep out so long.

PROFESSIONAL TALENT

Some few miles out of Hobart Harbour a place is pointed out where an escaped convict was discovered after being away several weeks. He escaped with three others, and when found here, dying, had by his side the remains

now only signs of industry, prosperity, and happiness. Mining and agriculture are the principal industries, especially mining; and gold, silver, copper, tin, and coal are found in great quantities. Fruit-growing is also much upon the increase, and is being developed very largely. One orchard we saw covered an area of nearly fifteen acres; it was laid out some few years ago by three Germans, and their enterprise has now been rewarded by a grand show of magnificent fruit-trees and a good income.

FLIRTING ON DECK

There is a very large and fine park in Hobart, and the harbour is reckoned amongst the finest in the world. There is also a great eucalyptus-oil establishment to be seen; and there are prospects of a big future trade, for the opinion seems to be

New Zealand in our minds—it seemed that the island was parched in a way, and seemed to lack the benefit of those nice night-dews which do such service in the other colony. We did not stay very long in Tasmania; there seemed to be a lack of excitement about the place. My friend didn't notice it, because he had his young lady friend to look after; and as she and her party were going over the same ground as we were, and then on to Melbourne, why, I didn't see much of him. After leaving Tasmania we had a good look at the coast, and it certainly looks very dangerous—very much like the Giant's Causeway; and the sailors said they always had to keep as far off land as possible because of the numerous snags of rocks which were just hidden by the water. Luckily we had no 'squalls' on this trip, and two days after leaving Hobart were safely made fast to a pier in the harbour of 'marvellous Melbourne,' of which we had heard so much.

From Our Colonies.

AUSTRALIA

CHAPTER XII

Snakes and a Shock—Melbourne—Australian Hospitality—A Picnic—Yarns, Mosquitoes, and a Snake—Rabbits — To Sydney by Train — Changing Trains — The Heat—Sydney—My Friend's Concert-party—To Hong-Kong.

AMONGST the many truisms written by Shakespeare is the one that

'Oft expectation fails, and most oft there
Where most it promises.'

This, however, cannot be said of Melbourne, although I must say, after all I had heard about it, I was in a way prepared to be disappointed. Of all the tales I had heard of Australia, there was not one unconnected with a snake; and these all came crowding into my brain as we neared the pier, and made me wonder where the snakes commenced. I was pleased to see the sailors on land used good old-fashioned hawsers for securing the boat, instead of defunct reptiles, as I had almost expected; but still, when I tripped off the gangway, and got on shore, I must say I kept my eyes steadfastly fixed on the ground for a little bit, for fear a ten or twenty feet long serpent should be wandering around and I accidentally treed on him. Nothing was to be seen of them how-

time a steamer close by let off steam, not with a whistle, but
with a 'hiss'; not only this, but a man some way off who was
coiling up this rope gave it a pull just at the moment my
foot got on it.   Pheugh! It was a shock!   For a moment I
thought I had been bitten in a thousand places, and felt just
about at hot and cold, one after the other, as many times in
the space of a second as I had been during the previous twelve
months.   It is all very well to laugh; but most people feel a
little nervous when they first enter a country where they have
been led to believe it is an everyday occurrence to find a little
snake taking his *siesta* in your waistcoat pocket when you
put your hand in for your watch to see how the time is,
or that it is nothing to find one curled round your feet for
warmth when you awake in the morning, or a dozen other
things that we are not used to in England or Scotland, or
indeed in Ireland since the days when St. Patrick 'closured
and named them,' and so got the whole lot out of the
place.   I was surprised soon after landing to find that I had
been somewhat misinformed before leaving home about these
wretched reptiles, for I think I only saw one during the whole
of my stay there; but that one—well, he'll be accounted for
later on.

But so far as Melbourne itself went, I found it everything—
indeed, perhaps more than—I had anticipated.   The approach
is strange, but impressive; for after steaming through a very
narrow opening called 'The Heads,' each side of which is
strongly fortified, an immense land-locked bay, called Port
Philip Bay, bursts into view.   The first land of Australia has

twenty years after—1861—close upon 200,000 was the total, while according to the census of 1891 the inhabitants were over 490,000. Of course, coming after spending so much time in the Pacific, New Zealand, etc., such a large and different kind of town would strike one as impressive at first; but even after I got used to it my opinion was the same—that it was a well-arranged, well-built, clean city, with good streets, and a cable-car system which was as perfect as any I had experienced. The systems at Washington and 'Frisco are 'real excellent'; but Melbourne comes as an improvement on both. From the width of the streets and the height of the sky-scraper houses, the place might easily be taken for an American city; but everything else about is 'quite English, you know,' and, looking into the shop-windows and different stores, one is able to realise something of the market for English goods. But why in the world the free and independent colonial, who, presumably, cares for 'nothing and nobody,' should go in so much for imitating Londoners as to wear a tall silk hat in his sweltering climate, is—well, there, it is one of those things that no fellow can understand. There are some fine parks in and about the city; also a first-class university, with three affiliated colleges. The Houses of Parliament form a magnificent pile of buildings; they were completed in 1891 at a cost of close upon one million sterling. Then there is a very fine and well-appointed public library containing about 200,000 volumes. Cathedrals (two), churches, public buildings, law-courts, all are well and substantially built; and it only takes a short stay in the place to see how it is it has acquired its title of 'Marvellous Melbourne.' All honour to those men who took the matter so well in hand, and

Melbourne, but Victoria, from the financial ruin that threatened them.

One thing I must say about colonial people, and that is, they are downright hospitable. Melbourne society I found very jolly and gay, and I believe if I had stayed in the city twelve months I could have gone to a different house every day. As it was, I had far more invitations than I could accept; and my friend and I had, as he expressed it, 'a real good time.' Houses are not considered complete without a ball-room, and most families have one night a week for a sort of open house, when there is a dance, or a dinner, or a supper, or perhaps all three. And very jolly entertainments they are, too. There is a freedom about the colonial girls that is very good. The 'insular stiffness' so prevalent in England is entirely absent; and the easy, buoyant manner which they all seem to possess adds an additional charm to them. What wonder, then, that my poor susceptible friend once more lost his head, and in more than one direction? He would even disturb them at their studies to have a talk. I must confess I had hard work to keep myself from falling in love with at least a dozen, especially Georgie, to whom a number of others were also rather attached.

One day we had a water-picnic up the river Yarra. This is where the great floods were some time ago; and I got a very good idea of what a disastrous affair the whole business was, for, when going up the river, at times we saw rails from fences,

all clear, and I got into serious trouble by remarking how muddy it was. I was soundly rated by the young ladies, and made to dip a tumbler in the water and see what it was like. Wonderful! it was quite clear! The fact was accounted for from the bed of the river being a dark reddish clay. I suppose it was just by way of making my friend and me feel at home and comfortable that all these young ladies talked so much. Their talking was very nice, their pretty, laughing voices being particularly pleasant to hear; but, then, the things they talked about!

PICNIC UP THE YARRA

think they must be. For instance, one young lady said she
had a little snake at home that she had a great liking for,
because some time ago, when her little brother was sitting out
in the garden trying to do a sum in addition, this little snake
coiled up on his shoulder, then let his tail down, and 'slimed'
out the correct answer on the slate. I naturally wanted to
know the name of this marvellous reptile, and when in reply
to my query she said it was an 'adder,' and everybody laughed,
I came to the conclusion I had been made a fool of somehow.
Still, I laughed like every one else, and thought it a good joke;
but up to the present have not quite fathomed it. However,
I believe there is one, if any one cares to look it out. When
we landed and selected a shady nook in which to locate ourselves, we found that, bad as the mosquitoes had been all the
way up the river, they were far worse on land. Flies are bad
enough to people who don't like being tickled in England, but
mosquitoes give them a good beating. It is a wonderful thing
how a man can keep his temper and tongue under control
when ladies are present, even under such trying circumstances
as a cloud of mosquitoes. I certainly did say 'Bother!' once or
twice, and with a good emphasis; but that was all, although a
word of one syllable would have relieved me better. Still, I was
like the sailor's parrot, and thought a lot more. We had to
make a good fire and get plenty of smoke in order to keep the
little wretches off, for, luckily, they are very fastidious, and like
a pure atmosphere. But I don't know which was the worst,
the malady or the cure; for the smoke was awful, and having
to be near a big fire on a sweltering day such as that was was

thrush by the crazy melody of the laughing jackass, and the dulcet voice of the cuckoo by the entrancing scream of the mynah. There is a fine of £20 for leaving a fire on the banks of the river; so while the others were fixing things up in the boat, I stayed behind with one of the men of the party to put our fire out; and it was at this time that I saw a snake, the only one during my tour in Australia. It was what is called a black snake, and there seems to be some kind of unwritten law declaring it to be high treason to see a black snake and not kill it, or at least try to do so. Being rather a student of natural history, as soon as I heard the man who was with me call out, 'By Jove, there's a black snake!' I left the fire and got up a tree as quickly as I could, to get a good view of what he did. The whole proceeding was very strange, and showed the artfulness and reasoning power of the snake. Run-

companion looked round, and saw the snake (about ten feet long) would reach the hole it was making for before he had time to get the rail and interview the reptile with it; so, rushing back, he was just able to catch hold with both hands of about the last twenty inches of the snake, and then he began to pull. It was a struggle; but having the advantage of leverage, he managed to pull Mr. Snake from the hole and by a dexterous movement send him flying over his head some distance backward, and then rush off again for the rail; but he wasn't quite quick enough, and had to hurry up to repeat performance number one. This time he threw the snake much further back—in fact, in far too close proximity to my tree than I cared for, for I can always see things better at a distance—and then, going at a great speed, managed to get hold of the rail and make for the snake. But Mr. Snake by this time had got hold of some idea of what was likely to happen, and, when he reached the hole, faced round, found the opening with his tail, and went home tail first, hissing and looking very dangerous, and thoroughly keeping my friend at bay, so that, after all, there was no killing done. This was the only snake I ever saw, and therefore the only snake story I can relate from experience.

I felt very sorry for little Australian boys, for they are not allowed to keep pet rabbits; in fact, the fine is £20 for each one. When I was small I wasn't allowed to keep pet rabbits, but I did. The penalty, if I were found out, was only an

was quite pitiable to see strong, able-bodied men begging. I remember one evening, while I was sitting on the verandah of

time I was in Melbourne, as he was anxious to get on to Sydney, so went round by boat, leaving me to join him later on. I went to Sydney some time after by train, and was rather sorry for it afterwards, for the journey was a perfect nuisance. We left Melbourne at five o'clock in the afternoon ; and at 11 P.M., just when every one was thoroughly tired and ready to 'turn in,' we had to 'turn out.' This was at a place called Albury, just on the borders of New South Wales; and as Victoria goes in for the narrow-gauge railways, and New South Wales patronises the broad - gauge system, a change here is inevitable. Why on earth the two colonies cannot go in for the same thing, and so save every one the bother and nuisance of being hustled out just when they are ready to go to sleep, I cannot make out. Perhaps when that much-to-be-desired result, Imperial Federation, becomes

A BEGGAR

fortable, for the carriages were 'Pullman.' At eleven next
morning we arrived at Sydney; but, really, from the heat I
thought that the engine-driver had altered the route, and
taken us to another destination. I was quite prepared to find
a little heat at Sydney, but not quite so much as there really
was, for it was awful. It puzzled me how water could be kept
from boiling, or meat from being cooked. I didn't try it, but
I am quite sure if I had stuck a slice of bread in the sun, it
would have been toast in no time. The houses give off the
heat tremendously, and the pavements are like hot bricks; if
the free-spitting American were about, one would see nothing
but little phizzing geysers all over the pavement. Even the
asphalte is soft, and retains the impression of one's boots,
as well as sometimes the heel of the boot. No, I did not
like Sydney; it was too hot, far too hot. Otherwise, it
was not half a bad place, although the huge donkey-engine
pulling a clumsy-looking lot of carriages up the middle of the
street—playing at steam-tramways as it were—looks so ridiculous. This must be dangerous for traffic; for, although a man
stands at the corner of streets with a big red flag to warn anyone coming along, horses are sensitive creatures, and object to
red flags, just as they do to other things of a peculiar nature
calculated to upset any one's highly-strung nerves. Melbourne
is far ahead of Sydney in the matter of streets; but Sydney
Harbour, or, to be more correct, Port Jackson, is simply
magnificent from a picturesque point of view. Botany Bay is
close handy—a name which conjures up all manner of visions
of the old convict days for here the members of the firm of

hospitals, etc. etc., and 'larrikinism' holds its own. The people of Sydney are no doubt pretty well accustomed to this most objectionable feature of life in their city, but to a stranger it is absolutely detestable.

A surprise awaited me in Sydney in connection with my irrepressible Yankee friend, for he had struck out in a new line

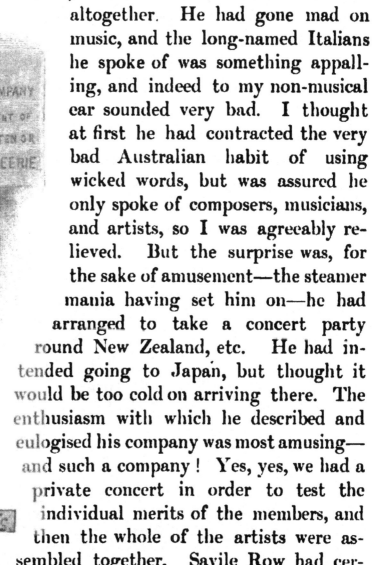

ONE OF THE COMPANY

altogether. He had gone mad on music, and the long-named Italians he spoke of was something appalling, and indeed to my non-musical ear sounded very bad. I thought at first he had contracted the very bad Australian habit of using wicked words, but was assured he only spoke of composers, musicians, and artists, so I was agreeably relieved. But the surprise was, for the sake of amusement—the steamer mania having set him on—he had arranged to take a concert party round New Zealand, etc. He had intended going to Japan, but thought it would be too cold on arriving there. The enthusiasm with which he described and eulogised his company was most amusing—and such a company! Yes, yes, we had a private concert in order to test the individual merits of the members, and then the whole of the artists were assembled together. Savile Row had cer-

arrangement of their long and somewhat greasy locks, and through constant practice had acquired a noble artistic finish in the manner in which they gracefully passed their fingers through their sleeky hair, in order to keep it in position. They were also more partial to clay pipes than cigars, and certainly seemed more at home with them. I presume all these little peculiarities were but signs of talent, so I must not jest about them, for talent in any form is always to be commended.

As I really couldn't stand the heat of Sydney, I didn't stay there long, and, after having a good look round the place, got on the move once more and started for Hong-Kong.

CHAPTER XIII

Port Jackson—Scenery and Sharks—Cockroaches and Rats—Chinamen on board—A Rat Hunt—On a Coral Reef—Thursday Island—A False Alarm—A 'Celestial' Fight—Port Darwin—Frightening Chinamen—Cockfighting—Earthquakes—A Shark in the Saloon—Musical Portuguese—Tackling a Monsoon—Propitiating the Josses—Shipping Corpses—Hong-Kong in sight.

THE voyage to Hong-Kong!—Yes, it was a voyage and no mistake, and it was also an experience I have no wish to repeat. But of that later on. The name of the boat I went by was the s.s. ———. Well, it was a name I shall long remember; but, with the terrors of the libel law rising before me, I will refrain from mentioning it. I heard of a bankrupt once living in grand style in a huge mansion kept up by his wife's money, and who, in a way to appease his creditors, invited them all to a musical evening; they went; he sang 'You'll remember me,' and there was an almost unanimous chorus of 'We'll never forget you.' That's how I feel about this boat.

natural and land-locked ; but, good as I had thought the two former, they paled immeasurably before the grand, the unique, the magnificent harbour of Port Jackson.

The hour's run down to the Heads is anything but an uninteresting passage, for the scenery on both sides is most attractive, and keeps the mind well occupied during the whole time. There are sharks, too, in Port Jackson, and not in small numbers

'YOU'LL REMEMBER ME.'

Out once more on the open sea, the breeze comes with most refreshing delightfulness after the intense and suffocating heat of Sydney, and although it may be a bit rough, the change is grand, for one feels that at last it is possible to breathe. A feeling of laziness came over me though, and from that time I have discarded razors, letting my beard grow *à la Nazarite.*

Now, however, began that month's experience, which I never want again.

The assortment of travellers was varied in the extreme, including both those who had and those who had not paid their passage. Fourteen days before sailing I had booked a cabin which was said to be the best on the ship and next to the captain's. However, at the last moment I was advised by the manager of the company to exchange into another which had just been forfeited, as it was so much better than the one I had originally selected.

I changed.

On retiring to rest, I began to think what an excellent article a boy John Chinaman was, for the one told off to look after me had laid out my sleeping-attire most carefully.

I began to unrobe. Coming to my necktie, I threw it down, and it went on to the floor; but it didn't lie still. No, it moved most perceptibly. Watching to discern the cause, my eye came in contact with a movement on the part of the left leg of my pyjamas so carefully laid out. This was very strange— and yes, my pyjama jacket made a movement as though it had heaved a sigh. Then the necktie moved again *en bloc* at least an

After putting on my slippers, and executing a wild war-dance over the floor, each step being accompanied by a crunch and a swish, I perceived the endeavour to lessen the multitude was vain, so I resigned myself to the inevitable, and slept. Yes, I slept, dreaming that I was a Maori chief ruling over the destinies of a large country, which was a kind of amalgamation ot Fiji, the Highlands of Scotland, Seven Dials, American Prairie, Sydney and New Zealand geysers, and that all my subjects were cockroaches, beetles, and snakes. But my rest was not for long, neither were my dreams to be undisturbed.

After reaching a point where a military tourna-ment was being held in a stalactite cave of huge proportions, and a grand tug-of-war was going on between fourteen snakes of immense length and 173 brobdingnagian cock-roaches, I awoke with a start, and the impression that a steeplechase of some kind was being held on the floor of my cabin. I was not far wrong, for upon getting my match-box from under the pillow, and striking a light, I beheld a by no means small assembly of

COCKROACHES

man of the meeting making a hasty drive for somewhere, and disappearing. The rest followed his example with all speed, and once more I slept.

At daylight I was awake again, and a chattering noise as though ten thousand monkeys were discussing some important question came floating through the open portholes of my state-room, which looked towards the hold. Cockroaches had worried me, rats had disturbed, but it was left for about 250 Chinamen to put on the finishing touch. I looked through the porthole, and within a few yards a strange scene came to view. A whole crowd of Chinamen, lying and sitting about, some asleep, some smoking opium, but the majority squabbling over their 'chow,' were all mixed up with the thirty sheep, the cow, and the calf that had been brought on board for catering purposes. This was the climax, and I got up. It appeared this party were returning to their fatherland, taking with them all the gold they could, and had engaged part of the hold for the voyage. The shipping company don't mind them doing this, as they pay better than freight, and only eat rice, fish, and such like !

After the first night's experience I moved aft—another nautical expression—and got into the cabin I engaged in the first instance. Here the things were not quite so bad, for the Chinamen and smell of opium were further away, and the cockroaches were fewer in number. The first evening here was uneventful, and the second commenced quietly, but ended uproariously at daybreak. A heavy thump on my chest brought me quickly from the land of dreams to find the grey dawn creeping in through my porthole, and a huge rat, which

too quick, and after a wriggle and a squeal he sprang to the floor. Then the fun began. Seizing a stick, I went for him round my cabin. He got into the saloon; I chased him round there, and up on to the deck where six or eight people were sleeping. I fell over one of these, rather disturbing the lower regions of another as I went down, and the rat put his foot in the mouth of another, so it was only a few seconds before all were awake, and joining in the chase. The light was better on

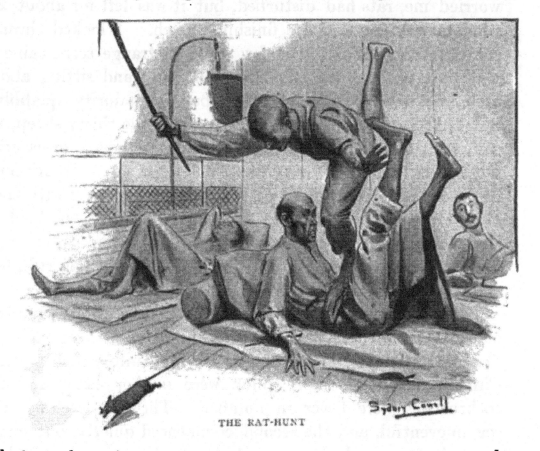

THE RAT-HUNT

It seemed that we were to have nothing else but experiences on this voyage, for just about the Torres Straits, where coral reefs are plentiful, the good ship—which shall be nameless—steered right into one of these, and stuck there for about four hours.   The sight, looking into the water from the bow of the vessel, was very beautiful, for there was coral all round, and it really looked like some magnificent garden and grotto below the surface of the sea, with a kind of pinky whiteness pervading the whole.   In fact, one young lady was so entranced she wanted to get out and take a dive, but the captain didn't approve.   We only cut into about nine feet of coral, but still all efforts to back off were fruitless, and cargo had to be moved before any impression could be made; then, with the aid of the tide, and the engineer putting on full pressure (he was great on full pressure) about 900 lbs.—or perhaps it was 90 lbs.—and going astern, we got safely off.

Thursday Island is a very primitive-looking place, and also unattractive; but, looking at it from the sea, it is rather pretty.   Pearl fishing goes on rather extensively about here, and we saw the upper part of a smack that had been sunk. One of the sailors, who had heard me give vent to my feelings and prescribe a remedy for ridding the ship we were on of its cargo of rats and cockroaches, pointed to this vessel, and said : 'Ah, they kill rats and cockroaches.'   In fact, I was told that such things were often done in these parts.

By the way, just before reaching Thursday Island, I had another impression we were going to the bottom.   It was early morning—that's the worst of these things, they always happen when one wants to be asleep, or something of that kind—it was rough, the wind was blowing pretty stiffly, while the rain was coming down—well, the fire-engine hose kind that

going for the boats,' so before I was properly awake I sprang out of my berth—nearly killing a rat that I stepped on—and, clutching a spare suit of pyjamas with one hand, and a pair of trousers with the other, rushed out on deck to be almost drowned with the sea and rain, nearly blown overboard by the terrific wind, and to find that all the noise and shouting came

A FIGHT BETWEEN TWO CELESTIALS

from the Chinamen's quarters, consequent upon a fight between two Celestials!

and as fast as the rolling and pitching and tossing of the boat would let them. The belligerents were so astonished they ceased their strife, and I went back to my cabin 'a sadder and wetter man' than I left it. Never again, if I can help it, will I sail in a vessel that also contains a parcel of inhabitants of John Chinaman's land. They were at it all day long—noise, squabbling, and fighting—with an occasional rest for a few whiffs at the opium pipe, and then at it again. Morning was the time, though, when rice was served out. That was the time for noise and fighting, and I really thought more than once that we should only land about half the original number alive; but, somehow, the fights never ended in a fatal manner. Then, again, the smell of dirt and opium was awful, and once I suggested to Mr. Speedy, the chief engineer, that the hose should be turned on to the whole crowd; but he knew more about the nature of a Celestial than I did, and said: 'No, no, mon; water will kill a Chinaman!' By the way, this chief engineer was a very nice fellow—came from Perth, in Scotland, a place famous for 'Fair Maids,' at least, so we read in books—and he was always talking of the girls he'd left behind him.

On the map it doesn't look very far from Thursday Island to Port Darwin, but it is a three days' trip; and the Gulf of Carpentaria, which is passed, suggests something to do with carpenters, but we didn't see any. On the way Melville Island is passed—a most interesting place, or would be if it were not for the blacks, who are particularly pugnacious, and greet any one wishing to land with a shower of spears. Needless to say, I did not court this delicate little attention.

What Port Darwin would really be if it were not the point where the cable comes on shore is not very easy to guess, although under present circumstances it is certainly an impor-

there have migrated from Threadneedle Street, Broad Street and neighbourhood, in the city of London, but have had to leave the habits, manners, and customs of the 'city man' behind them. It would do incalculable good to some of you immaculate young gentlemen at home, to whom frock coats, silk hats, tall collars, and cigarettes are of most vital importance, if you just went over to Port Darwin to see how your *confrères* worked. The work has to be done, and done in the sweltering heat of the tropics—but where is the tall hat? where the frock coat? where the light trousers and patent leather shoes? Again to quote the classics, they are 'far, far away!' The lightest of gear for head and feet is called into play; flannel pants do service for the well-cut trousers, and the long frock coat is cast aside for a singlet only. This is how business has to be done in Port Darwin, and how the gentlemen of the place have to array themselves for doing it.

John Chinaman is very much in evidence in Port Darwin, and, as in other places, he is always ready to do laundry work for the passengers on board a boat, though he doesn't care to do it so much for folks on shore, making the excuse that there is not sufficient rain. The night before our boat arrived with its passengers and freight of rats and cockroaches, there had been five inches of rain in two and a-half hours (the greatest on record for about ten years, I was told), so that how much is really wanted to satisfy the gentlemen must remain a question —I am not going to attempt to answer it. However, we managed to get some fun out of the place while we stayed there, some of the blacks being always ready to sing even the

his legs on dry land, the happy thought struck him : he would try and frighten a few Celestials.   He succeeded, and succeeded so well that the authorities on shore took charge of him for the night.   It was very funny to see John so frightened.   Our colleague started by stopping in front of one and smiling. The Chinaman smiled also.

FRIGHTENING CELESTIALS

indescribable horror and fright, and with a terrified scream he turned and fled. This proceeding was repeated in a shop where some six or eight Chinamen were making purchases, and with a much funnier result. The Celestials forgot their purchases, and in their wild fright and hurry to clear out of the place nearly all came to the ground, and the floor seemed to be covered with a kicking, screaming, and struggling mass of Chinamen.

Dilly, the capital of Timor, was the next place we touched at, and a very miserable place it was. The natives here are awfully keen on cockfighting, and numbers of them walk about with a bird under their arm, and a 'quid' of tobacco in their upper lip, ready at any moment to set their bird against another. An acquaintance of mine has since told me that this can be seen at any time within a mile of Bow Street, in a back cellar. Well, if so, it only shows that London can supply anything. When we were anchored here, or rather moored to a tree on the coast, we experienced —to use an Irishism—an earthquake at sea! The sensation was very peculiar, to say the least of it. The ship shook as though the screw were out of the water, and the cries of the natives were distinctly heard. It seems they are rather good at earthquakes here, and do not think very much of one that only lasts a little time. I was told that about two months previous to this there had been one that kept the earth on the move for eight days! Of course I was not there, so would not really care to vouch for the absolute truthfulness of the fact; but as it was told to me by the same individual who told me that once out there during a terrific cyclone, every feather was blown out of the fowls he used to keep, just as though they had

here, for he 'knew the ropes' a bit, and we soon saw all
there was to see, including one of the very few men who
spoke English, and he happened to be a Scotchman, and
spoke Scotch! He had been sent out by a syndicate from
Hong-Kong to explore for kerosene, and had just been
successful in finding it. He had not been there very long,
but had already been 'down' with fever five times. While
we were there, a few of the inhabitants came on board to
lunch, including Mr. Scottie, who was placed next to a
Chinese judge, one of our passengers, whom we had nick-
named the Lord High Executioner. Now any one who has
been in the East for about six months won't sit next to a
Chinaman, so Mr. Scottie went out, and off the boat,
followed by a look from the judge which showed plainly
what would have happened had they been in Chinaland.

We met with Scotchmen everywhere we went—they seemed
to be all over the place—and I never called down into the
engine-room of any steamer I was on, 'Hey, Mac!' without
getting a reply in broad Scotch that Mac would come up.

An interesting gentleman we saw here took a great fancy
to us, and in order to show us special attention, made his
black boy scale a cocoa-nut tree to get us some nuts. I've
always heard there's a special providence over drunken men
and children, and this climbing business proved it fairly
successfully, for to see a youngster almost run up and down
trees of about 100 feet in height, and throw down cocoa-nuts
without breaking his own juvenile neck, is rather remarkable.
Rambling about the beach was a good change to being cooped

way into the saloon, but only to find it already occupied. A large shark was having a look round, and swimming about inside, so Mr. Diver postponed his operations, and politely withdrew. I don't know, of course, what I should have done under similar circumstances, but I dare say I should have been about as polite as the diver was, and not have interfered with the tenant in possession.

Others of the new comers were Portuguese, and they were rather a rough lot, sleeping in all their clothes, and not even removing their boots and spurs. They were musical—in a way—and for a time we had plenty of music, such as comes from bad musical boxes, and that soul-scaring horror, which is a sort of a cross between a piano and a concertina, such as is used in the English streets by imitation blind men, while their half-starved dog runs about with half an old coffee-tin in his mouth, trying to collect coppers. Luckily the wind sprang up to rather a brisk tune, and the noble Portuguese had to drop the instrumental music and go in for vocal. This was extremely guttural, but as they kept to their cabins during this exercise they didn't annoy any one. The wind freshened up more, and my friend Speedy told me in a most cold-blooded manner, 'We'll have to look about us now, for we're going to tackle a monsoon!'

We did tackle it, or rather perhaps I should say it tackled us, and for over two days we had a very lively time of it. The poor Celestials were awfully frightened, and the scared look they had on their faces was quite comical to behold. The second night of the monsoon they took the matter into their own hands, and held a kind of prayer-meeting—supplicating their 'Josses' to send fair weather. It was a very strange sight to see the whole 250 of them on their knees

sea, and then resumed the happy and contented smile that is peculiarly John Chinaman's own, for they were quite certain they had appeased the wrath of their 'Josses,' and that fine weather would soon follow. And so it did—the next day. But I don't think the tapers and potatoes had anything to do with it. The first officer very artfully made out that he had the most to do with it, for he knew how long he would

A CHINESE PRAYER-MEETING

be steering through this pretty monsoon, and that evening

Chinaman's land by the next boat any Chinamen are sailing in, after his decease. These religiously see to the safe transit of the remains, as the Josses credit them above for this, but they are not over scrupulous as to how they get them on board. Now, in the present instance, one Celestial, perhaps more timid than the rest, told the officer quietly and mysteriously that the 'Josses' sent the storm because some of the Chinamen had smuggled some corpses on board without paying freight for them. He told him who they were, but begged and prayed most piteously that the source of information should not be divulged. The subject of the officer's harangue was the wickedness of displeasing the 'Josses' by being dishonest, and he said he was quite certain that they had amongst their baggage some that had not been paid for, and that until the money had been paid over, bad weather would continue. All the luggage was examined, and sure enough in one carpet bag three skulls were found, in a dilapidated chest two or three limbs, and in an old champagne case an assortment of limbs and a skull. To teach them a lesson, he made them all pay something, and collected a good few pounds, then rated them very soundly, and said the 'Josses' would send fine weather in the morning. By the early morning we had got clear of the monsoon, and were in lovely weather, and as soon as the first officer made his appearance on deck, the whole of the Chinamen approached him, and thanked him for teaching them their duty. 'It was so nice of them, I thought,' said a lady passenger, 'and didn't they look pleased?' Pleased? whoever saw a Chinaman look other than pleased? Why, his round shining face with a big smile on it would be a fortune to him in England if he could

been in the tropics.   It is not quite so comfortable, perhaps, sleeping on deck, but it is decidedly cooler. A Carlton Club gentleman who was amongst our passengers soon got used to sleeping on the floor, although no doubt he would have preferred the luxury of the palatial edifice in Pall Mall.   As for my friend Speedy, he could sleep anywhere, or at any time.   A berth, the floor, a rope, it didn't matter what it was, or how the weather was.   If Speedy wanted to sleep, why, he just slept there and then, and would say, 'Mon, it's a' richt up to noo!'

At last Hong-Kong hove in sight, and the scene was rather an imposing one, although there was such a tremendous drop in

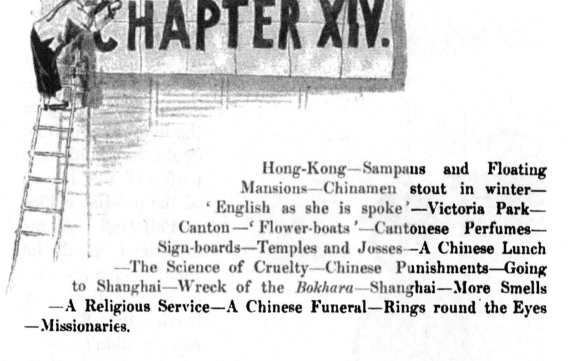

CHAPTER XIV.

Hong-Kong—Sampans and Floating
Mansions—Chinamen stout in winter—
'English as she is spoke'—Victoria Park—
Canton—'Flower-boats'—Cantonese Perfumes—
Sign-boards—Temples and Josses—A Chinese Lunch
—The Science of Cruelty—Chinese Punishments—Going
to Shanghai—Wreck of the *Bokhara*—Shanghai—More Smells
—A Religious Service—A Chinese Funeral—Rings round the Eyes
—Missionaries.

AFTER touring for so long amongst the islands of the East
Indian Archipelago, and seeing so much of the apparently
half-civilised, the downright lazy, and all-round lethargic
Portuguese, it was really a treat to think that once more
there was a chance of being amongst civilisation, and at home
in a British colony.

Watching from the bridge of the rat- and cockroach-laden
boat as she neared the harbour of Hong-Kong, the gradually
developing scenery attracted greater and greater attention,
until, at the time the anchor was dropped, the scene was one
that only a painter or a poet could adequately describe.
Imagine a high background of rock, half barren and half
studded with trees, and, rising in terraces amongst this, good-

merchantmen, men-of-war, passenger boats, and mail steamers. steam-launches darting here and there and everywhere, with their screeching whistles going all over the place, the rough business-like appearance of the whole being pleasantly broken by quaint Chinese junks flitting hither and thither, and a goodly collection of the almost clumsy-looking sampan, and there you have some idea of the view of Hong-Kong, after passing through the famous Ly-ce-moon Pass. As a Portuguese captain exclaimed, it was a sight to give any one an idea of England's power in colonising ; but, apart from that, quaintness, novelty, and thorough picturesqueness all lend themselves to give an additional charm to the scene.

Then, again, thoughts of very diversified character rise in one's mind. Here are we, approaching a corner of John Chinaman's land, and a place which, although a British colony, is also largely peopled by a very good supply of Chinamen.

What is he like at home ? It is all very well to have seen John in 'Frisco, Honolulu, Australia, and other places, but what are his semi-heathen ways at home ? Now comes a chance of seeing the Celestial ' in his habit, as he lives,' and almost in the midst of his native surroundings.

But to digress a little. Hong-Kong, or, to put it more correctly, Hiang-Kiang, which, being interpreted, means ' the place of sweet waters '—the waters may have been sweet, but I didn't try them—may really be taken as a very fine example of British enterprise and energy ; for, when we visited the island, and came to stop in 1841, there were only about 5000 people there, but in 1851 there were 37,000 and a gradually increasing trade, both export and import. Matters continued to prosper, and such was the importance of the place in 1871 its population numbered over 123,000 while at the time of writing it is close

sway, for in these things are in such a wretched state they
have advanced scarcely one iota since they were occupied some
three hundred years ago. The Portuguese captain just mentioned was very bitter against his people for not making more
progress, and their laziness in letting things take their own
course, as they were doing in Timor and their other possessions
around, but consoled himself by saying it was all very well to
talk, but that enterprise and prosperity followed the British
flag wherever it went, and there was no country in the world
that could stand against, or compete with, the English.

Our boat did not anchor close up to the quay, so we had
to be taken off in sampans, and the short trip from the vessel
to the shore gave me an insight of a very peculiar part of
Chinese life—the manners and customs of the floating population. The boat was not much more than twenty feet long, and
although I did not measure, I should say its depth would not
be more than two feet, or its beam over five feet, and yet it was
not only used as a means of conveyance, but it was the domi-
cile, home, and family mansion of the owner, his wife, and
family of three children! We heard that the previous night
two men had been suffocated in such a similar hold, the cold
being so intense they had shut themselves in, but that such
things were by no means of any uncommon occurrence—and I
can quite believe it.

The forepart of these boats is decked over, and this forms the
' house '—certainly not a commodious domain, for the measure-
ments couldn't possibly be more than five feet by four ; but

—a concern rather after the style of a nursery mail-cart or a miniature hansom, and drawn by a Chinese coolie.

Hong-Kong contains a large number of Europeans and Americans, but the majority of the people are Chinese, and to be thrown right into the middle of them, all at once, is very strange. I don't wish to infer that my coolie came to grief,

A JINRICKSHA

and that I had a spill while travelling to the hotel in this— to me—novel conveyance, because the journey was performed without mishap, although once or twice I did fancy there was a chance of my leaving the concern rather suddenly and the

things so reverse of European, makes one think they have been suddenly transported to Drury Lane stage, with a pantomime of 'Aladdin' in full swing, or else to one of those fancy fairs, bazaars, 'religious swindles,' or whatever may be their correct name, where young ladies and even men take such a delight in 'dressing up' and then try their hardest to sell things at most exorbitant prices, 'all for charity.'

My first night in Hong-Kong—it was the end of January—happened to be the coldest (so the people said) ever experienced, and yet the thermometer only went down to 26°. My, how people did complain of the cold in the morning! To tell the truth, though, I joined them, and was well to the front in my grumbling; but then there was an excuse for me, because only two days before I had been sweltering in 95°—rather a sudden drop. I couldn't quite make out how it was all the Chinese people looked so stout, until it was explained to me, and some one said, 'Man, they can't walk for clothes.' It appears that as the weather gets colder, these interesting and ingenious people just stick on another suit of clothes—if that be the correct term to apply to the wonderful arrangements with which they clothe themselves—and there they leave them until the warm weather turns up again. It often happens that a Chinaman will be carrying his whole wardrobe on his back. Curious people!

John prides himself very much on his English; but it can hardly be called 'English as she is spoke,' especially judging from the signboards, one of which, I noticed, read, 'Dealer in tailor and draper, Manila cigar, all kind silk handkerchief out-

frightened to go to bed, for fear he should turn round in his sleep and roll over into the sea, but I didn't feel nervous on this score in the slightest degree when in Hong-Kong. The island is very mountainous, although so small, and Victoria Peak, the highest point, has an altitude of somewhere about 1825 feet. Of course the proper thing to do is to go to the top of this, so, wishing to be always proper, I ascended. I wasn't sorry when I had reached the top, and my thanksgiving was fervent when I was once more on the level of the sea. You don't walk up, neither do you ride on donkeys or mules ; a cable car is the conveyance that takes you up, and it seems more like going up a great height in a lift with the sides out, so that you can see all round. It is decidedly not the kind of recreation I should advise to any one of nervous temperament, or any one whose appetite suddenly disappears at the sight of the matutinal frizzled bacon. Still, although the ascent is made by means of such an almost sensationally vertical tram, it is worth the fright when the summit is reached, for the picture all round is a perfectly grand one. In the air, at an elevation of about a third of a mile ; below is seen the whole of the island, but most distinctly the splendid harbour of Hong-Kong, with its crowds of shipping. On every hand is the sea, while away to the north is the mainland of China itself. It is really a glorious sight, and such a one as perhaps it is impossible to see elsewhere.

Well, after a fairly long stay at this place, I got a bit restless, and wanted to be off to somewhere else, so decided to go to Canton, as I thought I should there have a better chance of really studying the manners and customs of the Celestials.

pattern plate.   It is not a very rapid voyage from Hong-Kong
to Canton, for although the distance is only ninety-five miles,
it takes close upon fourteen hours to do the passage.   But
when the place is reached at last—what a sight ! Junks, boats,
and sampans of every description, shape, and size are moored
in long lines, and almost give any one the idea of the place
being composed of streets of water, with boats for houses.
They really are houses, too, for each one has a family on board,
and it is supposed that the river population here numbers
about 300,000.   Some of these boats are a kind of floating
restaurant, and are called 'flower-boats.'   Pretty name, but
there the prettiness stops.   They are hardly the places that a
young lady would take her mother to if in need of refreshment,
for I am sorry to say that some of them are very much in want
of a thorough 'London County Councilising.'   My sensitive
feelings were upset very much at some of the manners and
customs of the gay natives as depicted in some of these boats,
and I had to whisper to my guide in the best ' pidgeon ' I could
command, ' Me wantee go away ; me catchee too much blushee.'
I don't know whether he understood me or no, but we went
away.

Talking this ' pidgeon ' English is very funny, and seems very
much like talking to babies, like mothers and nursemaids do
when they say ' Catchee, catchee, catchee,' or something like
that, finishing up with a ' boo '; and then, when the baby gives
a semi-idiotic grin, does a gurgling sort of chuckle, and dribbles
so that it wants a new—feeder on, they say, ' Isn't it a dear ?'
but Chinamen really understand it, and one gets used to the
seeming absurdity of it in time.

Canton itself is—well, as the costermonger said when he was
so flabbergasted he couldn't even swear, ' there ain't no word

lump of camphor to our moustaches, we managed to make things a little more pleasant; but even then it was the most horrible, abominable, and disgusting conglomeration of vile smells that any one can possibly imagine. John Chinaman must be tough indeed to be able to live through all this.

Going into Canton puts one in mind of the very old, or even barbaric period, for it has a big wall all round it, and the gates in this are shut all night. This wall is a wondrous affair; it is about twenty-five feet high, on the average, although at places it goes much higher; it is twenty feet thick, and there are twelve gates for ordinary traffic and two water gates. There are over six hundred streets in the city, and every one of these is awfully narrow. Why, when we were doing our tour—it was certainly not a very wide chair we were in—we happened to meet another chair coming in the opposite direction in a rather narrow street, and, as there was not room to pass, both parties had to get out, in order that one chair could be lifted over the other. Some of the streets are really very peculiar, for they are not only narrow, and have tallish houses on each side, but they are covered with a kind of bamboo wicker-work, so that they look more like the arcades we know in England rather than streets, though not quite up to the Burlington in Piccadilly; and then the signboards, or flag advertisements, as one man told me they were called, which hang about from the various windows, make them look more like bazaars. Talk about 'dangerous structures,' why, they are nothing else. To understand what all the peculiar signs and things mean that are marked on those swinging signs may be all very well for a Chinaman, but

The largest covers about seven acres of ground, and is called Hai-chwang-sze, which means the Temple of the Ocean Banner; then there are such names as Temple of Filial Duty, the Temple of Longevity, the Temple of the Five Hundred Genii, etc. etc. This latter is a marvellous place, and contains five hundred images, life size, set out in rows for the natives to go and bow down to, and to say their prayers to, and otherwise worship. The whole five hundred seem to be on very amicable terms, for internal dissensions are never heard of, and one Joss never quarrels with another.

Getting to a more salubrious and less smelly part of the place about the middle of the day, our guide inquired, 'Can do Chow Chow?' (are you able to eat?) We made another shot at the 'pidgeon' language, and said, 'Yes, yes, hab catchee topside hungry.' He evidently understood, although I do not think it is quite real 'pidgeon,' and we were 'chaired' to a very fair restaurant, in order that we might try a real, genuine Chinese dinner. With a heroism worthy of far greater deeds, I stuck to my guns, and went through the whole lot of courses, although at times I must say I nearly gave in. The hedgehog soup was very passable, but I can't say I quite relished the boiled owl with beetle sauce; the fricasseed kittens were not at all bad, but I soon left off when the stewed puppy dog was put in front of me. I had a try at it, though, just to say I had some. It is not a dish I should encourage my friends to try, although they might do worse than get familiar with grilled horse steak. We did not try that peculiarly Chinese epicurean dish 'blind mice,' and I don't think I should care to do so either. They call this 'Milhi,' which really means 'mice'; they are placed alive on a small tray before each guest, who, taking them one by one by the tail, dips them in honey, then

feature in Canton, for it is really a very good building, although rather like a prison, and the students are guarded by soldiers during the time they are in the cells at their work.

Not being subject to any English or European influence, Canton is not the place it should be by a very long way, especially as regards her treatment of prisoners, etc., for the Chinese seem to have studied cruelty till they have brought it almost to an art, and I am very much inclined to think with others that for the real *science* of cruelty in the way of punishment you must go to China.

It makes one feel quite 'crawley' to *hear* what is done; but what it would be to witness any of the scenes I leave to the imagination. I understand a favourite diversion used to be to strip a criminal, seat him in a barrel, fill the barrel with lime till it reached the victim's chin, then secure him so that he could not get out, place the barrel facing the sun, cut off the poor wretch's eyelids, and pour water into the barrel! Horrible as is such treatment, it is mild compared with other 'treatments' I heard of, but would be sorry to repeat here. Amongst the milder 'discipline' is a barbarous fashion of hanging a victim upon a bamboo pole by his hands and feet, face downward, and then, he being clothed simply in nature's garments, thrashing him with a split bamboo.

When a criminal is sentenced to death, he is lucky if the sentence is carried out by his head being 'chop chop,' as they say, or lopped off while he is kneeling on the ground, although such punishment is considered a terrible disgrace, and all chance of going to heaven is lost. The head being gone, the pigtail also is gone, and therefore there is nothing left whereby the head Joss or his assistants can draw the deceased up to brighter realms. As a rule, various rather excruciating preliminaries

seventy-fourth cut, and then despatching him. They are called *cuts*, but really that is hardly the word, for the eyelids go, then the ears, and so on, until the wretched victim, lacerated, mutilated, and gashed in every quarter, is put out of his misery by the last and most merciful stroke of the knife.

At times, when the culprit has money, or his friends have anything to spare, an arrangement is made with the executioner to give only a light punishment, consisting of about twenty-one cuts or less! While I am on the horrible, let me explain how at times evidence is got out of a witness in a court of justice (?). The all supreme mandarin (whose tyrannical sway is far greater than was that of any of our old feudal lords) has his idea of what a witness ought to say, and takes means that the same shall be said. In many cases that simple means is resorted to that most of us have experienced in our earlier days of school life—the birch; but in some instances, where the witness persists in telling his own tale, thumb-screws are used, or he is suspended in the air by his thumbs and big toes, until the truth is extracted, or else he has to undergo the awful ordeal of 'knee-grinding.' The agony of this may be better imagined than described. The poor wretch is made to kneel on a stone, or tiled floor, his arms are put out at full length, and fastened to a horizontal bar of bamboo, while his legs are secured together by a chain, and a long and by no means light pole is placed inside the bend of the knee. Then, until he gives answers *to the satisfaction of the Court,* a weighty man stands at each end of the pole, and the pair play at what we know as 'see-saw'!

Such is the Chinese mode of extracting 'the truth, the whole truth, and nothing but the truth' from unwilling witnesses and prisoners. All this is in full swing in the present day in

be off again back to Hong-Kong, and from there take a boat to Japan, calling in at Shanghai on the way up. The ninety-five miles between heathenism and civilisation is safely traversed, and then, after transhipping, I am once more under weigh. The voyage to Shanghai from Hong-Kong takes about three days and a-half, but unfortunately it is at parts rather a dangerous one in more ways than one; for instance, the wretched heathen Chinee sailors will run their junks as close under the bows of a steamer as they possibly can, as they have an idiotic idea that if they do this their 'Joss' will be pleased, and send them fine weather and plenty of fish. In fact, the closer they can get the finer will be the weather, and the more plentiful the fish. They all fish, and turn their hand to a little bit of piracy when it can be done with tolerable safety. However, the Chinese Government recently gave them a bit of a lesson—some say after a hint from John Bull—and one fine morning as many as forty, who had been caught pirating, were removed from the face of this earth, and sent to realms above, or elsewhere. Some people do say that the Admiral simply went up the coast and collected the pirates from anywhere, saying that if they had not been at piracy that day they had been previously, or else would turn to it some day, so that it didn't matter.

Then, again, the fish-traps which are laid about here are an intolerable nuisance, and by no means devoid of danger to passing steamers, as, should the spars or net get mixed up with the screw, something would be bound to go wrong. The traps are an ingenious contrivance of bamboo spars, ropes, and nets, and made so that the fish get hopelessly entangled, and are

the awfulness of that night, when, after bravely fighting a typhoon for two days, three terrific seas struck the vessel·in succession, and smashing through the stokehole doors put out the fires, thus destroying the last ray of hope, and putting the ship entirely at the mercy of the waves, not only in one of the most dangerous parts of the ocean thereabouts, but in the midst of a raging typhoon. After this any chance of weathering the gale was perfectly hopeless, and it was not long before, with a terrible crash, the good ship *Bokhara* was dashed upon the reef. Within about two minutes of striking—so we are told by the few survivors—all was over, the vessel had disappeared, and the lives of some hundred and twenty-five persons were lost. Terrible, indeed, as was such a death, almost worse were the sufferings of the twenty-three survivors for the next two days before they were discovered and rescued by some natives; but all these details are, no doubt, still so fresh in the minds of all that I need not go further into them.

Shanghai is on the Woosung River, before entering which a rather awkward 'bar' has to be crossed, and there are times when some steamers cannot get across unless the tide is high. As luck would have it, we were not detained outside, owing to an accident that had happened about two months previously. A steamer was run down, and sunk in mid stream on this bar, making such a rush of water one side that the waterway had been deepened by four feet or more.

On landing, our impressions were very good, for the aspect of the place was thoroughly business-like and prosperous. As usual we found a big river population, the number being put

are closed, and the majority of the people go to the club, which is for the time being a kind of Exchange. The members are a very jolly set of fellows, and I soon felt quite at home there.

It was cold here, colder than even the oldest inhabitant could remember, and so it ought to be, for 10 below zero is all very well now and then, but to have it as a regular thing every winter would get very monotonous. There was a lot of snow as well, and a number of large lumps of ice were drifting down the river.

A British Supreme Court for China and Japan sits here, and this has jurisdiction over all British subjects in Shanghai, and is also a Court of Appeal from all British Consular reports in China and Japan.

Of course I went to the Chinese city, and was very much surprised at the reception I got there, for, from one or two things I had read, and a few more I had heard, I quite expected the chances of my returning in anything but a battered condition were very few, but—of course putting aside the question of smells, which I must say almost equalled those of Canton—really I did not meet with the slightest incivility from any one. My experience was that the natives seemed only too pleased if you took notice of their work. Quaint, very quaint, were some of the parts of the place, as were also the stuffy little workshops. In one shop, about ten or twelve feet square, I counted eleven workmen—tailors, tinsmiths, shoemakers, etc.—all trades were represented in these small shops— and the workmen seemed very comfortable. One reason of this is, there are no trades unions or large monopolies. In many cases I found the master gave his men, who were generally relatives, an interest in the work, lived with them under the same roof, and fed with them out of the same bowl

a most peculiar and eccentric performance was going on in one of those I visited. Three priests were arrayed in robes, of most glorious and astounding magnificence, and reading or rather howling something from a board, very much after the shape of a huge razor strop, which was held in front of them; then everybody in the place would moan terribly, after which all would bawl out their loudest, and every now and again the monotony of this was broken by an awful clashing of cymbals, making me think I was in London once more, and that some milkman outside had upset his milk-barrow, and spilt his tins on the pavement; or that I was at Waterloo Station when a country milk-train was being loaded. Every one was most solemn and earnest over the business, which I found out was going 'Chin-chin' to the Joss for warmer weather! If that Joss had a sensitive ear, or in any way suffered from nerves, he would have at once ordered up a blazing sun, and sent the temperature with a gallop up to about 120° in the shade, in order to put a stop to the horrible din; but as the weather continued cold all the time I was in Shanghai, I presume his 'Joss-ship' was either remarkably deaf, or else he had moved to warmer quarters himself, and had forgotten to leave a deputy behind to attend to business.

Just before completing my round of the city, I thought my last hour had arrived, for all at once a most frightful noise arose about twenty yards in front of me; a bonfire was also lighted, and upon this, boxes, boots, papers—in fact, all manner of things were being thrown. 'Here' thought I 'is another

brain him and fly? My fears—no, not my fears, because I was not afraid; no, my determination was altered—that's better—by the soothing tones of the gentle Chinee, as he pointed to the place and said, 'Ah! one piecee man hab catchee die!' I thought as he hadn't caught me, the 'piecee man' could catch just whatever he liked; but I found after that the meaning of the phrase was that *a man had died!* Yes, so it was; a man had died and in order to propitiate, or 'Chin-chin' the Joss to send his soul somewhere where it would be comfortable, all this noise was being made. The *paid* mourners, wrapped in sackcloth, were lying in the gutter wallowing in all the filth—wailing, moaning, and groaning to such an extent that I got fairly bewildered, so went off without waiting to see the finish of the performance.

Like Canton and other Chinese cities, this Chinese part of Shanghai is walled in with an enormously thick and high wall, in which are, I think, seven great gates that are shut and guarded at night. By the way, a wholesale wine merchant in the English settlement told me that a Chinaman made the best of all warehousemen in a wine merchant's establishment, not only because they did not drink very much, but that if they did,

AN AMERICAN WHO WORE
A PIGTAIL

be told by looking at the rings of the trunk or the horn, but this way of telling how much a man has had to drink was quite new to me. It would be a good thing sometimes if this were the case with Englishmen, and would assist most materially in 'drunk and disorderly' cases. Imagine a man denying before a magistrate at Bow Street that he had been drunk; how easy it would be for his worship to say, 'Constable, did you examine his eyes?' 'Yes, your wusship; but the rings all round each eye were so mixed up over 'is nose, and went right under the 'air of 'is 'ead, we couldn't count how many there really was!' 'Ten shillings or seven days!' Why the whole thing would be as easy as A B C.

Missionaries are very thick about Shanghai, and some of them —in fact, a good number—have gone to the ridiculous extreme of wearing pigtails. One of them, an American, who wore a pigtail, said that if you didn't have one, and dressed European fashion, over three-quarters of your time was taken up in answering questions as to the price of your clothes, where did the boots come from, and all such like, instead of propounding the gospel.

CHAPTER XV.

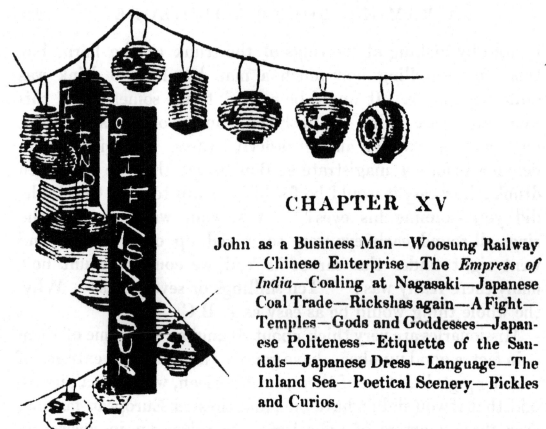

CHAPTER XV

John as a Business Man—Woosung Railway
—Chinese Enterprise—The *Empress of
India*—Coaling at Nagasaki—Japanese
Coal Trade—Rickshas again—A Fight—
Temples—Gods and Goddesses—Japan-
ese Politeness—Etiquette of the San-
dals—Japanese Dress—Language—The
Inland Sea—Poetical Scenery—Pickles
and Curios.

LEAVING Shanghai in the tender in order to get
outside the bar to board the *Empress of India*, although
there was some fog about, looking at the banks of the river
every evidence could be seen of the Chinaman's industry, for
there hardly seemed an inch of ground that was not cultivated.
It is said that the Chinese make the best gardeners in the world,
and from what I saw, I should really think this was correct ; in
fact, I almost agreed with those people who called Shanghai
the 'Garden of China.' Of course, I had not seen much of
the Celestial empire ; but it must be something very good
indeed to beat what I saw here. For once in a way while I

possible to find, is, in his own estimation, far superior to any European, whom he considers, if anything, just a shade lower than street mud !

The general opinion is that the Chinese, as a race, are born thieves and swindlers, and on no account to be trusted. Well, in striking a bargain with any one, one has to ' keep the weather-eye open,' and perhaps it is a little more necessary to do this in dealing with a Chinaman, for (although I am told there are honest ones) if they can do you, they certainly will. But then, who won't ? Is our standard of commercial morality so high at home that we can take everything for gospel that is told us in trade ? As I said, a Chinaman will do you if he can ; but he will do it in a straightforward way. Still, they are very intelligent and clear-headed, and if they know that they are well looked after, are as honest as any one can find man. They will stick to a bargain when once made, whatever may be the consequences; but, again, against this we have to put the

was first used as a horse tramway, then kind of donkey-engines made their appearance, till at length, I am told, it developed into almost a regular railway. Then the Chinese Government bought the whole concern, and tore up the rails, some say because they declared they only granted the concession for a horse-tramway, and that they were of opinion that had been 'got over.' The trades union theory comes in very strongly here, for the great reason given was that it threw thousands out of work, by taking away from them the trade they used to do by bringing up goods in junks, etc. However, whatever the reason may have been, the railway has been destroyed, and now every one has to put up with the inconvenience and loss of time in waiting for tenders or rickshas.

One instance of Chinese enterprise amused me very considerably. The previous day I had been out in a ricksha the best part of the day, and the next morning when I left the hotel there was a grand rush of about a dozen coolies shouting, 'Ha, ha, me belong you!' just like our cabbies sing out 'Cab, sir?' I shouted back, 'No, no, me walkee'; but that didn't suffice—a procession of 'crawlers' followed me for some time, my man of the previous day being amongst the number. One by one they gradually dropped off; but he remained, and followed me about for hours from shop to shop and place to place. If I stood still for a bit to have a look round, so would he; if I sat down anywhere, down he would squat about ten yards off, and all this just for the chance of getting a fare. After an hour or two of this sort of thing, I took compassion on him and got trundled back to the hotel. The look of

On the high seas once more, and on board a boat—*The Empress of India*; I can give the name this time, for she is a boat of which any company might well feel proud. Ah, what a difference to the last one I was on! Everything here nice,

clean, tidy—in fact, downright spick and span. Again it is possible to sleep well, for the rats have ceased from worrying, and cockroaches are at rest. At least, that is, if there are any on board, for certainly I never saw or heard of either of these abominable pests.

Out on the open sea again, I am bound for that most interesting country, 'the land of the Rising Sun,' the home of the jolly little Japs. Nagasaki is the first place reached, and a prettier harbour could not be found anywhere. It is rather narrow; in fact, the entrance would, I suppose, be about a

sampans, junks, and immense barges come floating towards us, as though we were in Venice, containing scores of men and women, boys and girls, and as soon as they reach the side they commence building a sort of hanging scaffolding. This is completed with marvellous dexterity and speed, and, when finished,

LEAVING THE BOAT IN A HURRY

looks a huge erection of steps. Every one is busy running

coal are passed along lines of some twenty-five or thirty Japs, and in this way two thousand tons is got on board. Ten hours is given

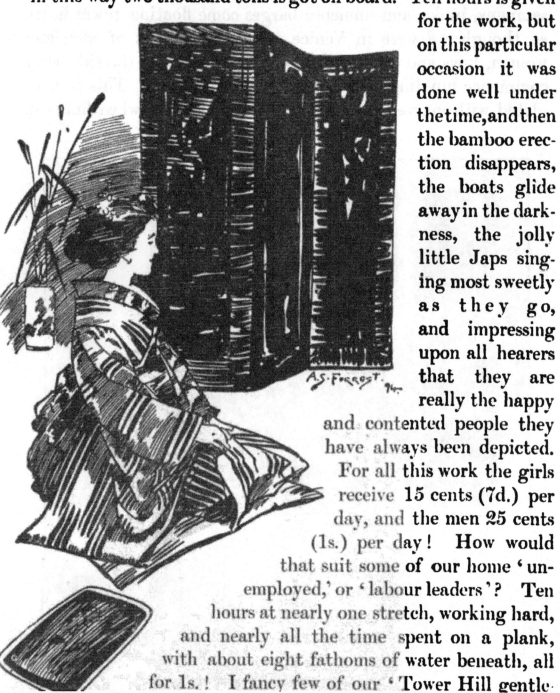

for the work, but on this particular occasion it was done well under the time, and then the bamboo erection disappears, the boats glide away in the darkness, the jolly little Japs singing most sweetly as they go, and impressing upon all hearers that they are really the happy and contented people they have always been depicted. For all this work the girls receive 15 cents (7d.) per day, and the men 25 cents (1s.) per day! How would that suit some of our home 'unemployed,' or 'labour leaders'? Ten hours at nearly one stretch, working hard, and nearly all the time spent on a plank, with about eight fathoms of water beneath, all for 1s.! I fancy few of our 'Tower Hill gentle-

chattering all the time, reminding me very much of the monkeys in the trees when I was in Africa some years ago.

By the way, the coal trade of Japan has largely developed in recent years, and perhaps chiefly from a cause that it would be as well for 'trades unionists' and 'labour leaders' in other parts to look at. Some time ago the whole coal trade in these parts was in the hands of Australia, but when the labour disputes arose, and strikes took place, of necessity steamship companies and others had to look elsewhere for their supplies, and consequently the trade was, as it were, forced on the Japanese, causing Australia to lose a large and lucrative trade in the East, which, in all probability, will never return. Radical statesmen and trades union leaders could take a good lesson from this, for it should show them the futility of trying to enforce such measures as eight hours days and such like. Capital and labour should be more sympathetic towards each other, and not by their antagonism force trade elsewhere, and thereby irretrievably damage the interests of both. Moreover, returning to Australia again, the coal trade is damaged, not only by the—shall we call it 'boycotting' by the steamship companies; but knowing what the resources are China and other

lost, as other countries will lose too, unless the labour party bring common-sense to bear on their actions and alter their present mode of procedure.

The sampan conveyance was used for transporting us from ship to shore, and my first impression of Japs on land was that they were an uncommonly peculiar lot. A body of about twenty ricksha men rushed at me almost before I was landed, and I found myself seized by the lot. The atmosphere became somewhat azure round about for a little time, then I managed to shake a few off, and say, 'Who talk English?' This brought the whole pack back, and amidst the noise, I heard several shouts of 'Me talk English!' This was getting a bit too warm, so, with a struggle, I got one arm free, and then 'landed out.' Five of the party were on the floor in no time, and during a bit of a pause, I jumped into the nearest ricksha, and yelled to the man to go like — well, very fast, up to the hotel. Then there was another

hullabaloo the

to do it in anything like the way it should be done—like the Hawaiian Islands—it ought to have a book to itself. Miles have been, and could still be written, on this most interesting country, and then the whole subject could be turned up again fresh.

So far as the towns go, they are all pretty much of a muchness —good thriving places, with every one happy and contented, and working hard. Starting at Nagasaki, one can go through the whole island if they wish, looking at nothing else but temples ; for they are about as thick all over the place as 'real estate' offices are in America, while 'kirks' in Scotland, and public-houses in Sydney, are simply not in it. They are not ordinary sort of places either, for some of them cover a lot of ground. I got rather tired of ' doing temples,' so generally told my guide to just switch me on to something else, as the almost innumer-able tales of the various gods and god-desses I was hearing from morning to night were beginning to have a confusing effect on my brain. Some of the pictures of these deities show them to be most mar-vellous conceptions, and so are some of the images themselves ; for instance, the figures of Nio, which stand at the outer gates of most temples to keep guard, and frighten away any demons who

Kompira, another deity, must be somewhat of a gentle look-ing creature. There was no life-size model of him on view, but he is supposed to have 1000 heads, 1000 arms, and to be

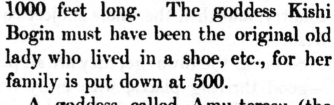

1000 feet long. The goddess Kishi Bogin must have been the original old lady who lived in a shoe, etc., for her family is put down at 500.

A goddess called Amu-terasu (the Heaven-shiner, or Sun Goddess) was pos-sessed of undoubted feminine instincts. After a tiff with her brother, Susa-ho-o, this lady deity retired to a large cavern in a fit of temper. This was very awkward for the other gods and goddesses, because, of course, she being the Sun Goddess, when she was not in evidence there was nothing but dark-ness about, for gas had not been in-vented in those days, so a musical evening was improvised at the mouth of the cave, all the deities getting there as well as they could in the dark. Naturally Amu-terasu came to see what all the noise was about, when a very artful god held a large look-ing-glass in front of her. This was too much for the lady, the sight of herself in the mirror made her forget all about the quarrel; and instead of going back to the cavern, she went

all day long, what wonder if the thing should get a bit monotonous. I heard such a lot about these gods and goddesses, I half expected to meet a few every now and then.

The turtle has a happy time of it in Japan, for he is a sacred animal—query, though, is he an animal? He certainly isn't a fish. Well, whatever he may be, he is held sacred.

A VERY ARTFUL GOD HELD A LARGE LOOKING-GLASS BEFORE HER

Great attention is paid to him by many thousands of people in our own country, but of a different nature.

For thorough downright (outward) politeness, commend me to the Japanese. They beat the French out and out, for they

manners and general habits, John Chinaman is miles and miles away behind the jolly Jap. John Chinaman has a crude practical roughness about him, while the Jap is more refined. To make a homely comparison — the difference between the Japanese and the Chinese is about the same as that between our real aristocrat and a gentleman resident of Whitechapel. It is the same with all classes, high and low, courtesy is the rule, and bowing, curtseying, and hat-raising goes on continuously.

One custom which prevails, though, is rather awkward to a beginner, and that is taking off one's shoes before entering a house. Of course, the idea of this is not to soil the mats that lie about the floor, and are used for sitting on, instead of the ordinary Christian-like chairs. When making a call, you can always tell how many people are in the house by counting the sandals at the door. This would be a very good idea for the authorities here at the next taking of the census, and it would certainly save a lot of expense, if, instead of filling up papers and all that kind of thing, people were simply sent round to count the pairs of boots on the door steps. Some plan would have to be devised though, to keep Messrs. Sykes & Co. asleep.

socks, that have a special place for the big toe, and a pair of sandals—they were called sandals, but in reality they were more like—well, say clogs on stilts. With these I thought it would be all right paying calls, because it would be so easy just to kick them off and hang them on the hat-peg. I tried them first in my room at the hotel, and gradually got used to walking in them. At first my carriage was hardly what one would expect to see in Hyde Park, but I soon got into the 'swing' of the thing, and was pre-pared to sally forth in these 'new boots,' when my friend, who was 'showing me round,' gravely told me that the previous day he had only been joking when advising me to buy sandals, and that the difficulty could be got over by carrying about a pair of cloth kind of goloshes to slip over the boots. My practice and my purchase had been thus in vain.

However, in the best tea-houses the boots have to come off. My ricksha man took me out to one of these one day, and when I got there, I almost fancied it

chairs or tables in evidence—in fact, the whole place looked like a well swept granary or malt barn. While wondering what to do, four little Jap girls suddenly appeared, and pounced on to my boots. I have had fox-terriers and puppies worrying at my laces, but I could not understand what these four little Japs were doing. Being too amused to ask questions, I submitted quietly, and listened to them chattering, till at last I had to lift up one foot, and off came the boot, up went the other foot, and off came the other boot; then two girls dodged from behind me, went down on their knees, and each one adjusted a slipper. When these were properly fixed on my feet, the six little Japs ushered me into the matted room. There was still no tea, but a large and elaborate cushion was brought and placed on the floor by me, also a kind of small brass bucket containing about a handful of charcoal fire in a

amusement was caused to the young ladies, but discomfiture to myself. All this time a most sage and austere Japanese chaperon had been superintending operations, and now she summoned music. Tom-tom things, like mandolines, were brought in, and while these were being played (?), half a dozen little Japs danced to me, while I was occasionally asked, 'You piecee 'Merican man? You piecee English man?' Then green tea without sugar or milk was brought, and I *had* to drink it! Then lumps of dough or suet, with sugar on, were brought round, as well as pastry and toffee. Oh, this was *so* nice! Awfully nice! But

THERE IS AN ART IN SQUATTING

there always is a but, it was about the most awfully indi-

tainment I gave two dollars, and thought it cheap, but next day I heard I had paid three times too much ! Still, what did it matter to me, when for an hour I had been fancying myself Nebuchadnezzar or some Eastern potentate surrounded by his court, and at the same time wondering what my London friends, 12,000 miles away, would think of me if they saw me in such luxuriousness ?

By the way, 'squatting' is another art that should be practised well in private before being attempted in public. The jolly little Japs seem to sink down on the floor with all the ease imaginable, and rise up again with the same freedom of action, but the first attempts at it by other than a native are not graceful. I began to practise it at the hotel, but came down with a run the first time, and caused a little consternation in the place, timid people thinking there was an earthquake coming along, so at a very polite request from the landlord I desisted. Otherwise I fell in with all the manners and customs of the country so well, I really believe that had I stayed much longer the Emperor would have wanted to create me an extraordinary Knight of the Grand Chrysanthemum, or in other ways signify his appreciation of my readiness to adapt myself to the usages of his country. However, I did not stay long enough, so this did not happen.

It is a great pity that the Japanese are taking so much to European customs and dress, for they don't suit them, especially the dress. The native costume is very becoming, and the people are built for it, but to see a man walking about arrayed

her suite, it will gradually become more and more worn by others.

The language of the place is not at all bad, although I did not try to acquire it. It takes rather a long time, though, to get round some of the phrases; for instance, 'How far is it to the next town?' is, in Japanese, 'Koro kara, saki no shuku made ri-su wa dono kurai desu?' One would think that, instead of taking up so much time over a question like that, it would be a saving to just walk over to the next town and see what the distance really was. Letters of introduction are most formidable affairs. A friend in Nagasaki gave me one to a gentleman Jap in Kobe—it was about a yard long, and I had not the slightest idea what it meant.

In going to Kobe from Nagasaki, we go through the Inland Sea, and this is really worth all the trouble of travelling, for it is incomparably lovely. From end to end—that is, from point to point where it communicates with the open sea—it is nearly 240 miles long, and although in one part it widens out to about forty miles, in others it narrows to somewhere about eight or less, and in parts where there are little islands, shoals, rocks, etc., the navigable part is only two or three hundred yards wide. The beauty of the surrounding scenery is superb:

leaving the rough and boisterous sea, a most perfect picture

A BLEND OF COLOURED
SILK

Wooded hills and well cultivated land are on all sides; above, a clear blue sky; below, this peaceful sea, studded all over with the quaint and attractive Japanese junks and vessels of various sizes and shapes, many containing fishermen fishing. As we proceed, for hour after hour, we watch this magnificent panorama, which seems to get more and more beautiful—in fact, the scene is poetry itself, and in poetry alone it should be described. My artistic feelings got the better of me, and I attempted a sketch, but could not get the light quite right, so made the whole thing darker, and called it moonlight. I am rather pleased with it. It is almost with feelings of regret we find that at last Kobe is reached, the anchor dropt, and the scene over.

Kobe is a favourite port, and a good business place; the climate also is very good. It is for this latter reason much visited, and another attraction to it is that there are so many places of interest in the immediate neighbourhood that can very easily be reached. The Nunobiki Waterfalls are worth seeing. There are two, called respectively Male and Female Fall—the first being eighty-two feet high, and the latter only forty-three feet. Quaint little tea-houses are dotted about here and the

It was in Kobe European habits seemed to be most obtrusive, upsetting the charm of the place; for to see in shop windows,

Scotch marmalade, or packets of English packed tobacco, is not nice, and all the poetry and romance is knocked clean out of the situation at once. Let the Japs sell English pickles and marmalade and anything else they like; but, my dear people, for goodness sake don't mix them all up with your own pretty wares.

Osaka, Kioto, Tokyo, all have their attractions; but the latter, being the capital, is naturally looked upon with most interest. Here the Parliament House is situated, and there are several large and interesting public and other buildings in the place. Then comes Yokohama, which is practically the port for Tokyo, and after a tour round this town and neighbourhood, having sampled so many different climates, and feeling so thoroughly well, I decide to close my tour and return home.

CHAPTER XVI

BEFORE I got to Yokohama, I had come very decidedly to the opinion that in wandering through Japan I had collected far more curios than I could ever dispose of, and my mind was made up that 'finis' should be put at the foot of the list, but when I reached here my good resolutions vanished far quicker than they were arrived at. It's a funny thing, most resolutions have that way about them. They take some considerable

nothing left but to go home, with a proud feeling of 'duty nobly done,' I strolled forth into the streets of Yokohama.

Alas for resolution! The first curio shop that intercepted

must say is very attractive. Their artless ways are particularly winning, and if they are at all inclined to be pretty—well, they are pretty, and this, with the peculiar style of doing the hair, and quaint but becoming costume, produces an effect almost irresistible. During my journey across the island, I had seen a great many pretty little lady Japs, but here in this curio shop was the prettiest of all. When he had showed me one or two things, told me the price, and smiled—what could a fellow do but buy! What resolution can stand against laughing, sparkling eyes, a winning smile that just shows the daintiest of white teeth, and a soft musical voice that discourses pretty broken English? St. Anthony himself couldn't have withstood the seductive wiles of this sweet little Jap. I gave in at once; it was no use trying to battle against it. Had I made a whole shipload of resolutions, they would have had to go and look after themselves. Before I really knew where

was, I was the possessor of goodness knows how many bronzes,

I had so rapidly soared whilst gazing on the lovely face of this angelic little charmer.   It is, as it always used to be—

> ' Poor Wisdom's chance,
> Against a glance,
> Is now as weak as ever.'

With this seraphic vision indelibly impressed upon my mind, with a beating heart and a regular tornado of peculiar feelings,

'POOR WISDOM'S CHANCE'

in my best Japanese, and with the neatest of bows, I bade fare-well to this fascinating little Jap, and went away to a Japanese lunch.   It was a very good lunch.   We began with Miso-shiru, then had some Sakana-no-shioyaki and Unagi-meshi, after this

It took me some little time to get all my things packed, and arrange with shipping-agents to have the numerous cases sent home; but it was all done at last, and then, after a final look round, I took up my quarters on board the Messageries Maritimes s.s. *Sagalion*, bound for Marseilles. I wanted to try this line, but had my doubts about it, as rumours were afloat that cholera was having a fine time at Marseilles. However, the officials at the Company's office soon restored my confidence, and said: 'Zare ise no cholera in Marseilles. It ise a cablegram sent by ze opposition Companie to say so, so zey get more passengaire. Cholera? Mon dieu! Zare ise no cholera in Marseilles, M'sieur!' Taking this as gospel, my passage was booked, and I was by no means sorry afterwards at the decision I came to.

It seemed strange, after knocking about so much, seeing so many different countries, and knowing

'ZARE ISE NO CHOLERA AT MARSEILLES'

that there was still a six or seven weeks' voyage ahead, that I was going home at last. That word home sounds very different on different occasions, and this was one of the times when the full meaning comes strongly to the front. Here was I, consider-

and started on my way home to spend my holidays in the best way I could.

I always used to enjoy those holidays, more so than the rest of the family, I believe. There were certain neighbours, too, who never seemed to look on those holidays with pleasure. One in particular, I remember, who didn't like them, and only just because I would at times get up early in the morning and try my hand at reducing the game and vermin in the district. Most ridiculous, I thought at the time (but I can understand it now), because I didn't kill much. He said that was just it; in fact his words were: It isn't what he kills, it's what the little

Sydney Cowell

BOTHERED BY THESE

these men so, because I wasn't a poacher—only an amateur
sportsman. Still there are some people who will not see any
idea different to the one fixed in their own mind. More
than once, I verily believe, I should have been most ignominiously removed by these objectionable gentlemen, had it not
been for my most faithful red dog, who had the same rooted
antipathy to gamekeepers as myself, and could smell them a
mile off, and so give me warning that perhaps it would be as
well to change the base of our operations.

Well, the ' going home for the holidays ' kind of feeling came
over me as I stepped on board the *Sagalion*, and I almost felt
inclined to shout, but on second thoughts came to

the conclusion
that it would
hardly be the
correct thing
to do amongst
the excitable
Frenchmen and
Japs, so re-
frained.

Is it wicked to laugh at the misfortunes of
others, or wrong to be amused at them ? If so, I am afraid I
must plead guilty of being both wicked and wrong, but not so
wrong as wicked. Still, I can't help it, for the sight on board
just before leaving Yokohama was without doubt the funniest
and most laughable scene I had witnessed during the whole of
the many thousands of miles I had travelled.

If the reader will bear in mind what I have said about the

on coming on board they took off their sandals, and left them lying on deck while they went below to have a final leave-taking over one of the large variety of beverages stored downstairs, and it was only natural that a long row of these should prove a little in the way of the sailors. Not for a minute would I infer that the sailors and middies of the *Sagalion* purposely found those sandals in their way. They had their duty to perform, and if in the execution of that duty one, two, or three came in contact with their feet, and made a rapid flight towards various parts of the deck, who was to blame? Surely not the sailors and middies. But at anyrate, somehow or other the majority of the sandals, so carefully placed on the deck, finding themselves getting mixed with the feet of various people, endeavoured to adopt the politeness of their owners and get out of the way, so distributed themselves over a very wide area.

Now came the time for starting, and those who had to return to shore, knowing full well the punctuality of the French boats, were frantically tearing about the deck endeavouring to find their sandals! The scramble was awful, and, although the sight was most ludicrous, it did seem to be hard upon the poor offenceless Japs. An individual would possibly find one sandal, and see another some yards off, looking like its fellow, rush at it, make a grab at it, but at that moment it would probably come in contact with some one's foot, and move off some yards, with the result that the anxious owner would overbalance himself, and cut a somewhat

ever, the last jolly Jap and the last pair of sandals were eventually safely transported overboard on to the tender, and then the erstwhile worried victims showed that they had thoroughly enjoyed the joke.

The ways and habits of the French ships are very similar to those of other countries When every one is on board, and the gangway is pulled up, up comes the anchor, a lot of smoke goes out of the funnels, there is a big noise, a cross between a

SANDAL-HUNT ON BOARD THE 'SAGALION'

burr-ur-ur and thud, thud, thud, and a commotion in the water at the stern of the boat as the screw goes round, and the big vessel gradually moves away, amidst cheering, handkerchief waving, and—yes, and weeping. I didn't weep, although

Gradually that little island, the visit to which had proved none the least interesting part of my travels, got dimmer in the distance, and, as it disappeared, I said good-bye to it with an earnest hope that I might some day see it and its clever, interesting, intelligent, and industrious people again.

Then came the settling down for the long voyage, and a casual look round to see who was who. In that look round there was a chance of having a good look at the boat, and it didn't take very long to find out that the directors of the Messageries Maritimes de France studied the comfort of their passengers in every possible way, for all the arrangements were most excellent. This opinion, formed at the commencement of the voyage, was confirmed and strengthened each day, and I must say that I should never wish for greater comfort or attention than that I experienced on board the *Sagalion*. In fact, it would be useless to wish it, because you couldn't get it.

The day after leaving Yokohama, we experienced one of those lively little things called Monsoons, and for nearly two days the waves played with the big boat in great style, but we weathered it all right, and there were not many invalids. The seas are very nasty about here ; in fact, in some parts it seems to be hardly sea at all, for it is more like liquid mud flying about, and some of the officers and crew coming off duty don't look altogether unlike a London policeman after he has been directing traffic for a few hours in Piccadilly on a good wet muddy day.

It was getting rather dark as we approached the mouth of

—a habit, I believe, common to Dutchmen—he said, 'Good Heavens, yes! It seems funny, ch? but de Engleesh language, do you know, is always de very best to use in extremities. De very best!' That mud-bank didn't detain us long, and by night we were safely anchored off the bar.

Hearing in the morning that a lot of festivities were going on in

BLOWING HARD—ON THE 'SAGALION

Henley Regatta was not in it for 'bunting.'   I tried a different way to get to Shanghai this time, and had a nine miles' run in a ricksha, in order to see where that notorious railway had been pulled up.   Dear me!   The journey was very interesting—extremely so to those whose sense of smell is deficient or absent altogether!   There were overground graves—that's all right, although it does look rather Irish—all along the route,

and at Shanghai itself were some fifteen or twenty boxes containing corpses, awaiting a fine day for a good royal burial!   I wondered at this, because funerals don't cost very much; in fact, they are so cheap, I could not help thinking of an advertisement I saw once, at the time influenza was raging, in the window of a Whitechapel under-taker, ' Why walk about in misery when you can be comfortably buried for £3, 10s. 0d. ? '   ' Kniffy' is a peculiar word, but it is really the proper one to describe the atmos-phere in the neighbourhood of these boxes.

On my previous visit to Shanghai, I had only seen the native 'force'

time, as in our country. In the evening, a friend of mine and I visited a theatre in the Chinese quarter, not much patronised by Europeans, as they don't care to run the risk, but we were paid marked attention, and had no cause for complaint, although we were very conspicuous, being the only Europeans present. Yes, yes; it was an experience, and reminded one of the Scotchman's remark, after his first visit to Sandie Thompson's back parlour in Edinburgh, that it was the nearest to

bliss it was possible to get, for there were five-and-twenty pipers all playing different tunes at the same time. Really, as far as we were concerned, each of the actors might have been acting different plays, for everything was to us simply downright unintelligible. Just like in our London Music Halls, all classes of the community were represented, from the Celestial masher to the ditto 'Arry, and all seemed to be thoroughly enjoying themselves, especially when some particularly typical element was introduced, and this was every few minutes, for in almost

all the acts there was an execution with knives of all sorts, shapes, and sizes flying about. The programme was as the

was the handing round of small cups of tea and a pipe. It was a public pipe, and the man who handed this round also carried a hot cloth, with which he wiped the mouthpiece every time any one had had a whiff. It was a good wipe round, and then bang it went into the nearest Celestial mouth. He also had a hot cloth to wipe faces with. I had been watching this, while my friend was engrossed with the performance on the stage, and when my turn came I said most politely, 'No, my friend catchee pipee first,' whereupon he took it, and was putting it into his mouth when he caught sight of a smile on my face, and dropped the whole thing like a hot potato, much to the consternation of Mr. Chinaman pipe-bearer.

The *Sagalion* was to start early in the morning, and I had requested to be called at 7 A.M., and just about this time I was roused up by a noise, then saw a beaming face, the owner of which was pulling at my clothes to get me up, and shouting, 'You piecee man b'long Flench boat; Flench boat go chop-chop.' What on earth did that mean? It was evidently something important, so up I got, and got the whole sentence off by heart while I was dressing, to find, when I got downstairs, that it meant that the French boat was really the only one that started to time, so that passengers had better 'hurry up,' if they didn't want to be left behind.

Very soon I 'chop-chopped' off to the tug, as I had no particular wish to wait for another steamer.

Dear me, there was an enormous crowd on board this tug, and, from the look of the people, it almost seemed that every dispenser of the gospel was clearing out of the neighbourhood

certain pigtailed gentlemen displayed an unmistakably Oxford cultured language, and then the ladies! 'Next, please!' To describe the eccentric, the pronounced fanatical, the æsthetical, and otherwise peculiar specimens of feminine nature on board that tug is beyond me, so 'I pass.'

By the time we reached Hong-Kong, where we just made a call, the passengers had begun to feel more at home with each other, and flirting, and deck-games had already commenced—especially the former. Wonderful place for flirting, a large ocean-going boat! And they all do it, even down to the little girls and boys on board. I suppose it's human nature, and will always be the same. And why shouldn't it? It passes away the time, and is very good fun into the bargain—at least, so I've been told. Please do not think for one moment, gentle reader—dear me, I like that term 'gentle reader,' and to think I have never used it once before! perhaps it is the reminiscence of the soothing influence of the China missionaries that brought it out!—no, no, please, do not think that I speak on this subject from any personal experience, for it would be an error on your part, and almost as great a one as it would have been on mine, had I so far forgotten myself as to take part in such sport. No, I was very much amused at the whole business, but there I drew the line.

There was a large crowd of passengers between Shanghai and Hong-Kong, simply because there were going to be some races at the latter place, and the Shanghai people were trooping down to witness two days' racing with very inferior ponies. Well, every one to their taste, but that is certainly not mine. I never even go to Sandown Park, although, like all costers, I have been to the Derby and Ascot, and perhaps Goodwood, because every well-regulated individual goes to these

typhoons just to see a few races lasting two days, is an enthusiasm I could not possibly work myself up to.

Of course it would not have been right to be anchored at Hong-Kong and not go ashore, so, as much as anything to have what I thought would be a final jaunt in a sampan and ricksha, I took a turn on dry land.

Hong-Kong looked just like it did when I left it a few weeks before, and John Chinaman was just as smiling; but even here, where he is so much in contact with English influence, the contrast between him and the Japs was very marked. Having studied the two nationalities in their own countries, I came to the conclusion, after having another good look at the Celestials here, that the two people cannot be compared; both have their good qualities and special merits, but the Japanese are the superior social people.

Leaving Hong - Kong, our next stopping-place was Saigon, which we found to be a lovely spot, and every one was charmed with it. The Botanical Gardens here are very fine, and contain more

STORKS

to see them in gardens, but quite a different matter to dream that while an assortment of pelicans are 'going for you' from behind, some six or eight storks of different sizes are prodding at you with their beaks in front.

It is a thoroughly tropical place, not badly situated for trading purposes, and altogether the French did well to select it for the capital of their Cochin-Chinese settlements. The town itself is quite French, but still it seems to lack that bustle and business-like atmosphere so noticeable at Hong-Kong, and one almost thinks what a pity it is John Bull hasn't got the little place, so as to put some more commercial activity into it. It is only a passing thought, though, for really we ought to be satisfied, as we have about every corner of the world that is worth having.

Some Americans talk very largely about eventually owning the universe, but up to now the preponderance of the British flag, flying as it does in every quarter of the globe, and on every sea, does not point very clearly to this. It is not right that we should compete with our Ameri-

marked partiality to mud-banks, for on leaving Saigon something went a little bit wrong with the steering-gear, and all at once she found herself some thirty feet or more in a bank. Had warning been given to the passengers that something was going to happen, results would have been more pleasant ; but these things all come off when you least expect them. In the present instance I was just enjoying the delights of a bath when the shock came, and I suddenly found myself on the floor outside the bath ! Most people are naturally inquisitive, but when anything of this kind happens on board it is wonderful how quickly every one gets on deck to see what is the matter. It didn't take me long to slip on my pyjamas, and get up aloft to make inquiries. Having been assured it was only a mud-bank that had got in the way of the ship, I returned below and completed my toilet.

Having recovered from the shock of imaginary shipwreck, our well assorted party of passengers began to settle down for the voyage to Singapore, our next stopping-place. The general subject of conversation seemed to be the bad colonisation of the French, and the comparison to be drawn between that country's efforts in foreign parts and those of England. There were plenty of Germans on board, and they, while decrying the French system very much (they would naturally do this), were bound to put in a heap of praise for the 'Vaterland' and the taming influence of the sausage and the onion on the savage mind. I simply listened to all this, but at the same time must

fun we availed ourselves of it, either on board or on shore, and we made game of the 'flirters.' More than once we turned a bright lantern on to a dark corner on deck rather unexpectedly and disturbed a couple who seemed to be evidently rehearsing lovemaking or some tender scene in a novel or a play, and perhaps this had something to do with it; I don't know. This harmless amusement ought not to have earned for us the reputation necessary to be acquired before being called such names, because, after all, it was very innocent amusement. Is there anything wrong in kissing a girl? I don't know at all, because I never did it; but if it's all right, why should any one object to having a bright light thrown on them just as they are going through the process? This is a mystery to me altogether

THE EFFECT WAS AWFUL

raised wrath within his fevered soul. He considered himself a bit of a poet, and now and then when opportunity
arose, would avail himself of it, and give off most doggerel
rhymes.

One night, after leaving Saigon, there was an impromptu
concert on board, and, just before this commenced, he was on
deck with one or two of the 'blackguard' party. We had
secured our horror-striking lantern, and, while chaffing him
about his flirty companion, suddenly turned on the light to
discover her and a missionary in a loving embrace in a dark
recess behind the wheel.

The effect was awful. There was a screech, and a—well, not
a religious word—from the quarter the light struck on, and no
end of gurgling and smothered exclamations, reminding me of
the geyser district of New Zealand, from the poet; and then
everybody tried to laugh. The 'blackguard' party laughed
most genuinely, but the others only did it in a sickly sort of
way. However, it seemed to have been all forgotten by the time
the concert commenced ; but it hadn't. During the evening the
poet was called on for something. 'Something of your own, Mr.
Rhymer,' said the skittish one. With a withering glance at the
fair frivoller, the poet arose, and putting himself into an atti-
tude presumably imposing if not eminently graceful, he gave
off some lines which showed that his busy brain had been at
work since being present at our exploit with the lantern of all-
penetrating rays. Whether or no, when he was fairly estab-
lished in a position on the saloon carpet, with a second

showered so much devoted attention, he thus delivered himself: 'The small item I intend giving you this evening
has been brought from my brain from viewing many amor-

GOT A BIT HURT IN TRYING TO LEAVE

I was given to understand afterwards that there were five or six verses like this ; but the first was quite enough for me. 'Enough of this, begone !' something seemed to scream in my ear, and evidently into the ears of several of my fellow-passengers ; for there was a wild rush for the door, and a fairish amount of squeezing was necessary in order to 'get out.' Some people said they got a bit hurt in trying to leave the saloon and get on deck.

The time was wiled away somehow or other, and the usual 'sweep' on the run of the vessel was started, with a very jolly gallant Major as auctioneer. I liked this Major, although there are some army men who are not very entertaining, especially the younger ones, for they seem so eaten up with their own importance, they cannot allow any one to have any ideas at all that do not coincide with their own, and they will talk upon

A VERY JOLLY MAJOR

CHAPTER XVII

Dressed for Landing—Singapore—**The Silver Question—A Cab Strike—' Home, sweet Home '—The New Passengers—Busybodies—The Smoke-room Party—French Politeness—Colombo—Singhalese Tradesmen—Bargaining—The Twenty-Dollar Piece—An Impromptu Sale—Messageries Maritimes Punctuality—Female Friendliness.**

THE day before we reached Singapore there was naturally a little excitement about, as here we were to see an almost entirely different country—in fact, get into the land of the Malays. Information was given that we should in all probability be able to land at about 11 o'clock in the morning, and the consequence was 7 A.M. saw nearly every one on deck preparing to land at a port, like an old lady or gentleman trying to catch a train, three hours before it starts—but what a change to the previous day. The fashionable promenade of any large city might suddenly have been transported on to the deck of the *Sagalion*.

and trim waists were *de rigueur*. Being on board a French ship is answerable for that expression. The passengers whose intention it was to land were determined that the natives of Singapore should not have cause to complain of their wearing-apparel, and the Japanese certainly took first prize, for their European garb was simply faultless, even to the tall hat. One Japanese was a perfect picture. Above the ordinary height of his countrymen, and of little stouter build, he was not altogether a bad figure—and he knew it. He was arrayed in orthodox frock-coat, light trousers, patent leather boots, and a real lovely church-parade tall hat. Apparelled thus, he wandered up and down the deck, with a smile here, a nod there, a sweeping bow now and then to a lady, but all the time followed by the sorrowfully envious glances of his fellow-Japs, whose headgear was so far inferior in magnificence to that beautiful, that splendid hat. The varied assortment of hats was really a study ; the well-known straw was much in evidence, and there were also straws with flexible brims some eight or twelve inches in width ; the 'bowler' was not altogether out of the hunt, while the soft felt put in an occasional appearance, as did also the somewhat æsthetic-looking lawn tennis hat, and those so much associated with the name of

IN SHORE TRIM

they strutted about waiting for 'landing time' to enable them to give a treat to the folks on shore.

Singapore is not a great distance from the 'line'—in fact, only about one degree north—so any one can imagine the climate

A SWEEPING BOW NOW AND THEN

thing ; but, like all other resolutions, they were not stuck to long—in fact, within about ten minutes of starting, the next time I saw any of them was when I got on board again. Goodness only knows where they got to.

Singapore is a very important place, and another specimen of British enterprise in the East. It is not a remarkably large place, although its population is somewhere about 170,000. All is bustle and business, and the place is really the grand junction for all outlying places, and up - country states, as Peterborough or Grantham, on the Great Northern Railway, or Swindon, on the Great Western, where every one has to stop. In fact, for almost every place lying eastward of it, Singapore must be a calling-place. It is a grand place, and its commercial prosperity is something to be proud of.

Stanley L Wood
94

SOME HATS

quite certain what it was all about. I am pretty safe on one point, though, and that is that if I really did understand it, it would be too weighty a subject to handle here.

It was not unlucky business for me, though, for all along I had been getting a little over seven dollars for the English sovereign ; consequently I had no right to complain. It is all very well for people to spend their money in the East, drawing

it from London in gold, and turning it then into dollars ; but for those who have fortunes in the East and spend them in London, the situation is exactly reversed. In fact, this latter is almost as ruinous as the 'bang went saxpence' story of times gone by, and the unfortunate individuals who are placed in this position ought to be almost as careful of their belongings as the other astute Scotchman, who, shortly after landing in London, at Euston, was met by a couple of those professional gentlemen who always seem so anxious to know what other people have in their pockets. These two gentlemen proceeded to interview Scottie in a somewhat rough manner, and were rather surprised to find themselves in the gutter four or five times during the proceedings, but at last, having managed to rifle his pockets, they rushed off to some quiet spot to divide the proceeds, but only to find one halfpenny. 'Thunder. Bill !' said one of the gentlemen. ' if it had been a

a sensation going through the city of London; but little vulgar boys might be rude enough to say it was something that had got lost out of a circus, and others might make matters unpleasant; so our good old dray-horse may go on his way rejoicing without any fear of being superseded by a humpbacked Singapore cow.

About the time for returning on board an alarming diffi-

IN THE GUTTER FOUR OR FIVE TIMES

culty arose, for there was something like an organised strike amongst the Chinamen in charge of what answered the purpose of our cabs, and, as during the London 'bus strike a few years

and we had a plaintive cable from him at Colombo, asking us to shortship his luggage there. The strike couldn't have been very well organised, otherwise the bribe I offered would not have stirred the striker's heart and induced him to run the gauntlet of his irate colleagues. Just before leaving Singapore, there was a very impressive scene enacted on the quay, if it were not altogether a quiet one. About fifty fellows stood round in a circle and sang several good old English songs, winding up with 'Home, sweet home!' This last was almost too much for several of them; in fact, one man, who, having been in Singapore for over ten years, was now returning home to try his fortune once more in the old country, fairly broke down. I am not at all a sentimental individual, and can laugh at most things when other people weep, but I never even thought of a smile at this, as I could so thoroughly understand it. It's really marvellous how everybody you meet abroad talks of going home, excepting in America. All English people, and even Colonials who have never seen the Mother country, seem to have one fixed idea, and that is, of some day or other 'going home,' meaning, of course, England. It's a nice feeling, and one to be encouraged, for it shows that however much some people may talk, there is an innate loyalty and love of home in the heart of the Britisher and Colonial that cannot be eradicated.

When fairly at sea again and settled down, we were able to see who had come aboard, and found them a very miscellaneous lot, coming from Batavia, Sumatra, Java, etc.; and even the

and all that sort of rubbish, just like at seaside hotels and those places. If people would only spend a little more time looking after their own affairs, instead of prying about, poking their noses into other people's business, slandering people before they know who they are, and in other ways making themselves downright objectionable by their interfering, they would soon find out that they were doing far more good both to themselves and others, and would be much happier generally.

Of course it didn't take long the first night to see who were the ones that had not been to sea much, for these people wandered quietly to their berths at a very early hour, and those who did try and 'brass it out' by turning up in the smoking-room, looked with anything but a kindly eye on both pipes and whisky. This wasn't a matter of sentiment, so of course we laughed. That smoking-room contained a most extraordinary cosmopolitan crowd; in fact, just about as fine a mixture as could well be imagined. A good quarter of the people could well be put down as English, and another quarter was composed of genuine 'parlez-vous's'; then the 'happy fatherland' laid claim to a fourth; and the remaining quarter was made

up of a variety of nationalities—Dutchmen from Java, Japs, Chinese, Malays, Portuguese, etc., not forgetting gentlemen who called themselves English, but who could not hide the traces of the 'smack of the tar-brush.' The clatter of dominoes on the marble-topped tables, as the French detach-

at least ten cases out of twelve I did not come off *second* best. Draughts again afforded me considerable amusement, but caused great consternation to an elderly gentleman, who considered himself 'a swell' at the game, for, when I was his opponent, he was annihilated every game. Lots of people don't like to think their fathers taught them anything; but I am always very proud to think my father taught me to play draughts, and the care and trouble he took over it then, have since thoroughly disconcerted many opponents who started the game with a free and easy air, and a kind of conscious-of - victory style about them. Then there were poker, nap, loo, etc., all of which games claimed

one objection to them, and that was the amount of absinthe they drank. Naturally they tried to convert us to the beauties of this stimulant; but, as far as I was concerned, I said, 'Get thee behind me, Satan! The Almighty has not given me much in the way of brains, but what little I have I will keep!' It would, perhaps, have been almost pardonable in the French passengers if they had assumed a certain amount of authority over the others, on board their own National liner; but this they did not do—in fact, it was the reverse. Every one was conscious they were on board the French National Line, the Messageries Maritimes (messages across the sea) and to the credit of the French party they seemed to so thoroughly recognise the fact that they appeared to think it their duty to do all in their power to please the other passengers, even to talking English. It was not altogether with feelings of pride that I watched the behaviour of some of my

STRONG ON 'ENGLAND'S IMPERTINENCE'

countrymen. There was a little too much of the 'Britisher abroad' about them, and the rude glare to which they treated every one who did not speak English was not a thing to rejoice at.

than I could; although, of course, there was an accent observable now and then.   This accent always gives any one away. It did me once when I was talking French with a volubility which surprised me, for I was told that I spoke beautiful French; but there was a very broad Scotch accent about it. This Chinaman was called Ching-Chang something or other; what it really was I never could make out; but all Chinamen

are Ching-Changs, Ah Sings, or something after that style.   He was a very shrewd man, well educated, and well informed on every topic. He was very strong on the matter of 'England's impertinence' in trying to teach everybody what they should do, when it was well known that China was in full swing many hundreds of years before any other place.   We often talked on this point; but I could never make him angry about it, although I often tried.   No; he was a most gentlemanly fellow, more so than any other Celestial I had met; he didn't even eat his rice with chop-sticks, and if it had not been for his green complexion, squat nose, broad features, and pigtail, he might well have been

Without anything remarkable happening on the way, we at last anchored at Colombo; and, as at other places, every one was 'dressed for the shore' hours before there was a chance of landing. Little native boys seemed to live in the water, and dived for any mortal thing that was thrown overboard. Of course, almost before we had anchored, men came on board for washing, and tried to sell things; and it was here that we got the first specimen of the European idea of Eastern —well, I was going to say cheating, but perhaps it should be called cunning! At every turn these Eastern gentlemen try to 'do' any one; and even when rowing us to shore they stopped half-way and wanted more money, which they did not get. On landing, the 'going-home' feeling came over us all again very strongly, and we wanted to send a cable home, although for no apparent reason.

Colombo is a beautiful place, and I was sorry we could not stay there longer so that we could have a look over the island of Ceylon, the golden world of tea-planters. The place was awfully hot, and the variety of outfits was 'most extwadinawy, weally.' First of all we started off to see Arabi Pasha, and found him a most agreeable

verandah, with coolies to bring iced drinks, etc., was grand; and to hear the residents raving about *hard times*, while they went in for iced champagne, was rather bewildering! Of course, it was not an uninterrupted journey to Arabi's or the hotel, for large numbers of the populace, consisting of Singhalese, Parsees, Arabs, Persians, Kaffirs, Afghans, etc., met the boats, and before we landed commenced pestering every

VISIT TO ARABI PASHA

one to buy something, and the selection ranged from native jam to sapphires.

After a rest at the hotel, I and half a dozen others started

were only Singhalese men, with beaming smiles on their
chalked faces, and long hair done up chignon fashion, who
crowded round you, pestering you to buy, and trying to push
you into their shops. Competition, from outward appearances,
seems very keen; but as all the lot are such awful rogues, I
doubt it, and believe they all work into each other's hands.
The amount of bad language they will stand if they think 'a

COOLING DRINKS ON THE VERANDAH

deal' is to follow is tremendous. England may be called a
nation of shopkeepers; but an Englishman can pick up a lot
of hints in smartness from these Singhalese, for no Q.C. in the

chalked foreheads, and swear in a way to their deity not to cheat; and then out come the lies just as fast and as thick as it is possible for them to talk. A favourite dodge at starting is to show a lot of dirty, greasy cards of persons who have done business at the shop, such as colonial governors, English nobility, etc. etc. I got tired of this, and yelled at the man whose shop I was in that I didn't come to see dirty cards, but to see what he had to sell; and if he couldn't show me any-thing, I would go elsewhere. 'Ah! master not know me. Only honest man here; all others robbers.' Then, having, as they think, gained confidence, they begin to swindle, or, as a friend of mine puts it, 'descend to common robbery,' but talk all the time about their valu-able stock of gems and jewels; and my shopman made a great feature of the fact that his father and grandfather had the business before him. He didn't care if I bought anything or not—oh, dear, no! but if I did, when I got to Eng-land I should be very sorry I didn't buy the whole stock. Money? oh, no, he didn't want money! If I hadn't brought any from the ship, a bill of exchange on London would do just as well. 'What would master like to see? Here

A COLOMBO DIAMOND
MERCHANT

up, dusky thieves, and keep even with them, 'takes a little bit of doing,' as they say in the classics. Three or four of us really intended buying, and we did the whole of the arcade to see what we could get. At one place I picked out a fairly good quantity of stones and put them into a heap, and then said, 'Now, then, you cunning Ananias, master want to buy. How much?' Several hundred sovereigns were mentioned. 'No, no—too dear.' Off came a hundred sovereigns at once. 'No, no—too dear. Master can't buy. He'll go somewhere

else.' 'No, no—master not go somewhere else. Master buy from honest man. Only honest man here. All others bad, robbers, wicked. Master must buy. What will master give?' I pulled out an American twenty-dollar piece, and then thought the term of my natural life was about run out, for, as I found out afterwards, these people will do almost anything for one of these coins to hang it round their dirty necks, or on their watch-chain, with other trinkets. Bargaining was forgotten, and like wildfire news spread round the place that I was the master with the big gold coin. The crowd began to get a little too attentive, and I got tired of being pulled about, so, with my friends backed out of the place, but only to find matters worse. Quite a crowd had collected and feeling

thicker, for everybody seemed to turn up to see what all the commotion was about ; then, feeling a bit like Tattersall selling best blood stock at Newmarket, when the folks got a little quiet I commenced the business, and had a very lively time of it too. With a tremendous flourish I started to harangue the crowd, and said : 'Gentlemen of bronze complexion, chalked foreheads, long hair, and generally unclean appearance, this sale, positively without reserve, will now commence, and I hope it will be conducted with due decorum and propriety on your part. I have here a twenty-dollar piece, bought by me in 'Frisco, and carried by me many thousands of miles, until it has arrived here, and I offer it——' I could get no further, for an excited would-be purchaser, eluding the vigilance of my 'guards,' jumped on the stone, caught hold of me, and cried, ' Master, how much ? how much ?' This was too much for the excited onlookers, and they charged the 'guards,' evicted the would-be purchaser, knocked me off the stone as well, and once more there was something like a fight, my friends and I using our fists very freely. Business all round the place was suspended, and the wildest excitement prevailed. Pulled first on one side, then on the other by a frantic crowd, offering me money in handfuls, yelling. 'How much, master ? how much ?' I was getting a bit

petitors in price, until at last I sold it in rupees for just three times its value! After that we went back to complete our purchases, and tried to get up some byways out of the way, but were followed by a large and admiring crowd, each member of which tried his hardest to monopolise our attention by telling what was this, that, and the other, and at the same time not forgetting to throw in business. Prices were getting lower and lower, and the man in whose shop I had selected the heap of stones kept a watchful eye on me, coming up to me every now and then, doing the confidence trick, advising me not to deal with others, and winding up by whispering a lower quotation. To get clear of the lot, notwithstanding the heat, we made a 'bolt' for the hotel, but were followed by the crowd, and the whole lot waited patiently outside until we had had lunch. Our boat was to go at seven P.M., and when we left the hotel we had about three hours; so, to get rid of our tagrag-and-bobtail following and make the best of our time, we went back to the arcade and settled with the merchants. My man came to terms, and parted with my selection when I offered him a handful of sovereigns (perhaps about £40), although at first he had held out for several hundreds. Bargains completed, the dusky tradesman wanted me to write him a letter testifying to his honesty in trading, my satisfaction at purchases made, etc. etc., so that he could show it to other customers; but although I am not altogether averse to a little advertisment now and then, judiciously done, I drew the line at this. Several more purchases were made, and then we rowed off to the boat, having had the most rollicking time on shore that we had yet experienced. The proverbial punctuality of the Messageries Maritimes was evidenced on leaving Colombo for the *Sagalien*

Australia coming in as we left.   The dinner that evening was a most lively one, for every one was most anxious to explain his or her experiences while on shore, and how they had 'done' the native traders in their bargains.   Very strange, in all these cases nobody ever gets 'done' himself—he always gets the best of the bargain.   I suppose it's natural, and I ought not to confess to being an exception, but I feel morally certain 'the

THEY ACTUALLY COMMENCED TO SQUABBLE

squabbles was that some people declared that they knew more about so-and-so than some one else did, and then the supposed to be inferiorly informed feminine mind asserted itself, and its owner endeavoured by all possible means to prove that nobody knew anything about anybody else but herself. Dear old busybodies! How they do love to meddle with other people's business, instead of looking after their own! It doesn't matter to them what mischief they cause through their meddlesomeness—not a bit of it; that's half the fun of being of an interfering disposition.

The sight of passing steamers showed us we were getting nearer home, and a slave-dhow that made its appearance threw us all into a great state of excitement. At last we got in sight of land again, and the idea of a walk on dry land once more stirred us all up to 'concert pitch.'

NEAR NEIGHBOURS

CHAPTER XVIII

Aden—Mutiny in a Boat—An Eastern Pickpocket—Buying Mementoes—
'Sold' over Ostrich Eggs—The Red Sea—Perim and Yarns—Suez
and Photo-merchants—Port Said a 'Hell upon Earth'—Thinking of
Children—Different Passengers—French Custom-house Officers—
Monte Carlo, Nice, Paris, and 'Home, Sweet Home.'

ADEN was the point we anchored at next, and that is a name
that never leaves the mind of any one who has once experienced
the pleasures and delights of a stay there, however short that
stay may have been; for it is there that sublimest of sublime
occupations, coaling, takes place. It is a fine place to get rid
of one's superfluous foreign coin, such as Chinese, Japanese,
American, and all that, for little imps of boys swarm round
the vessel like ducks, and dive for all the coins thrown over-

lived, and the crew of our boat was a most mongrel assortment. They numbered six, and represented almost as many nationalities, including a nigger with a mouth that looked as if it had been put on hot and run all over. About half-way to the shore the crew 'mutinied' for a higher fare than bargained for, and refused to move until we agreed. We tried volleys of Anglo-Saxon as at Colombo, but without avail, so had to resort to other means, especially as the 'crew' were getting insolent, and there were too many sharks about to make it pleasant for us to swim ashore. Words being of no use, a gentleman from the Fatherland, exclaiming, 'Stop, I vill kill der scoundrel!' brought his stick down on the head of the ringleader, I pushed another fellow off the seat and took his oar, while another passenger did ditto, and a Yankee, whipping out a six-shooter and firing in the air, guessed and swore by all that was blue he would shoot the whole lot rather than pay another cent. The effect was magical: four of the crew dived overboard, like seals off a rock, and swam ashore; the other two the Yankee, who assumed command, kept covered, while Mr. Fatherland, another man, and myself took the oars and rowed ashore. After landing, acting under in-

FORREST.

Aden is a peculiar place, and at times almost reminded me of the Scripture pictures I used to see in my juvenile days. Especially so was it to see camels going along in single file like horses at exercise in the early morning on the Heath at Newmarket ; but at the same time I should like to say I considered

The real men of commerce are found here—gentlemen straight from Jerusalem, Smyrna, etc. and they take a little bit of talking to. When we arrived on board with our cargo of purchases, there were still numbers of traders there, and we had to run the gauntlet again. Many nationalities were represented in this commercial crowd—in fact, even sufficient to remind one of that beautiful (I believe that is the correct adjective in such cases) hymn, known so well in one's childhood, 'From Greenland's icy mountains,' etc. Interviewing the Arabs on board was good fun, for all of them had a peculiar tale; some had been slaves, and some were sons of chieftains, and all of them had but one motive in trading, and that was, to make sufficient money to take them back to their chieftain fathers. Lies, most likely; for it seems a terribly hard matter for any of these Eastern beauties to even think the truth. I suppose it is, they tell the same story so often that, like most other liars all over the world, they actually believe it, and therefore 'lie like truth.' Whatever may be the price at which the articles these fellows, or indeed any others, sell, are offered, it is a great mistake to go buying things cheap, for if you don't want them they are always dear. I went buying away at all ports, just for friends at

HIS POCKETS PICKED

to know the cheapest market, I unhesitatingly say London. Of course, this may be open to contradiction; but I am speaking as a globe-trotter who, when on his walks abroad, sees pretty things and buys them, not as an expert who does the thing upon a commercial basis. However, my opinion is that anything is to be had better and cheaper in London than from cunning and artful natives, who lay themselves out to 'do' their customers at 'passenger prices,' and laugh when they have

done it. Be as 'cute as you like, you can't get the best of those fellows, for with them it is the result of a lifetime training. My advice is, go to a respectable tradesman in London, and pay him a fair and legitimate price for what you want; but, of course, the great objection to this is, that all the romance of the thing disappears, and a teapot bought in St. Mary Axe

mits to take them away. In fact, I bought no end of things. At Port Elizabeth I made a great bargain, and bought a number of ostrich eggs at an auction in the market-place, at about the same price as hen's eggs here, and gave a carpenter instructions to pack them and send off home to friends. Now, ostrich eggs are peculiar things when packed up, as I found out afterwards; for when I saw the immense crate into which they had been stowed, I certainly thought the carpenter had made a package of half-a-dozen pianos, instead of my bargain in eggs! My friends were in a white heat of excitement when the huge thing arrived in Scotland, and many were the conjectures as to the contents; but dire was the disappointment when it was found to contain eggs—only eggs! To add to this, on my arrival in London I saw ostrich eggs marked up at one shilling each; whereas, one way and another, not counting the bother, mine had cost me—well, I will never calculate what they did cost.

After leaving Aden, a certain gentleman of the genus Know-all, who, since Singapore, had been posing as a 'great authority' on all matters, began to assert himself very much. When we had been lying on deck, almost panting in the sweltering heat, he had strutted about saying, 'Nonsense! call this heat? Bosh! just wait till you get into the Red Sea, then you can talk about heat if you like!' Of course, I had heard all manner of tales of the heat in the Red Sea, such as there

tales; so when the 'great authority' commenced to talk, after passing Perim, about 'Now you'll find what heat is,' I was prepared for the worst.   Unfortunately for our learned friend, the excessive heat was taking a rest, and to his great discomfiture he, with others, was glad to put on an overcoat at night. However, this was, I was told, a very exceptional case.   The passage through the Red Sea is a dreary part of the voyage,

THE GENUS 'KNOW-ALL'

stone, as there is on Highgate Hill to mark the place where Dick Whittington sat down to listen to the bells before he and his cat took the tramp back to the City.

By the way, mention of Perim puts me in mind of a smoking-room story as to how it came into the possession of the English. It is, I know, a 'chestnut'—in fact, it is possible it may be approaching the bald-headed stage; but still, it was told in the smoking-room. Although the place looks like nothing but a cinder-heap, and doesn't seem to be worth anything to anybody, it is said that a French admiral, calling in at Aden, got friendly with the governor, and eventually told him he was on his way to Perim to hoist the French flag. The governor, congratulating him, invited him and his officers to dinner, but in the meantime gave instructions of a peculiar nature to a British gunboat; and the next day, when the admiral arrived at Perim, he was mightily surprised to find the Union Jack proudly floating there, and English bluejackets in possession! Some of the old travellers remembered no end of tales about this cinder-heap, and one of them I give just as I heard it, so hope no brother-author will think I want to hurt his feelings, or think me guilty of plagiarism if he has used

it before. It was of an officer who, in charge of a company of men, was stationed here; and, strange to say, although every one always objected to the post, he wrote on several occasions to have his stay prolonged, as the place suited him so well.

he ran right against the officer supposed to be in charge at Perim !

Then again, another story was about some outlandish British possession, where a newly appointed official over a certain district, who took it into his head to make a tour and become personally acquainted with the different consuls, was surprised to find at one place that the consul had been dead for three years, and that the business had been carried on by his widow since then, and indeed for some years previously.

Having finished this dismal tour through the Red Sea, we arrived at Suez about 1 A.M.; and I verily believe I should have known nothing about it, so soundly was I asleep, had I not been very unpleasantly awakened. Rousing myself with the idea that something horrible was going to happen, I became conscious that some one was in my cabin. A harsh, hoarse, croaking whisper, accompanied by most undeniable evidence of bad breath, assailed me as I raised myself in my berth. 'Master want to buy photographs?' I switched on the electric light, and for the second wondered if I were in this world or the next. I have had many bad dreams, but the worst of them pales indescribably before the shock I had then. Fancy being roused from a calm and peaceful sleep, to turn on the light, and then

the strongest and most effective words I could from my vocabulary, but all to no purpose. They wanted so much in shillings, francs, or rupees—I forget which—for a large bundle of photographs; and eventually, to get rid of them, I gave them about one-third of the price, and then kicked them out of the place. It is always as well to buy under such circumstances, otherwise the gentlemen are very apt to *find* things.

However, sleep was a stranger to me for the rest of the night, for, as I dozed off, the recollection of those hideous, devilish faces came to me, and all idea of slumber vanished.

Port Said is an awfully busy place and I had not been there half-an-hour before I found that its appellation, 'a true hell upon earth,' was by no means a misnomer. I once considered Paris bad, Berlin and Vienna shocking, and I had put in my diary up to this, 'Frisco was about the most wicked place I could possibly imagine; but there I had to alter my opinion, and, with apologies to 'Frisco, confess I had been mistaken. If the inhabitants about are human beings, they are certainly of the lowest type that can be conceived. There appears to be no law in the place, and the gambling dens

KICKED OUT

Lot and his family when they hurried away from another place.

Arrived in the Mediterranean, everything seemed to assume

a different aspect, and we became conscious that, having left behind us the rough, half-civilised, and even savage races of various kinds, we were at last re-entering the zone of civilisation. At Alexandria I met some military friends of mine, and enjoyed a good chat and a stroll with them, and got so excited over their description of the bombardment that whenever I heard a noise I would duck my head, fancying it was a shell.

Alexandria is not at all a bad place, and I liked it immensely. There are an awful lot of blackguards about, but they are almost immaculate compared with the demons of Port Said. The place was very lively when we called, for the crew of a British man-o'-war were holding a regatta in the harbour.

More purchases were made on shore, and on returning to the vessel there were a lot of traders on board, so we were compelled to submit to an interview from all of them, and buy more things; I purchased some Egyptian, or perhaps I should say Turkish, delight, and a few fezes for my little nephews at home. It is strange how every one thinks of children when

for them, is worth far more to any onlooker with even a little bit
of a soul, than it would be if I had bought them costly presents
that they could not appreciate.

As we left Alexandria there was such salute-firing and flying
up and down of flags, I almost
thought I had been mistaken
for some mighty potentate in
disguise, but afterwards thought
it was on account of the regatta.
It was rather rough and choppy
in the Mediterranean, and we
had not left the harbour very
long before we discovered we
had swells on the sea, and also

on board.   Our cargo of passengers had been considerably
augmented, and some of them were of an amusing type.   There
were a lot of the regular 'Haw, haw!' style, the kind of people
who have a different way of shaking hands about every six
months—sometimes over the head, sometimes just touching
the hand and dropping
it, sometimes a suspicion
of a shake about the
level of the nose, some-
times a little below the level
of the chin, with the elbows
raised as high as possible, and
all that sort of nonsense ; and
there were also a lot of the
'Really, doncher know,' 'Oh, yes!

Lawn, or in Hyde Park. I am not talking of the genuine good family people, but those who try to ape them; and the whole thing grated terribly on the nerves of the homely kind of folks like ourselves who had been going through the genuine colonies, and had got used to things so different.

It did not seem far to Marseilles, and as we neared this port there was a certain sadness mixed up with our feelings of pleasure, for the happy and jolly time we had had together was

HOW THEY SHAKE HANDS

now at an end, and our long sea-voyage was over. So far, on the voyage, when touching at different places, we had been

men approached me and most politely raised their hats. I saw
they were officials of some sort, so, to be equally polite, I bowed
and raised my hat. Bowing again, and pointing to my baggage,
one asked, 'Tabac?' I bowed and said, 'No.' 'Speerits?'
'No'; and imagine my surprise when my things were chalked,
and I was free! The polite gentlemen were custom-house
officers! Fancy a British exciseman raising his hat or bowing,
or a railway booking-clerk saying 'sir,' or 'madam'! Such

'TABAC? SPEERITS?'

things are not in our country; but why they should not be I
do not know. Some people have an insane notion that it is
foolish to be polite to all classes, but I stoutly oppose this

now, the excitement to get nearer grew stronger, and indeed some people got almost beyond themselves. One man in particular was downright amusing; he had been in China for fifteen years, and to be so near home was almost too much for him, and he unconsciously insisted upon shaking hands with

everybody over and over again every time any one met him who had been on board with him. Of course, we had a look round Marseilles, and went over to Monte Carlo to see 'the tables'; and, much to my astonishment, after having put a twenty-franc piece on a square on the table, another was shuffled towards me, and I fancy I won, for I picked both up, and nothing was said about it. I didn't try again. Nice was very nice, and the journey from there to Paris very comfortable. From Paris to Calais, and from Calais to Dover, and Old England was reached at last. At Dover the almost ludicrous, but at first surprising, thing is to get London papers the day they are issued! Weeks old had been the usual thing for so long, that to see the actual date on the paper, and know it had only just been issued, caused at first a most peculiar sensation. Heaps of papers were bought by every one just to see the date; but, leaving Dover, and getting into the regular neatly kept hedgerows, the old familiar fields, the truly rustic spots so well known to all lovers of country life ; the hop-poles and hop-fields of Kent ; the open villages, happy in the security of a free country, minus the walls and guards to which the eye of the foreign traveller becomes accustomed ; and, in fact, on every hand are signs of peace, of happiness, and of prosperity that not only make one's breast swell with pardonable pride, but ejacu-

ARRIVAL AT CHARING CROSS

are friends to greet me, and, vigilant as ever, my old valet Dobson, who has since passed away to that land from which there is no return. Here once more I stand in London, dear old London, home again safe and well. The smart, quick, and businesslike Customs officers, although so different from the Frenchmen, get through their work; and once more I go out into the streets of the greatest and most marvellous city on this earth, to be assailed with the true London cries that fall almost as music on the returned wanderer's ear, 'Piccadilly, 'Yde Park, 'Ammersmith,' ' Paper. extira speshul, all the winners,' and the other old familiar cries, and to see once more the bustle and the rush which is simply unequalled in its genuineness! Yes, I am at home once more; and the substantial superiority over everything I have seen, which seems to pervade the very air, comes before me like a flash. Republics, kingdoms, empires, all are good; but Old England beats the lot, and London (ignoring Macaulay) says as with Tennyson in ' The Brook':

' Men may come, and men may go,
But I go on for ever.'

CHATTO & WINDUS'S
LIST OF CHEAP POPULAR NOVELS
BY THE BEST AUTHORS.
Picture Covers, TWO SHILLINGS each.

BY EDMOND ABOUT.
The Fellah.

BY HAMILTON AÏDÉ.
Carr of Carrlyon.
Confidences.

BY MARY ALBERT.
Brooke Finchley's Daughter.

BY MRS. ALEXANDER.
Maid, Wife, or Widow?
Valerie's Fate.

BY GRANT ALLEN.
Strange Stories.
Philistia.
Babylon.
The Beckoning Hand.
In All Shades.
For Maimie's Sake.
The Devil's Die.
This Mortal Coil.
The Tents of Shem.
The Great Taboo.
Dumaresq's Daughter.
The Duchess of Powysland.
Blood-Royal.

BY EDWIN LESTER ARNOLD.
Phra the Phœnician.

BY FRANK BARRETT.
A Recoiling Vengeance.
For Love and Honour.
John Ford; & His Helpmate.
Honest Davie.
A Prodigal's Progress.
Folly Morrison.
Lieutenant Barnabas.
Found Guilty.
Fettered for Life.
Between Life and Death.
The Sin of Olga Zassoulich.
Little Lady Linton.

BY SHELSLEY BEAUCHAMP.
Grantley Grange.

BY BESANT AND RICE.
Ready-Money Mortiboy.
With Harp and Crown.
This Son of Vulcan.
My Little Girl.
The Case of Mr. Lucraft.
The Golden Butterfly.
By Celia's Arbour.
The Monks of Thelema.
Twas in Trafalgar's Bay.

BY WALTER BESANT.
All Sorts and Conditions of
Men.
The Captains' Room.
All in a Garden Fair.
Dorothy Forster.
Uncle Jack.
Children of Gibeon.
World went very well then.
Herr Paulus.
For Faith and Freedom.
To Call her Mine.
The Bell of St. Paul's.
The Holy Rose.
Armorel of Lyonesse.
St. Katherine's by the Tower.
The Ivory Gate.
Verbena Camellia Stephanotis

BY AMBROSE BIERCE.
In the Midst of Life.

BY FREDERICK BOYLE.
Camp Notes.
Savage Life.
Chronicles of No-Man's Land.

BY HAROLD BRYDGES.
Uncle Sam at Home.

BY ROBERT BUCHANAN.
The Shadow of the Sword.
A Child of Nature.
God and the Man.
Annan Water.
The New Abelard.
The Martyrdom of Madeline.
Love Me for Ever.
Matt: a Story of a Caravan.
Foxglove Manor.
The Master of the Mine.
The Heir of Linne.

BY HALL CAINE.
The Shadow of a Crime.
A Son of Hagar.
The Deemster.

BY COMMANDER CAMERON.
Cruise of the 'Black Prince.'

BY MRS. LOVETT CAMERON.
Deceivers Ever.
Juliet's Guardian.

BY EX-CHIEF INSPECTOR CAVANAGH.
Scotland Yard, Past and Present.

BY AUSTIN CLARE.
For the Love of a Lass.

BY MACLAREN COBBAN.
The Cure of Souls.

BY C. ALLSTON COLLINS.
The Bar Sinister.

BY WILKIE COLLINS.
Armadale.
After Dark.
No Name.
A Rogue's Life.
Antonina.
Basil.
Hide and Seek.
The Dead Secret.
Queen of Hearts.
My Miscellanies.
The Woman in White.
The Moonstone.
Man and Wife.
Poor Miss Finch.
Miss or Mrs.?
The New Magdalen.
The Frozen Deep.
The Law and the Lady.
The Two Destinies.
The Haunted Hotel.
The Fallen Leaves.
Jezebel's Daughter.
The Black Robe.
Heart and Science.
'I say No.'
The Evil Genius.
Little Novels.
The Legacy of Cain.
Blind Love.

BY MORTIMER COLLINS.
Sweet Anne Page.
Transmigration.
From Midnight to Midnight.
A Fight with Fortune.

MORT. AND FRANCES COLLINS.
Sweet and Twenty.
Frances.
The Village Comedy.
You Play Me False.
Blacksmith and Scholar.

BY M. J. COLQUHOUN.
Every Inch a Soldier.

BY DUTTON COOK.
Leo.
Paul Foster's Daughter.

BY C. EGBERT CRADDOCK

BY MATT CRIM.
Adventures of a Fair Rebel.

BY B. M. CROKER.
Pretty Miss Neville.
Proper Pride.
A Bird of Passage.
Diana Barrington.
'To Let.'
A Family Likeness.

BY WILLIAM CYPLES.
Hearts of Gold.

BY ALPHONSE DAUDET.
The Evangelist.

BY ERASMUS DAWSON.
The Fountain of Youth.

BY JAMES DE MILLE.
A Castle in Spain.

BY J. LEITH DERWENT.
Our Lady of Tears.
Circe's Lovers.

BY CHARLES DICKENS.
Sketches by Boz.
The Pickwick Papers.
Oliver Twist.
Nicholas Nickleby.

BY DICK DONOVAN.
The Man-hunter.
Caught at Last!
Tracked and Taken.
Who Poisoned Hetty Duncan?
The Man from Manchester.
A Detective's Triumphs.
In the Grip of the Law.
Wanted!
From Information Received.
Tracked to Doom.
Link by Link.
Suspicion Aroused.

BY MRS. ANNIE EDWARDES.
A Point of Honour.
Archie Lovell.

BY M. BETHAM-EDWARDS.
Felicia.
Kitty.

BY EDWARD EGGLESTON.
Roxy.

BY G. MANVILLE FENN.
The New Mistress.

BY PERCY FITZGERALD.
Bella Donna.
Polly.
The Second Mrs. Tillotson.
Seventy-five Brooke Street.
Never Forgotten.
The Lady of Brantome.
Fatal Zero.

BY R. E. FRANCILLON.
Olympia.
One by One.
Queen Cophetua.
A Real Queen.
King or Knave.
Romances of the Law.

BY HAROLD FREDERIC.
Seth's Brother's Wife.
The Lawton Girl.

PREFACED BY BARTLE FRERE.
Pandurang Hári.

BY HAIN FRISWELL.
One of Two.

BY EDWARD GARRETT.
The Capel Girls.

BY GILBERT GAUL.
A Strange Manuscript Found
in a Copper Cylinder.

BY CHARLES GIBBON.
Robin Gray.
For Lack of Gold.
What will the World Say?
In Honour Bound.
In Love and War.
For the King.
Queen of the Meadow.
In Pastures Green.
The Flower of the Forest.
A Heart's Problem.
The Braes of Yarrow.
The Golden Shaft.
Of High Degree.
The Dead Heart.
By Mead and Stream.
Heart's Delight.
Fancy Free.
Loving a Dream.
A Hard Knot.
Blood-Money.

BY WILLIAM GILBERT.
James Duke.
Dr. Austin's Guests.
The Wizard of the Mountain.

BY ERNEST GLANVILLE.
The Lost Heiress.
The Fossicker.

BY REV. S. BARING GOULD.
Eve.
Red Spider.

BY HENRY GREVILLE.
A Noble Woman.
Nikanor.

BY CECIL GRIFFITH.
Corinthia Marazion.

BY JOHN HABBERTON.
Brueton's Bayou.

BY THOMAS HARDY.
Under the Greenwood Tree.

BY BRET HARTE.
An Heiress of Red Dog.
The Luck of Roaring Camp.
Californian Stories.
Gabriel Conroy.
Flip.
Maruja.
A Phyllis of the Sierras.

BY J. BERWICK HARWOOD.
The Tenth Earl.

BY JULIAN HAWTHORNE.
Garth.
Ellice Quentin.
Sebastian Strome.
Dust.
Fortune's Fool.
Beatrix Randolph.
Miss Cadogna.
Love—or a Name.
David Poindexter's Disappearance.
The Spectre of the Camera.

BY SIR ARTHUR HELPS.
Ivan de Biron.

BY HENRY HERMAN.
A Leading Lady.

BY HEADON HILL.
Zambra the Detective.

BY JOHN HILL.
Treason-Felony.

BY MRS. CASHEL HOEY.
The Lover's Creed.

BY MRS. GEORGE HOOPER.
The House of Raby.

BY TIGHE HOPKINS.
'Twixt Love and Duty.

BY MRS. HUNGERFORD.
In Durance Vile.
A Maiden all Forlorn.
A Mental Struggle.
Marvel.
A Modern Circe.

BY MRS. ALFRED HUNT.
Thornicroft's Model.
The Leaden Casket.
Self-Condemned.
That Other Person.

BY JEAN INGELOW.
Fated to be Free.

BY WILLIAM JAMESON.
My Dead Self.

BY HARRIETT JAY

BY R. ASHE KING.
A Drawn Game.
'The Wearing of the Green.'
Passion's Slave.
Bell Barry.

BY JOHN LEYS.
The Lindsays.

BY E. LYNN LINTON.
Patricia Kemball.
Atonement of Leam Dundas.
The World Well Lost.
Under which Lord ?
With a Silken Thread.
The Rebel of the Family.
'My Love!'
Ione.
Paston Carew.
Sowing the Wind.

BY HENRY W. LUCY.
Gideon Fleyce.

BY JUSTIN McCARTHY.
Dear Lady Disdain.
The Waterdale Neighbours.
My Enemy's Daughter.
A Fair Saxon.
Linley Rochford.
Miss Misanthrope.
Donna Quixota.
The Comet of a Season.
Maid of Athens.
Camiola : a Girl with Fortune.

BY HUGH MacCOLL.
Mr. Stranger's Sealed Packet.

BY MRS. MACDONELL.
Quaker Cousins.

BY KATHARINE S. MACQUOID.
The Evil Eye.
Lost Rose.

BY W. H. MALLOCK.
The New Republic.
A Romance of the Nineteenth
  Century.

BY FLORENCE MARRYAT.
Fighting the Air.
Written in Fire.
A Harvest of Wild Oats.
Open! Sesame!

BY J. MASTERMAN.
Half-a-dozen Daughters.

BY BRANDER MATTHEWS.
A Secret of the Sea.

BY LEONARD MERRICK.
The Man who was Good.

BY JEAN MIDDLEMASS.

BY J. E. MUDDOCK.
Stories Weird and Wonderful.
The Dead Man's Secret.
From the Bosom of the Deep.

BY D. CHRISTIE MURRAY.
A Life's Atonement.
Joseph's Coat.
Val Strange.
A Model Father.
Coals of Fire.
Hearts.
By the Gate of the Sea.
The Way of the World.
A Bit of Human Nature.
First Person Singular.
Cynic Fortune.
Old Blazer's Hero.
Bob Martin's Little Girl.

BY D. CHRISTIE MURRAY AND HENRY HERMAN.
One Traveller Returns.
Paul Jones's Alias.
The Bishops' Bible.

BY HENRY MURRAY.
A Game of Bluff.
A Song of Sixpence.

BY HUME NISBET.
'Bail Up!'
Dr. Bernard St. Vincent.

BY ALICE O'HANLON.
The Unforeseen.
Chance ? or Fate ?

BY GEORGES OHNET.
Doctor Rameau.
A Last Love.
A Weird Gift.

BY MRS. OLIPHANT.
Whiteladies.
The Primrose Path.
Greatest Heiress in England.

BY MRS. ROBERT O'REILLY.
Phœbe's Fortunes.

BY OUIDA.
Held in Bondage.
Strathmore.
Chandos.
Under Two Flags.
Idalia.
Cecil Castlemaine's Gage.
Tricotrin.
Puck.
Folle Farine.
A Dog of Flanders.
Pascarél.
Signa.
In a Winter City.
Ariadnê.

BY OUIDA—continued.
Wanda.
Frescoes.
Princess Napraxine.
Two Little Wooden Shoes.
A Village Commune.
Othmar.
Guilderoy.
Ruffino.
Syrlin.
Santa Barbara.
Wisdom, Wit, and Pathos.

BY MARGARET AGNES PAUL.
Gentle and Simple.

BY JAMES PAYN.
Lost Sir Massingberd.
A Perfect Treasure.
Bentinck's Tutor.
Murphy's Master.
A County Family.
At Her Mercy.
A Woman's Vengeance.
Cecil's Tryst.
The Clyffards of Clyffe.
The Family Scapegrace.
The Foster Brothers.
The Best of Husbands.
Found Dead.
Walter's Word.
Halves.
Fallen Fortunes.
What He Cost Her.
Humorous Stories.
Gwendoline's Harvest.
Like Father, Like Son.
A Marine Residence.
Married Beneath Him.
Mirk Abbey.
Not Wooed, but Won.
£200 Reward.
Less Black than Painted.
By Proxy.
High Spirits.
Under One Roof.
Carlyon's Year.
A Confidential Agent.
Some Private Views.
A Grape from a Thorn.
From Exile.
Kit : a Memory.
For Cash Only.
The Canon's Ward.
The Talk of the Town.
Holiday Tasks.
Glow-worm Tales.
The Mystery of Mirbridge.
The Burnt Million.
The Word and the Will.
A Prince of the Blood.
Sunny Stories.

TWO-SHILLING POPULAR NOVELS.

BY MRS. CAMPBELL PRAED.
The Romance of a Station.
The Soul of Countess Adrian.

BY E. C. PRICE.
Valentina.
Gerald.
Mrs. Lancaster's Rival.
The Foreigners.

BY RICHARD PRYCE.
Miss Maxwell's Affections.

BY CHARLES READE.
It is Never Too Late to Mend.
Hard Cash.
Peg Woffington.
Christie Johnstone.
Griffith Gaunt.
Put Yourself in His Place.
The Double Marriage.
Love Me Little, Love Me Long.
Foul Play.
The Cloister and the Hearth.
The Course of True Love.
The Autobiography of a Thief.
A Terrible Temptation.
The Wandering Heir.
A Simpleton.
A Woman-Hater.
Singleheart and Doubleface.
Good Stories of Men, &c.
The Jilt.
A Perilous Secret.
Readiana.

BY MRS. J. H. RIDDELL.
Her Mother's Darling.
The Uninhabited House.
Weird Stories.
Fairy Water.
Prince Wales's Garden Party.
Mystery in Palace Gardens.
The Nun's Curse.
Idle Tales.

BY AMÉLIE RIVES.
Barbara Dering.

BY F. W. ROBINSON.
Women are Strange.
The Hands of Justice.

BY JAMES RUNCIMAN.
Skippers and Shellbacks.
Grace Balmaign's Sweetheart.

BY ALAN ST. AUBYN.
A Fellow of Trinity.
The Junior Dean.
The Master of St. Benedict's.

BY GEORGE AUGUSTUS SALA.
Gaslight and Daylight.

BY JOHN SAUNDERS.
Guy Waterman.
The Lion in the Path.
The Two Dreamers.

BY KATHARINE SAUNDERS.
Joan Merryweather.
The High Mills.
Margaret and Elizabeth.
Sebastian.
Heart Salvage.

BY GEORGE R. SIMS.
Rogues and Vagabonds.
The Ring o' Bells.
Mary Jane's Memoirs.
Mary Jane Married.
Tales of To-day.
Dramas of Life.
Tinkletop's Crime.
Zeph: a Circus Story.
My Two Wives.

BY ARTHUR SKETCHLEY.
A Match in the Dark.

BY HAWLEY SMART.
Without Love or Licence.

BY T. W. SPEIGHT.
The Mysteries of Heron Dyke.
The Golden Hoop.
By Devious Ways.
Hoodwinked.
Back to Life.
The Loudwater Tragedy.
Burgo's Romance.

BY R. A. STERNDALE.
The Afghan Knife.

BY R. LOUIS STEVENSON.
New Arabian Nights.
Prince Otto.

BY BERTHA THOMAS.
Proud Maisie.
The Violin-player.
Cressida.

BY WALTER THORNBURY.

BY FRANCES E. TROLLOPE.
Anne Furness.
Mabel's Progress.
Like Ships upon the Sea.

BY T. ADOLPHUS TROLLOPE.
Diamond Cut Diamond.

BY J. T. TROWBRIDGE.
Farnell's Folly.

BY IVAN TURGENIEFF, &c.
Stories from Foreign Novels.

BY MARK TWAIN.
Tom Sawyer.
A Tramp Abroad.
The Stolen White Elephant.
Pleasure Trip on Continent.
The Gilded Age.
Huckleberry Finn.
Life on the Mississippi.
The Prince and the Pauper.
Mark Twain's Sketches.
A Yankee at the Court of
King Arthur.

BY SARAH TYTLER.
Noblesse Oblige.
Citoyenne Jacqueline.
The Huguenot Family.
What She Came Through.
Beauty and the Beast.
The Bride's Pass.
Saint Mungo's City.
Disappeared.
Lady Bell.
Buried Diamonds.
The Blackhall Ghosts.

BY C. C. FRASER-TYTLER.
Mistress Judith.

BY ARTEMUS WARD.
Artemus Ward Complete.

**BY AARON WATSON AND
LILLIAS WASSERMANN.**
The Marquis of Carabas.

BY WILLIAM WESTALL.
Trust-Money.

BY MRS. F. H. WILLIAMSON.
A Child Widow.

BY J. S. WINTER.
Cavalry Life.
Regimental Legends.

[Sept. 1894.

A List of Books Published by
CHATTO & WINDUS
214, Piccadilly, London, W.

ABOUT.—THE FELLAH: An Egyptian Novel. By EDMOND ABOUT. Translated by Sir RANDAL ROBERTS. Post 8vo, illustrated boards, **2s.**

ADAMS (W. DAVENPORT), WORKS BY.
A DICTIONARY OF THE DRAMA: The Plays, Playwrights, Players, and Playhouses of the United Kingdom and America. Cr. 8vo, half-bound, **12s. 6d.** [*Preparing.*
QUIPS AND QUIDDITIES. Selected by W. D. ADAMS. Post 8vo, cloth limp, **2s. 6d.**

AGONY COLUMN (THE) OF "THE TIMES," from 1800 to 1870. Edited, with an Introduction, by ALICE CLAY. Post 8vo, cloth limp, **2s. 6d.**

AIDÉ (HAMILTON), WORKS BY. Post 8vo, illustrated boards, **2s.** each.
CARR OF CARRLYON. | CONFIDENCES.

ALBERT.—BROOKE FINCHLEY'S DAUGHTER. By MARY ALBERT. Post 8vo, picture boards, **2s.**; cloth limp, **2s. 6d.**

ALDEN.—A LOST SOUL. By W. L. ALDEN. Fcap. 8vo, cl. bds., **1s. 6d.**

ALEXANDER (MRS.), NOVELS BY. Post 8vo, illustrated boards, **2s.** each.
MAID, WIFE, OR WIDOW? | VALERIE'S FATE.

ALLEN (F. M.).—GREEN AS GRASS. By F. M. ALLEN, Author of "Through Green Glasses." Frontispiece by J. SMYTH. Cr. 8vo, cloth ex., **3s. 6d.**

ALLEN (GRANT), WORKS BY. Crown 8vo, cloth extra, **6s.** each.
THE EVOLUTIONIST AT LARGE. | COLIN CLOUT'S CALENDAR.
POST-PRANDIAL PHILOSOPHY. Crown 8vo, linen, **3s. 6d.**

Crown 8vo, cloth extra, **3s. 6d.** each; post 8vo, illustrated boards, **2s.** each.

PHILISTIA.	IN ALL SHADES.	DUMARESQ'S DAUGHTER.
BABYLON.	THE DEVIL'S DIE.	THE DUCHESS OF
STRANGE STORIES.	THIS MORTAL COIL.	POWYSLAND.
BECKONING HAND.	THE TENTS OF SHEM.	BLOOD ROYAL.
FOR MAIMIE'S SAKE.	THE GREAT TABOO.	

Crown 8vo, cloth extra, **3s. 6d.** each.
IVAN GREET'S MASTERPIECE, &c. With a Frontispiece by STANLEY L. WOOD.
THE SCALLYWAG. With a Frontispiece.
DR. PALLISER'S PATIENT. Fcap. 8vo, cloth extra, **1s. 6d.**
AT MARKET VALUE. Two Vols., crown 8vo, cloth, **10s.** net.

ARCHITECTURAL STYLES, A HANDBOOK OF. By A. ROSENGARTEN. Translated by W. COLLETT-SANDARS. With 639 Illusts. Cr. 8vo, cl. ex., **7s. 6d.**

ASHTON (JOHN), WORKS BY. Crown 8vo, cloth extra, **7s. 6d.** each.
HISTORY OF THE CHAP-BOOKS OF THE 18th CENTURY. With 334 Illusts.
SOCIAL LIFE IN THE REIGN OF QUEEN ANNE. With 85 Illustrations.
HUMOUR, WIT, AND SATIRE OF SEVENTEENTH CENTURY. With 82 Illusts.
ENGLISH CARICATURE AND SATIRE ON NAPOLEON THE FIRST. 115 Illusts.
MODERN STREET BALLADS. With 57 Illustrations.

BACTERIA, YEAST FUNGI, AND ALLIED SPECIES, A SYNOPSIS
OF. By W. B. GROVE, B.A. With 87 Illustrations, Crown 8vo, cloth extra, **3s. 6d.**

BARDSLEY (REV. C. W.), WORKS BY.
ENGLISH SURNAMES: Their Sources and Significations. Cr. 8vo, cloth, **7s. 6d.**
CURIOSITIES OF PURITAN NOMENCLATURE. Crown 8vo, cloth extra, **6s.**

BARING GOULD (S., Author of "John Herring," &c.), NOVELS BY.
Crown 8vo, cloth extra, **3s. 6d.** each; post 8vo, illustrated boards, **2s.** each.
RED SPIDER. | EVE.

BARR (ROBERT: LUKE SHARP), STORIES BY. Cr. 8vo, cl., **3s. 6d.** ea.
IN A STEAMER CHAIR. With Frontispiece and Vignette by DEMAIN HAMMOND.
FROM WHOSE BOURNE, &c. With 47 Illustrations.

BARRETT (FRANK, Author of "Lady Biddy Fane,") NOVELS BY.
Post 8vo, illustrated boards, **2s.** each; cloth, **2s. 6d.** each.

FETTERED FOR LIFE.	A PRODIGAL'S PROGRESS.
THE SIN OF OLGA ZASSOULICH.	JOHN FORD; and HIS HELPMATE.
BETWEEN LIFE AND DEATH.	A RECOILING VENGEANCE.
POLLY MORRISON.	HONEST DAVIE.	LIEUT. BARNABAS.	FOUND GUILTY.
LITTLE LADY LINTON.	FOR LOVE AND HONOUR.

- THE WOMAN OF THE IRON BRACELETS. Crown 8vo, cloth. **3s. 6d.**

BEACONSFIELD, LORD. By T. P. O'CONNOR, M.P. Cr. 8vo, cloth, **5s.**

BEAUCHAMP (S).—GRANTLEY GRANGE. Post 8vo, illust. boards, **2s.**

BEAUTIFUL PICTURES BY BRITISH ARTISTS: A Gathering from
the Picture Galleries, engraved on Steel. Imperial 4to, cloth extra, gilt edges, **21s.**

BECHSTEIN.—AS PRETTY AS SEVEN, and other German Stories.
Collected by LUDWIG BECHSTEIN. With Additional Tales by the Brothers GRIMM,
and 98 Illustrations by RICHTER. Square 8vo, cloth extra, **6s. 6d.**; gilt edges, **7s. 6d.**

BEERBOHM.—WANDERINGS IN PATAGONIA; or, Life among the
Ostrich Hunters. By JULIUS BEERBOHM. With Illusts. Cr. 8vo, cl. extra, **3s. 6d.**

BENNETT (W. C., LL.D.), WORKS BY. Post 8vo, cloth limp. **2s.** each.
A BALLAD HISTORY OF ENGLAND. | SONGS FOR SAILORS.

BESANT (WALTER), NOVELS BY.
Cr. 8vo, cl. ex., **3s. 6d.** each; post 8vo, illust. bds., **2s.** each; cl. limp, **2s. 6d.** each.
ALL SORTS AND CONDITIONS OF MEN. With Illustrations by FRED. BARNARD.
THE CAPTAINS' ROOM, &c. With Frontispiece by E. J. WHEELER.
ALL IN A GARDEN FAIR. With 6 Illustrations by HARRY FURNISS.
DOROTHY FORSTER. With Frontispiece by CHARLES GREEN.
UNCLE JACK, and other Stories. | CHILDREN OF GIBEON.
THE WORLD WENT VERY WELL THEN. With 12 Illustrations by A. FORESTIER.
HERR PAULUS: His Rise, his Greatness, and his Fall.
FOR FAITH AND FREEDOM. With Illustrations by A. FORESTIER and F. WADDY.
TO CALL HER MINE, &c. With 9 Illustrations by A. FORESTIER.
THE BELL OF ST. PAUL'S.
THE HOLY ROSE, &c. With Frontispiece by F. BARNARD.
ARMOREL OF LYONESSE: A Romance of To-day. With 12 Illusts. by F. BARNARD.
ST. KATHERINE'S BY THE TOWER. With 12 page Illustrations by C. GREEN.
YERBENA CAMELLIA STEPHANOTIS, &c. | THE IVORY GATE: A Novel.
Crown 8vo, cloth extra, **3s. 6d.** each.
THE REBEL QUEEN. | IN DEACON'S ORDERS. [Shortly.
BEYOND THE DREAMS OF AVARICE. Three Vols., cr. 8vo, **15s.** net. [Shortly.
FIFTY YEARS AGO. With 144 Plates and Woodcuts. Crown 8vo. cloth extra. **5s.**

BESANT (WALTER) AND JAMES RICE, NOVELS BY.
Cr. 8vo, cl. ex., **3s. 6d.** each; post 8vo, illust. bds., **2s.** each; cl. limp, **2s. 6d.** each.

READY-MONEY MORTIBOY.	BY CELIA'S ARBOUR.
MY LITTLE GIRL.	THE CHAPLAIN OF THE FLEET.
WITH HARP AND CROWN.	THE SEAMY SIDE.
THIS SON OF VULCAN.	THE CASE OF MR. LUCRAFT, &c.
THE GOLDEN BUTTERFLY.	'TWAS IN TRAFALGAR'S BAY, &c.
THE MONKS OF THELEMA.	THE TEN YEARS' TENANT, &c.

** There is also a LIBRARY EDITION of the above Twelve Volumes, handsomely
set in new type, on a large crown 8vo page, and bound in cloth extra, **6s.** each.

BEWICK (THOMAS) AND HIS PUPILS. By AUSTIN DOBSON. With
95 Illustrations. Square 8vo, cloth extra, **6s.**

BIERCE.—IN THE MIDST OF LIFE : Tales of Soldiers and Civilians,
By AMBROSE BIERCE. Crown 8vo, cloth extra, **6s.**; post 8vo, illustrated boards, **2s.**

BILL NYE'S HISTORY OF THE UNITED STATES. With 146 Illustrations by F. OPPER. Crown 8vo, cloth extra, **3s. 6d.**

BLACKBURN'S (HENRY) ART HANDBOOKS.

ACADEMY NOTES, 1875, 1877-86, 1889, 1890, 1892-1894, each 1s.	GROSVENOR NOTES, Vol. III., 1888-90. With 230 Illusts. Demy 8vo, cloth, **3s. 6d.**
ACADEMY NOTES, 1875-79. Complete in One Vol., with 600 Illusts. Cloth, **6s.**	THE NEW GALLERY, 1888-1894. With numerous Illustrations, each 1s.
ACADEMY NOTES, 1880-84. Complete in One Vol., with 700 Illusts. Cloth, **6s.**	THE NEW GALLERY, Vol. I., 1888-1892. With 250 Illustrations. Demy 8vo, cloth, **6s.**
GROSVENOR NOTES, 1877. 6d.	ENGLISH PICTURES at the NATIONAL
GROSVENOR NOTES, separate years, from 1878-1890, each 1s.	GALLERY. With 114 Illustrations. 1s.
GROSVENOR NOTES, Vol. I., 1877-82. With 300 Illusts. Demy 8vo, cloth, **6s.**	OLD MASTERS AT THE NATIONAL GALLERY. With 128 Illustrations. 1s. 6d.
GROSVENOR NOTES, Vol. II., 1883-87. With 300 Illusts. Demy 8vo, cloth, **6s.**	ILLUSTRATED CATALOGUE TO THE NATIONAL GALLERY. 242 Illusts., cl., **3s.**

THE PARIS SALON, 1894. With Facsimile Sketches. **3s.**
THE PARIS SOCIETY OF FINE ARTS, 1894. With Sketches. **3s. 6d.**

BLAKE (WILLIAM) : India-proof Etchings from his Works by WILLIAM
BELL SCOTT. With descriptive Text. Folio, half-bound boards, **21s.**

BLIND (MATHILDE), Poems by. Crown 8vo, cloth extra, **5s.** each.
THE ASCENT OF MAN.
DRAMAS IN MINIATURE. With a Frontispiece by FORD MADOX BROWN.
SONGS AND SONNETS. Fcap. 8vo, vellum and gold.

BOURNE (H. R. FOX), WORKS BY.
ENGLISH MERCHANTS: Memoirs in Illustration of the Progress of British Com-
merce. With numerous Illustrations. Crown 8vo, cloth extra, **7s. 6d.**
ENGLISH NEWSPAPERS: The History of Journalism. Two Vols., demy 8vo, cl., **25s.**
THE OTHER SIDE OF THE EMIN PASHA RELIEF EXPEDITION. Cr. 8vo. **6s.**

BOWERS.—LEAVES FROM A HUNTING JOURNAL. By GEORGE
BOWERS. Oblong folio, half-bound, **21s.**

BOYLE (FREDERICK), WORKS BY. Post 8vo, illustrated boards, **2s.** each.
CHRONICLES OF NO-MAN'S LAND. | CAMP NOTES. | SAVAGE LIFE.

BRAND'S OBSERVATIONS ON POPULAR ANTIQUITIES ; chiefly

BRET HARTE, WORKS BY.

LIBRARY EDITION. In Seven Volumes, crown 8vo, cloth extra, 6s. each.

BRET HARTE'S COLLECTED WORKS. Arranged and Revised by the Author.

Vol.   I. COMPLETE POETICAL AND DRAMATIC WORKS. With Steel Portrait.
Vol. II. LUCK OF ROARING CAMP—BOHEMIAN PAPERS—AMERICAN LEGENDS.
Vol. III. TALES OF THE ARGONAUTS—EASTERN SKETCHES.
Vol. IV. GABRIEL CONROY. | Vol. V. STORIES—CONDENSED NOVELS, &c.
Vol. VI. TALES OF THE PACIFIC SLOPE.
Vol. VII. TALES OF THE PACIFIC SLOPE—II. With Portrait by JOHN PETTIE, R.A.
Vol.VIII. TALES OF THE PINE AND THE CYPRESS.

THE SELECT WORKS OF BRET HARTE, in Prose and Poetry With Introductory Essay by J. M. BELLEW, Portrait of Author, and 50 Illusts. Cr.8vo, cl. ex., 7s. 6d.

BRET HARTE'S POETICAL WORKS. Hand-made paper & buckram. Cr.8vo, 4s. 6d.

THE QUEEN OF THE PIRATE ISLE. With 28 original Drawings by KATE GREENAWAY, reproduced in Colours by EDMUND EVANS. Small 4to, cloth, 5s.

Crown 8vo, cloth extra, 3s. 6d. each.

A WAIF OF THE PLAINS. With 60 Illustrations by STANLEY L. WOOD.
A WARD OF THE GOLDEN GATE. With 59 Illustrations by STANLEY L. WOOD.
A SAPPHO OF GREEN SPRINGS, &c. With Two Illustrations by HUME NISBET.
COLONEL STARBOTTLE'S CLIENT, AND SOME OTHER PEOPLE. With a Frontispiece by FRED. BARNARD.
SUSY: A Novel. With Frontispiece and Vignette by J. A. CHRISTIE.
SALLY DOWS, &c. With 47 Illustrations by W. D. ALMOND, &c.
A PROTÉGÉE OF JACK HAMLIN'S. With 26 Illustrations by W. SMALL, &c.
THE BELL-RINGER OF ANGEL'S, &c. 39 Illusts. by DUDLEY HARDY, &c. [*Shortly.*

Post 8vo, illustrated boards, 2s. each.

GABRIEL CONROY. | THE LUCK OF ROARING CAMP, &c.
AN HEIRESS OF RED DOG, &c. | CALIFORNIAN STORIES.

Post 8vo, illustrated boards, 2s. each; cloth limp, 2s. 6d. each.

FLIP. | MARUJA. | A PHYLLIS OF THE SIERRAS.

Fcap. 8vo, picture cover, 1s. each.

SNOW-BOUND AT EAGLE'S. | JEFF BRIGGS'S LOVE STORY.

BRYDGES.—UNCLE SAM AT HOME. By HAROLD BRYDGES. Post

8vo, illustrated boards, 2s.; cloth limp, 2s. 6d.

BUCHANAN'S (ROBERT) WORKS. Crown 8vo, cloth extra, 6s. each.

SELECTED POEMS OF ROBERT BUCHANAN. With Frontispiece by T. DALZIEL.
THE EARTHQUAKE; or, Six Days and a Sabbath.
THE CITY OF DREAM: An Epic Poem. With Two Illustrations by P. MACNAB.
THE WANDERING JEW: A Christmas Carol. Second Edition.
THE OUTCAST: A Rhyme for the Time. With 15 Illustrations by RUDOLF BLIND, PETER MACNAB, and HUME NISBET. Small demy 8vo, cloth extra, 8s.
ROBERT BUCHANAN'S COMPLETE POETICAL WORKS. With Steel-plate Portrait. Crown 8vo, cloth extra, 7s. 6d.

Crown 8vo, cloth extra, 3s. 6d. each; post 8vo, illustrated boards, 2s. each.

THE SHADOW OF THE SWORD. | LOVE ME FOR EVER. Frontispiece.
A CHILD OF NATURE. Frontispiece. | ANNAN WATER. | FOXGLOVE MANOR.
GOD AND THE MAN. With 11 Illus- | THE NEW ABELARD.
  trations by FRED. BARNARD. | MATT: A Story of a Caravan. Front.
THE MARTYRDOM OF MADELINE. | THE MASTER OF THE MINE. Front.
  With Frontispiece by A. W. COOPER. | THE HEIR OF LINNE.

Crown 8vo, cloth extra, 3s. 6d. each.

WOMAN AND THE MAN. | RED AND WHITE HEATHER.

RACHEL DENE. Two Vols., crown 8vo, cloth, 10s. net.   [*Shortly.*

BURTON (CAPTAIN).—THE BOOK OF THE SWORD. By RICHARD

F. BURTON. With over 400 Illustrations. Demy 4to, cloth extra, 32s.

BURTON (ROBERT).

THE ANATOMY OF MELANCHOLY. Demy 8vo, cloth extra, 7s. 6d.

CARLYLE (THOMAS) ON THE CHOICE OF BOOKS. With Life by R. H. Shepherd, and Three Illustrations. Post 8vo, cloth extra, 1s. 6d.
CORRESPONDENCE OF THOMAS CARLYLE AND R. W. EMERSON, 1834 to 1872. Edited by C. E. Norton. With Portraits. Two Vols., crown 8vo, cloth, 24s.

CARLYLE (JANE WELSH), LIFE OF. By Mrs. Alexander Ireland. With Portrait and Facsimile Letter. Small demy 8vo, cloth extra, 7s. 6d.

CHAPMAN'S (GEORGE) WORKS.—Vol. I., Plays.—Vol. II., Poems and Minor Translations, with Essay by A. C. Swinburne.—Vol. III., Translations of the Iliad and Odyssey. Three Vols., crown 8vo. cloth, 6s. each.

CHATTO AND JACKSON.—A TREATISE ON WOOD ENGRAVING. By W. A. Chatto and J. Jackson. With 450 fine Illusts. Large 4to, hf.-bd., 28s.

CHAUCER FOR CHILDREN: A Golden Key. By Mrs. H. R. Haweis. With 8 Coloured Plates and 30 Woodcuts. Small 4to, cloth extra, 3s. 6d.
CHAUCER FOR SCHOOLS. By Mrs. H. R. Haweis. Demy 8vo. cloth limp. 2s. 6d.

CLARE (A.).—FOR THE LOVE OF A LASS. Post 8vo, 2s. ; cl., 2s. 6d.

CLIVE (MRS. ARCHER), NOVELS BY. Post 8vo, illust. boards, 2s. each.
PAUL FERROLL. | WHY PAUL FERROLL KILLED HIS WIFE.

CLODD.—MYTHS AND DREAMS. By Edward Clodd, F.R.A.S. Second Edition, Revised. Crown 8vo, cloth extra, 3s. 6d.

COBBAN (J. MACLAREN), NOVELS BY.
THE CURE OF SOULS. Post 8vo, illustrated boards, 2s.
Crown 8vo, cloth extra, 3s. 6d. each.
THE RED SULTAN. | THE BURDEN OF ISABEL. [Shortly.

COLEMAN (JOHN), WORKS BY.
PLAYERS AND PLAYWRIGHTS I HAVE KNOWN. Two Vols., 8vo, cloth, 24s.
CURLY: An Actor's Story. With 21 Illusts. by J. C. Dollman. Cr. 8vo, cl., 1s. 6d.

COLERIDGE.—THE SEVEN SLEEPERS OF EPHESUS. By M. E. Coleridge. Fcap. 8vo, cloth, 1s. 6d.

COLLINS (C. ALLSTON).—THE BAR SINISTER. Post 8vo, 2s.

COLLINS (MORTIMER AND FRANCES), NOVELS BY.
Crown 8vo, cloth extra, 3s. 6d. each; post 8vo, illustrated boards, 2s. each.
FROM MIDNIGHT TO MIDNIGHT. | BLACKSMITH AND SCHOLAR.
TRANSMIGRATION. | YOU PLAY ME FALSE. | A VILLAGE COMEDY.
Post 8vo, illustrated boards, 2s. each.
SWEET ANNE PAGE. | FIGHT WITH FORTUNE. | SWEET & TWENTY. | FRANCES.

COLLINS (WILKIE), NOVELS BY.
Cr. 8vo, cl. ex., 3s. 6d. each ; post 8vo, illust. bds., 2s. each; cl. limp, 2s. 6d. each.
ANTONINA. With a Frontispiece by Sir John Gilbert, R.A.
BASIL. Illustrated by Sir John Gilbert, R.A., and J. Mahoney.
HIDE AND SEEK. Illustrated by Sir John Gilbert, R.A., and J. Mahoney.
AFTER DARK. Illustrations by A. B. Houghton. | THE TWO DESTINIES.
THE DEAD SECRET. With a Frontispiece by Sir John Gilbert, R.A.
QUEEN OF HEARTS. With a Frontispiece by Sir John Gilbert, R.A.
THE WOMAN IN WHITE. With Illusts. by Sir J. Gilbert, R.A., and F. A. Fraser.
NO NAME. With Illustrations by Sir J. E. Millais, R.A., and A. W. Cooper.
MY MISCELLANIES. With a Steel-plate Portrait of Wilkie Collins.
ARMADALE. With Illustrations by G. H. Thomas.
THE MOONSTONE. With Illustrations by G. Du Maurier and F. A. Fraser.

COLMAN'S (GEORGE) HUMOROUS WORKS: "Broad Grins," "My
Nightgown and Slippers," &c. With Life and Frontis. Cr. 8vo, cl. extra, **7s. 6d.**

COLQUHOUN.—EVERY INCH A SOLDIER: A Novel. By M. J.
COLQUHOUN. Post 8vo, illustrated boards, **2s.**

CONVALESCENT COOKERY: A Family Handbook. By CATHERINE
RYAN. Crown 8vo, **1s.**; cloth limp, **1s. 6d.**

CONWAY (MONCURE D.), WORKS BY.
DEMONOLOGY AND DEVIL-LORE. 65 Illustrations. Two Vols., 8vo, cloth, **28s.**
GEORGE WASHINGTON'S RULES OF CIVILITY. Fcap. 8vo, Jap. vellum, **2s. 6d.**

COOK (DUTTON), NOVELS BY.
PAUL FOSTER'S DAUGHTER. Cr. 8vo, cl. ex., **3s. 6d.**; post 8vo, illust. boards, **2s.**
LEO. Post 8vo, illustrated boards, **2s.**

COOPER (EDWARD H.)—GEOFFORY HAMILTON. Cr. 8vo, **3s. 6d.**

**CORNWALL.—POPULAR ROMANCES OF THE WEST OF ENG-
LAND**; or, The Drolls, Traditions, and Superstitions of Old Cornwall. Collected
by ROBERT HUNT, F.R.S. Two Steel-plates by GEO. CRUIKSHANK. Cr. 8vo, cl., **7s. 6d.**

COTES.—TWO GIRLS ON A BARGE. By V. CECIL COTES. With
44 Illustrations by F. H. TOWNSEND. Post 8vo, cloth, **2s. 6d.**

CRADDOCK (C. EGBERT), STORIES BY.
PROPHET of the GREAT SMOKY MOUNTAINS. Post 8vo, illust. bds., **2s.**; cl., **2s. 6d.**
HIS VANISHED STAR. Crown 8vo, cloth extra, **3s. 6d.**   [*Shortly.*

CRELLIN (H. N.), BOOKS BY.
ROMANCES of the OLD SERAGLIO. 28 Illusts. by S. L. WOOD. Cr. 8vo, cl., **3s. 6d.**
THE NAZARENES: A Drama. Crown 8vo, **1s.**

CRIM.—ADVENTURES OF A FAIR REBEL. By MATT CRIM. With
a Frontispiece. Crown 8vo, cloth extra, **3s. 6d.**; post 8vo, illustrated boards, **2s.**

CROKER (B.M.), NOVELS BY. Crown 8vo, cloth extra, **3s. 6d.** each; post
8vo, illustrated boards, **2s.** each; cloth limp, **2s. 6d.** each.
PRETTY MISS NEVILLE.	**DIANA BARRINGTON.**
A BIRD OF PASSAGE.	**PROPER PRIDE.**
A FAMILY LIKENESS.	**"TO LET."**

MR. JERVIS. Three Vols., crown 8vo, cloth, **15s.** nett.

CRUIKSHANK'S COMIC ALMANACK. Complete in Two SERIES:
The FIRST from 1835 to 1843; the SECOND from 1844 to 1853. A Gathering of
the BEST HUMOUR of THACKERAY, HOOD, MAYHEW, ALBERT SMITH, A'BECKETT,
ROBERT BROUGH, &c. With numerous Steel Engravings and Woodcuts by CRUIK-
SHANK, HINE, LANDELLS, &c. Two Vols., crown 8vo, cloth gilt, **7s. 6d.** each.
THE LIFE OF GEORGE CRUIKSHANK. By BLANCHARD JERROLD. With 84
Illustrations and a Bibliography. Crown 8vo, cloth extra, **6s.**

CUMMING (C. F. GORDON), WORKS BY. Demy 8vo, cl. ex., **8s. 6d.** each.
IN THE HEBRIDES. With Autotype Facsimile and 23 Illustrations.
IN THE HIMALAYAS AND ON THE INDIAN PLAINS. With 42 Illustrations.
TWO HAPPY YEARS IN CEYLON. With 28 Illustrations.
VIA CORNWALL TO EGYPT. With Photogravure Frontis. Demy 8vo, cl., **7s. 6d.**

CUSSANS.—A HANDBOOK OF HERALDRY; with Instructions for
Tracing Pedigrees and Deciphering Ancient MSS., &c. By JOHN E. CUSSANS. With
408 Woodcuts and 2 Coloured Plates. Fourth edition, revised, crown 8vo, cloth, **6s.**

CYPLES (W.)—HEARTS of GOLD. Cr. 8vo, cl., **3s. 6d.**; post 8vo, bds., **2s.**

DANIEL.—MERRIE ENGLAND IN THE OLDEN TIME. By GEORGE
DANIEL. With Illustrations by ROBERT CRUIKSHANK. Crown 8vo, cloth extra, **3s. 6d.**

DAVIES' (SIR JOHN) COMPLETE POETICAL WORKS, for the first time Collected and Edited, with Memorial-Introduction and Notes, by the Rev. A. B. GROSART, D.D. Two Vols., crown 8vo. cloth boards, **12s.**

DAWSON.—THE FOUNTAIN OF YOUTH. By ERASMUS DAWSON, M.B. Crown 8vo, cloth extra, **3s. 6d.**; post 8vo, illustrated boards, **2s.**

DE GUERIN.—THE JOURNAL OF MAURICE DE GUERIN. Edited by G. S. TREBUTIEN. With a Memoir by SAINTE-BEUVE. Translated from the 20th French Edition by JESSIE P. FROTHINGHAM. Fcap. 8vo, half-bound, **2s. 6d.**

DE MAISTRE.—A JOURNEY ROUND MY ROOM. By XAVIER DE MAISTRE. Translated by HENRY ATTWELL. Post 8vo, cloth limp, **2s. 6d.**

DE MILLE.—A CASTLE IN SPAIN. By JAMES DE MILLE. With a Frontispiece. Crown 8vo, cloth extra, **3s. 6d.**; post 8vo, illustrated boards, **2s.**

DERBY (THE).—THE BLUE RIBBON OF THE TURF. With Brief Accounts of THE OAKS. By LOUIS HENRY CURZON. Cr. 8vo, cloth limp, **2s. 6d.**

DERWENT (LEITH), NOVELS BY. Cr. 8vo. cl., **3s. 6d.** ea.; post 8vo, bds., **2s.** ea.
OUR LADY OF TEARS. | CIRCE'S LOVERS.

DEWAR.—A RAMBLE ROUND THE GLOBE. By T. R. DEWAR. With 220 Illustrations by W. L. WYLLIE, A.R.A., SYDNEY COWELL, A. S. FORREST, S. L. WOOD, JAMES GREIG, &c. Crown 8vo, cloth extra, **7s. 6d.** [Shortly.

DICKENS (CHARLES), NOVELS BY. Post 8vo. illustrated boards, **2s.** each.
SKETCHES BY BOZ. | NICHOLAS NICKLEBY.
THE PICKWICK PAPERS. | OLIVER TWIST.
THE SPEECHES OF CHARLES DICKENS, 1841-1870. With a New Bibliography. Edited by RICHARD HERNE SHEPHERD. Crown 8vo, cloth extra. **6s.**
ABOUT ENGLAND WITH DICKENS. By ALFRED RIMMER. With 57 Illustrations by C. A. VANDERHOOF, ALFRED RIMMER, and others. Sq. 8vo, cloth extra, **7s. 6d.**

DICTIONARIES.
A DICTIONARY OF MIRACLES: Imitative, Realistic, and Dogmatic. By the Rev. E. C. BREWER, LL.D. Crown 8vo. cloth extra, **7s. 6d.**
THE READER'S HANDBOOK OF ALLUSIONS, REFERENCES, PLOTS, AND STORIES. By the Rev. E. C. BREWER, LL.D. With an ENGLISH BIBLIOGRAPHY. Fifteenth Thousand. Crown 8vo, cloth extra. **7s. 6d.**
AUTHORS AND THEIR WORKS, WITH THE DATES. Cr. 8vo, cloth limp, **2s.**
FAMILIAR SHORT SAYINGS OF GREAT MEN. With Historical and Explanatory Notes. By SAMUEL A. BENT, A M. Crown 8vo, cloth extra. **7s. 6d.**
SLANG DICTIONARY: Etymological, Historical, and Anecdotal. Cr. 8vo, cl., **6s. 6d.**
WOMEN OF THE DAY: A Biographical Dictionary. By F. HAYS. Cr. 8vo, cl., **5s.**
WORDS, FACTS, AND PHRASES: A Dictionary of Curious, Quaint, and Out-of-the-Way Matters. By ELIEZER EDWARDS. Crown 8vo, cloth extra, **7s. 6d.**

DIDEROT.—THE PARADOX OF ACTING. Translated, with Annotations, from Diderot's " Le Paradoxe sur le Comédien," by WALTER HERRIES POLLOCK. With a Preface by HENRY IRVING. Crown 8vo, parchment, **4s. 6d.**

DOBSON (AUSTIN), WORKS BY.
THOMAS BEWICK & HIS PUPILS. With 95 Illustrations. Square 8vo, cloth. **6s.**
FOUR FRENCHWOMEN. With 4 Portraits. Crown 8vo, buckram, gilt top, **6s.**
EIGHTEENTH CENTURY VIGNETTES. Two SERIES. Cr. 8vo, buckram, **6s.** each.

DRAMATISTS, THE OLD. With Vignette Portraits. Cr. 8vo, cl. ex., **6s.** per Vol.
     BEN JONSON'S WORKS. With Notes Critical and Explanatory, and a Biographical Memoir by WM. GIFFORD. Edited by Col. CUNNINGHAM. Three Vols.
     CHAPMAN'S WORKS. Complete in Three Vols. Vol. I. contains the Plays complete; Vol. II., Poems and Minor Translations, with an Introductory Essay by A. C. SWINBURNE; Vol. III., Translations of the Iliad and Odyssey.
     MARLOWE'S WORKS. Edited, with Notes, by Col. CUNNINGHAM. One Vol.
     MASSINGER'S PLAYS. From GIFFORD's Text. Edit by Col. CUNNINGHAM. One Vol.

DUNCAN (SARA JEANNETTE), WORKS BY. Cr. 8vo, cl., **7s. 6d.** each.
     A SOCIAL DEPARTURE: How Orthodocia and I Went round the World by Ourselves. With 111 Illustrations by F. H. TOWNSEND.
     AN AMERICAN GIRL IN LONDON. With 80 Illustrations by F. H. TOWNSEND.
     THE SIMPLE ADVENTURES OF A MEMSAHIB. Illustrated by F. H. TOWNSEND.
     A DAUGHTER OF TO-DAY. Two Vols., crown 8vo, **10s.** net.
     VERNON'S AUNT. With 47 Illusts. by HAL HURST. Cr. 8vo, cl. ex., **3s. 6d.** [Shortly.

DYER.—THE FOLK-LORE OF PLANTS. By Rev. T. F. THISELTON DYER, M.A. Crown 8vo, cloth extra, **6s.**

EARLY ENGLISH POETS. Edited, with Introductions and Annotations, by Rev. A. B. GROSART, D.D. Crown 8vo, cloth boards, **6s.** per Volume.
     FLETCHER'S (GILES) COMPLETE POEMS. One Vol.
     DAVIES' (SIR JOHN) COMPLETE POETICAL WORKS. Two Vols.
     HERRICK'S (ROBERT) COMPLETE COLLECTED POEMS. Three Vols.
     SIDNEY'S (SIR PHILIP) COMPLETE POETICAL WORKS. Three Vols.

EDGCUMBE.—ZEPHYRUS : A Holiday in Brazil and on the River Plate. By E. R. PEARCE EDGCUMBE. With 41 Illustrations. Crown 8vo, cloth extra, **5s.**

EDISON, THE LIFE & INVENTIONS OF THOMAS A. By W. K. L. and A. DICKSON. 250 Illusts. by R. F. OUTCALT, &c. Demy 4to, linen gilt, **18s.** [Shortly.

EDWARDES (MRS. ANNIE), NOVELS BY:
     A POINT OF HONOUR. Post 8vo, illustrated boards, **2s.**
     ARCHIE LOVELL. Crown 8vo, cloth extra, **3s. 6d.**; post 8vo, illust. boards, **2s.**

EDWARDS (ELIEZER).—WORDS, FACTS, AND PHRASES : A Dictionary of Quaint Matters. By ELIEZER EDWARDS. Crown 8vo, cloth, **7s. 6d.**

EDWARDS (M. BETHAM-), NOVELS BY.
     KITTY. Post 8vo, illustrated boards, **2s.**; cloth limp, **2s. 6d.**
     FELICIA. Post 8vo, illustrated boards, **2s.**

EGERTON.—SUSSEX FOLK & SUSSEX WAYS. By Rev. J. C. EGERTON. With Introduction by Rev. Dr. H. WACE, and 4 Illustrations. Cr. 8vo, cloth ex., **5s.**

EGGLESTON (EDWARD).—ROXY : A Novel. Post 8vo, illust. bds., 2s.

ENGLISHMAN'S HOUSE, THE : A Practical Guide to all interested in Selecting or Building a House; with Estimates of Cost, Quantities, &c. By C. J. RICHARDSON. With Coloured Frontispiece and 600 Illusts. Crown 8vo, cloth, **7s. 6d.**

EWALD (ALEX. CHARLES, F.S.A.), WORKS BY.
     THE LIFE AND TIMES OF PRINCE CHARLES STUART, Count of Albany (THE YOUNG PRETENDER). With a Portrait. Crown 8vo, cloth extra, **7s. 6d.**
     STORIES FROM THE STATE PAPERS. With an Autotype. Crown 8vo, cloth. **6s.**

EYES, OUR : How to Preserve Them from Infancy to Old Age. By JOHN BROWNING, F.R.A.S. With 70 Illusts. Eighteenth Thousand. Crown 8vo, **1s.**

FAMILIAR SHORT SAYINGS OF GREAT MEN. By SAMUEL ARTHUR BENT. A.M. Fifth Edition, Revised and Enlarged. Crown 8vo, cloth extra. **7s. 6d.**

FARADAY (MICHAEL), WORKS BY. Post 8vo, cloth extra, **4s. 6d.** each.

FIN-BEC.—THE CUPBOARD PAPERS: Observations on the Art of Living and Dining. By FIN-BEC. Post 8vo. cloth limp, 2s. 6d.

FIREWORKS, THE COMPLETE ART OF MAKING; or, The Pyrotechnist's Treasury. By THOMAS KENTISH. With 267 Illustrations. Cr. 8vo, cl., 5s.

FIRST BOOK, MY. By WALTER BESANT, J. K. JEROME, R. L. STEVENSON, and others. With a Prefatory Story by JEROME K. JEROME, and nearly 200 Illustrations. Small demy 8vo, cloth extra, 7s. 6d.

FITZGERALD (PERCY, M.A., F.S.A.), WORKS BY.
THE WORLD BEHIND THE SCENES. Crown 8vo, cloth extra, 3s. 6d.
LITTLE ESSAYS: Passages from Letters of CHARLES LAMB. Post 8vo, cl., 2s. 6d.
A DAY'S TOUR: Journey through France and Belgium. With Sketches. Cr. 4to, 1s.
FATAL ZERO. Crown 8vo, cloth extra, 3s. 6d.; post 8vo, illustrated boards, 2s.

Post 8vo, illustrated boards, 2s. each.
BELLA DONNA. | LADY OF BRANTOME. | THE SECOND MRS. TILLOTSON.
POLLY. | NEVER FORGOTTEN. | SEVENTY-FIVE BROOKE STREET.
LIFE OF JAMES BOSWELL (of Auchinleck). With an Account of his Sayings, Doings, and Writings; and Four Portraits. Two Vols., demy 8vo, cloth, 24s.
THE SAVOY OPERA. With 60 Illustrations and Portraits. Cr. 8vo, cloth, 3s. 6d.

FLAMMARION (CAMILLE), WORKS BY.
POPULAR ASTRONOMY: A General Description of the Heavens. Trans. by J. E. GORE, F.R.A.S. With 3 Plates and 288 Illusts. Medium 8vo, cloth, 16s. [Shortly.
URANIA: A Romance. With 87 Illustrations. Crown 8vo, cloth extra, 5s.

FLETCHER'S (GILES, B.D.) COMPLETE POEMS: Christ's Victorie in Heaven, Christ's Victorie on Earth, Christ's Triumph over Death, and Minor Poems. With Notes by Rev. A. B. GROSART, D.D. Crown 8vo, cloth boards, 6s.

FONBLANQUE (ALBANY).—FILTHY LUCRE. Post 8vo, illust. bds., 2s.

FRANCILLON (R. E.), NOVELS BY.
Crown 8vo, cloth extra, 3s. 6d. each; post 8vo, illustrated boards, 2s. each.
ONE BY ONE. | QUEEN COPHETUA. | A REAL QUEEN. | KING OR KNAVE?
Crown 8vo, cloth extra, 3s. 6d. each.
ROPES OF SAND. Illustrated. | JACK DOYLE'S DAUGHTER. [Shortly.
A DOG AND HIS SHADOW.
OLYMPIA. Post 8vo. illust. bds., 2s. | ESTHER'S GLOVE. Fcap. 8vo, pict. cover, 1s.
ROMANCES OF THE LAW. Post 8vo, illustrated boards, 2s.

FREDERIC (HAROLD), NOVELS BY. Post 8vo, illust. bds., 2s. each.
SETH'S BROTHER'S WIFE. | THE LAWTON GIRL.

FRENCH LITERATURE, A HISTORY OF. By HENRY VAN LAUN. Three Vols., demy 8vo, cloth boards, 7s. 6d. each.

FRERE.—PANDURANG HARI; or, Memoirs of a Hindoo. With Preface by Sir BARTLE FRERE. Crown 8vo, cloth, 3s. 6d.; post 8vo, illust. bds., 2s.

FRISWELL (HAIN).—ONE OF TWO: A Novel. Post 8vo, illust. bds., 2s.

FROST (THOMAS), WORKS BY. Crown 8vo, cloth extra, 3s. 6d. each.
CIRCUS LIFE AND CIRCUS CELEBRITIES. | LIVES OF THE CONJURERS.
THE OLD SHOWMEN AND THE OLD LONDON FAIRS.

FRY'S (HERBERT) ROYAL GUIDE TO THE LONDON CHARITIES. Edited by JOHN LANE. Published Annually. Crown 8vo, cloth, 1s. 6d.

GARDENING BOOKS. Post 8vo. 1s. each; cloth limp, 1s. 6d. each.
A YEAR'S WORK IN GARDEN AND GREENHOUSE. By GEORGE GLENNY.
HOUSEHOLD HORTICULTURE. By TOM and JANE JERROLD. Illustrated.
THE GARDEN THAT PAID THE RENT. By TOM JERROLD.
OUR KITCHEN GARDEN. By TOM JERROLD. Crown 8vo, cloth, 1s. 6d.
MY GARDEN WILD. By FRANCIS G. HEATH. Crown 8vo, cloth extra, 6s.

GARRETT.—THE CAPEL GIRLS: A Novel. By EDWARD GARRETT. Crown 8vo, cloth extra, 3s. 6d.; post 8vo, illustrated boards, 2s.

GERMAN POPULAR STORIES. Collected by the Brothers GRIMM and Translated by EDGAR TAYLOR. With Introduction by JOHN RUSKIN, and 22 Steel Plates after GEORGE CRUIKSHANK. Square 8vo, cloth, 6s. 6d.; gilt edges, 7s. 6d.

GIBBON (CHARLES), NOVELS BY.
Crown 8vo, cloth extra, 3s. 6d. each; post 8vo, illustrated boards, 2s. each.

ROBIN GRAY.	LOVING A DREAM.	THE GOLDEN SHAFT.
THE FLOWER OF THE FOREST.	OF HIGH DEGREE.

Post 8vo, illustrated boards, 2s. each.

THE DEAD HEART.	IN LOVE AND WAR.
FOR LACK OF GOLD.	A HEART'S PROBLEM.
WHAT WILL THE WORLD SAY?	BY MEAD AND STREAM.
FOR THE KING.	A HARD KNOT.	THE BRAES OF YARROW.
QUEEN OF THE MEADOW.	FANCY FREE.	IN HONOUR BOUND.
IN PASTURES GREEN.	HEART'S DELIGHT.	BLOOD-MONEY.

GIBNEY (SOMERVILLE).—SENTENCED! Cr. 8vo, 1s.; cl., 1s. 6d.

GILBERT (WILLIAM), NOVELS BY. Post 8vo, illustrated boards, 2s. each.
DR. AUSTIN'S GUESTS. | JAMES DUKE, COSTERMONGER.
THE WIZARD OF THE MOUNTAIN. |

GILBERT (W. S.), ORIGINAL PLAYS BY. Two Series, 2s. 6d. each.
The FIRST SERIES contains: The Wicked World—Pygmalion and Galatea—Charity—The Princess—The Palace of Truth—Trial by Jury.
The SECOND SERIES: Broken Hearts—Engaged—Sweethearts—Gretchen—Dan'l Druce—Tom Cobb—H.M.S. "Pinafore"—The Sorcerer—Pirates of Penzance.

EIGHT ORIGINAL COMIC OPERAS written by W. S. GILBERT. Containing: The Sorcerer—H.M.S. "Pinafore"—Pirates of Penzance—Iolanthe—Patience—Princess Ida—The Mikado—Trial by Jury. Demy 8vo, cloth limp, 2s. 6d.
THE "GILBERT AND SULLIVAN" BIRTHDAY BOOK: Quotations for Every Day in the Year, Selected from Plays by W. S. GILBERT set to Music by Sir A. SULLIVAN. Compiled by ALEX. WATSON. Royal 16mo, Jap. leather, 2s. 6d.

GLANVILLE (ERNEST), NOVELS BY.
Crown 8vo, cloth extra, 3s. 6d. each; post 8vo, illustrated boards, 2s. each.
THE LOST HEIRESS: A Tale of Love, Battle, and Adventure. With 2 Illusts.
THE FOSSICKER: A Romance of Mashonaland. With 2 Illusts. by HUME NISBET.
A FAIR COLONIST. With a Frontispiece. Cr. 8vo, cl. extra, 3s. 6d.

GLENNY.—A YEAR'S WORK IN GARDEN AND GREENHOUSE: Practical Advice to Amateur Gardeners as to the Management of the Flower, Fruit, and Frame Garden. By GEORGE GLENNY. Post 8vo, 1s.; cloth limp, 1s. 6d.

GODWIN.—LIVES OF THE NECROMANCERS. By WILLIAM GODWIN. Post 8vo, cloth limp, 2s.

GOLDEN TREASURY OF THOUGHT, THE: An Encyclopædia of QUOTATIONS. Edited by THEODORE TAYLOR. Crown 8vo, cloth gilt, 7s. 6d.

GONTAUT, MEMOIRS OF THE DUCHESSE DE, Gouvernante to the Children of France, 1773-1836. With Photogravure Frontispieces. Two Vols., small demy 8vo, cloth extra, 21s.

GOODMAN.—THE FATE OF HERBERT WAYNE. By E. J. GOODMAN, Author of "Too Curious." Crown 8vo, cloth, 3s. 6d.

GRAHAM.—THE PROFESSOR'S WIFE: A Story By LEONARD GRAHAM. Fcap. 8vo, picture cover, 1s.

HABBERTON (JOHN, Author of "Helen's Babies"), **NOVELS BY.**
Post 8vo, illustrated boards 2s. each; cloth limp, 2s. 6d. each.
BRUETON'S BAYOU.   . | COUNTRY LUCK.

HAIR, THE: Its Treatment in Health, Weakness, and Disease. Translated from the German of Dr. J. PINCUS. Crown 8vo. 1s.; cloth, 1s. 6d.

HAKE (DR. THOMAS GORDON), POEMS BY. Cr. 8vo, cl. ex., 6s. each.
NEW SYMBOLS. | LEGENDS OF THE MORROW. | THE SERPENT PLAY.
MAIDEN ECSTASY. Small 4to, cloth extra. 8s.

HALL.—SKETCHES OF IRISH CHARACTER. By Mrs. S. C. HALL.
With numerous Illustrations on Steel and Wood by MACLISE, GILBERT, HARVEY, and GEORGE CRUIKSHANK. Medium 8vo. cloth extra. 7s. 6d.

HALLIDAY (ANDR.).—EVERY-DAY PAPERS. Post 8vo, bds., 2s.

HANDWRITING, THE PHILOSOPHY OF. With over 100 Facsimiles and Explanatory Text. By DON FÉLIX DE SALAMANCA. Post 8vo. cloth limp. 2s. 6d.

HANKY-PANKY: Easy Tricks, White Magic, Sleight of Hand, &c. Edited by W. H. CREMER. With 200 Illustrations. Crown 8vo, cloth extra. 4s. 6d.

HARDY (LADY DUFFUS).—PAUL WYNTER'S SACRIFICE. 2s.

HARDY (THOMAS).—UNDER THE GREENWOOD TREE. By THOMAS HARDY, Author of "Tess." With Portrait and 15 Illustrations. Crown 8vo. cloth extra, 3s. 6d.; post 8vo, illustrated boards, 2s.; cloth limp, 2s. 6d.

HARPER (CHARLES G.), WORKS BY. Demy 8vo, cloth extra, 16s. each.
THE BRIGHTON ROAD. With Photogravure Frontispiece and 90 Illustrations.
FROM PADDINGTON TO PENZANCE: The Record of a Summer Tramp. 105 Illusts.

HARWOOD.—THE TENTH EARL. By J. BERWICK HARWOOD. Post 8vo, illustrated boards, 2s.

HAWEIS (MRS. H. R.), WORKS BY. Square 8vo, cloth extra, 6s. each.
THE ART OF BEAUTY. With Coloured Frontispiece and 91 Illustrations.
THE ART OF DECORATION. With Coloured Frontispiece and 74 Illustrations.
THE ART OF DRESS. With 32 Illustrations. Post 8vo, 1s.; cloth, 1s. 6d.
CHAUCER FOR SCHOOLS. Demy 8vo, cloth limp, 2s. 6d.
CHAUCER FOR CHILDREN. 38 Illusts. (8 Coloured). Sm. 4to, cl. extra, 3s. 6d.

HAWEIS (Rev. H. R., M.A.).—AMERICAN HUMORISTS: WASHINGTON IRVING, OLIVER WENDELL HOLMES, JAMES RUSSELL LOWELL, ARTEMUS WARD, MARK TWAIN, and BRET HARTE. Third Edition. Crown 8vo. cloth extra. 6s.

HAWLEY SMART.—WITHOUT LOVE OR LICENCE: A Novel. By HAWLEY SMART. Crown 8vo, cloth extra, 3s. 6d.; post 8vo, illustrated boards, 2s.

HAWTHORNE.—OUR OLD HOME. By NATHANIEL HAWTHORNE. Annotated with Passages from the Author's Note-book, and Illustrated with 31 Photogravures. Two Vols., crown 8vo. buckram, gilt top, 15s.

HAWTHORNE (JULIAN), NOVELS BY.
Crown 8vo, cloth extra, 3s. 6d. each; post 8vo, illustrated boards, 2s. each.
GARTH. | ELLICE QUENTIN. | BEATRIX RANDOLPH. | DUST.
SEBASTIAN STROME. | DAVID POINDEXTER.
FORTUNE'S FOOL. | THE SPECTRE OF THE CAMERA.
Post 8vo, illustrated boards, 2s. each.
MISS CADOGNA. | LOVE—OR A NAME.
MRS. GAINSBOROUGH'S DIAMONDS. Fcap. 8vo. illustrated cover, 1s.

HEATH.—MY GARDEN WILD, AND WHAT I GREW THERE. By FRANCIS GEORGE HEATH. Crown 8vo, cloth extra, gilt edges, 6s.

HELPS (SIR ARTHUR), WORKS BY. Post 8vo, cloth limp, 2s. 6d. each.
ANIMALS AND THEIR MASTERS. | SOCIAL PRESSURE.
IVAN DE BIRON: A Novel. Cr. 8vo cl. extra 3s. 6d.; post 8vo, illust. bds., 2s.

HERRICK'S (ROBERT) HESPERIDES, NOBLE NUMBERS, AND COMPLETE COLLECTED POEMS. With Memorial-Introduction and Notes by the Rev. A. B. Grosart, D.D.; Steel Portrait, &c. Three Vols., crown 8vo. cl. bds., 18s.

HERTZKA.—FREELAND: A Social Anticipation. By Dr. Theodor Hertzka. Translated by Arthur Ransom. Crown 8vo, cloth extra, 6s.

HESSE-WARTEGG.—TUNIS: The Land and the People. By Chevalier Ernst von Hesse-Wartegg. With 22 Illustrations. Cr. 8vo, cloth extra, 3s. 6d.

HILL (HEADON).—ZAMBRA THE DETECTIVE. By Headon Hill. Post 8vo, illustrated boards, 2s.; cloth, 2s. 6d.

HILL (JOHN, M.A.), WORKS BY.
TREASON-FELONY. Post 8vo, 2s. | THE COMMON ANCESTOR. Cr. 8vo, 3s. 6d.

HINDLEY (CHARLES), WORKS BY.
TAVERN ANECDOTES AND SAYINGS: Including Reminiscences connected with Coffee Houses, Clubs, &c. With Illustrations. Crown 8vo, cloth, 3s. 6d.
THE LIFE AND ADVENTURES OF A CHEAP JACK. Cr. 8vo, cloth ex., 3s. 6d.

HOEY.—THE LOVER'S CREED. By Mrs. Cashel Hoey. Post 8vo, 2s.

HOLLINGSHEAD (JOHN).—NIAGARA SPRAY. Crown 8vo, 1s.

HOLMES.—THE SCIENCE OF VOICE PRODUCTION AND VOICE PRESERVATION. By Gordon Holmes, M.D. Crown 8vo, 1s.; cloth, 1s. 6d.

HOLMES (OLIVER WENDELL), WORKS BY.
THE AUTOCRAT OF THE BREAKFAST-TABLE. Illustrated by J. Gordon Thomson. Post 8vo, cloth limp 2s. 6d.—Another Edition, post 8vo, cloth, 2s.
THE AUTOCRAT OF THE BREAKFAST-TABLE and THE PROFESSOR AT THE BREAKFAST-TABLE. In One Vol. Post 8vo, half-bound, 2s.

HOOD'S (THOMAS) CHOICE WORKS, in Prose and Verse. With Life of the Author, Portrait, and 200 Illustrations. Crown 8vo, cloth extra, 7s. 6d.
HOOD'S WHIMS AND ODDITIES. With 85 Illusts. Post 8vo, half-bound, 2s.

HOOD (TOM).—FROM NOWHERE TO THE NORTH POLE: A Noah's Arkæological Narrative. By Tom Hood. With 25 Illustrations by W. Brunton and E. C. Barnes. Square 8vo, cloth extra, gilt edges, 6s.

HOOK'S (THEODORE) CHOICE HUMOROUS WORKS; including his Ludicrous Adventures, Bons Mots, Puns, and Hoaxes. With Life of the Author, Portraits, Facsimiles, and Illustrations. Crown 8vo, cloth extra, 7s. 6d.

HOOPER.—THE HOUSE OF RABY: A Novel. By Mrs. George Hooper. Post 8vo, illustrated boards, 2s.

HOPKINS.—"'TWIXT LOVE AND DUTY:" A Novel. By Tighe Hopkins. Post 8vo, illustrated boards, 2s.

HORNE.—ORION: An Epic Poem. By Richard Hengist Horne. With Photographic Portrait by Summers. Tenth Edition. Cr. 8vo, cloth extra, 7s.

HUNGERFORD (MRS.), Author of "Molly Bawn," NOVELS BY.
Post 8vo, illustrated boards, 2s. each; cloth limp, 2s. 6d. each.
A MAIDEN ALL FORLORN. | IN DURANCE VILE. | A MENTAL STRUGGLE.
MARVEL. | A MODERN CIRCE.
Crown 8vo, cloth extra, 3s. 6d. each.
LADY VERNER'S FLIGHT. | THE RED-HOUSE MYSTERY.

ESSAYS BY LEIGH HUNT. A TALE FOR A CHIMNEY CORNER.

INGELOW (JEAN).—FATED TO BE FREE. Post 8vo, illustrated bds., **2s.**

INDOOR PAUPERS. By ONE OF THEM. Crown 8vo, 1s.; cloth, 1s. 6d.

INNKEEPER'S HANDBOOK (THE) AND LICENSED VICTUALLER'S MANUAL. By J. TREVOR-DAVIES. Crown 8vo, 1s.; cloth, 1s. 6d.

IRISH WIT AND HUMOUR, SONGS OF. Collected and Edited by A. PERCEVAL GRAVES. Post 8vo, cloth limp, 2s. 6d.

JAMES.—A ROMANCE OF THE QUEEN'S HOUNDS. By CHARLES JAMES. Post 8vo, picture cover, 1s.; cloth limp, 1s. 6d.

JAMESON.—MY DEAD SELF. By WILLIAM JAMESON. Post 8vo, illustrated boards, 2s.; cloth, 2s. 6d.

JAPP.—DRAMATIC PICTURES, SONNETS, &c. By A. H. JAPP, LL.D. Crown 8vo, cloth extra, 5s.

JAY (HARRIETT), NOVELS BY. Post 8vo, illustrated boards, 2s. each.
THE DARK COLLEEN. | THE QUEEN OF CONNAUGHT.

JEFFERIES (RICHARD), WORKS BY. Post 8vo, cloth limp, 2s. 6d. each.
NATURE NEAR LONDON.| THE LIFE OF THE FIELDS.| THE OPEN AIR.
. Also the HAND-MADE PAPER EDITION, crown 8vo, buckram, gilt top, 6s. each.
THE EULOGY OF RICHARD JEFFERIES. By WALTER BESANT. Second Edition With a Photograph Portrait. Crown 8vo, cloth extra, 6s.

JENNINGS (H. J.), WORKS BY.
CURIOSITIES OF CRITICISM. Post 8vo, cloth limp, 2s. 6d.
LORD TENNYSON: A Biographical Sketch. Post 8vo, 1s.; cloth, 1s. 6d.

JEROME.—STAGELAND. By JEROME K. JEROME. With 64 Illustrations by J. BERNARD PARTRIDGE. Square 8vo, picture cover, 1s.; cloth limp, 2s.

JERROLD.—THE BARBER'S CHAIR; & THE HEDGEHOG LETTERS. By DOUGLAS JERROLD. Post 8vo, printed on laid paper and half-bound, 2s.

JERROLD (TOM), WORKS BY. Post 8vo, 1s. each; cloth limp, 1s. 6d. each.
THE GARDEN THAT PAID THE RENT.
HOUSEHOLD HORTICULTURE: A Gossip about Flowers. Illustrated.
OUR KITCHEN GARDEN: The Plants, and How we Cook Them. Cr. 8vo, cl., 1s. 6d.

JESSE.—SCENES AND OCCUPATIONS OF A COUNTRY LIFE. By EDWARD JESSE. Post 8vo, cloth limp, 2s.

JONES (WILLIAM, F.S.A.), WORKS BY. Cr. 8vo, cl. extra, 7s. 6d. each.
FINGER-RING LORE: Historical, Legendary, and Anecdotal. With nearly 300 Illustrations. Second Edition, Revised and Enlarged.
CREDULITIES, PAST AND PRESENT. Including the Sea and Seamen, Miners, Talismans, Word and Letter Divination, Exorcising and Blessing of Animals, Birds, Eggs, Luck, &c. With an Etched Frontispiece.
CROWNS AND CORONATIONS: A History of Regalia. With 100 Illustrations.

JONSON'S (BEN) WORKS. With Notes Critical and Explanatory, and a Biographical Memoir by WILLIAM GIFFORD. Edited by Colonel CUNNINGHAM. Three Vols., crown 8vo, cloth extra, 6s. each.

JOSEPHUS, THE COMPLETE WORKS OF. Translated by WHISTON. Containing "The Antiquities of the Jews" and "The Wars of the Jews." With 52 Illustrations and Maps. Two Vols., demy 8vo, half-bound, 12s. 6d.

KEMPT.—PENCIL AND PALETTE: Chapters on Art and Artists. By ROBERT KEMPT. Post 8vo, cloth limp, 2s. 6d.

KERSHAW. — COLONIAL FACTS AND FICTIONS: Humorous Sketches. By MARK KERSHAW. Post 8vo, illustrated boards, 2s.; cloth, 2s. 6d.

KEYSER. — CUT BY THE MESS: A Novel. By ARTHUR KEYSER. Crown 8vo, picture cover, 1s.; cloth limp, 1s. 6d.

KING (R. ASHE), NOVELS BY. Cr. 8vo, cl., 3s. 6d. ea.; post 8vo, bds., 2s. ea.
| "THE WEARING OF THE GREEN."

KNIGHTS (THE) OF THE LION : A Romance of the Thirteenth Century.
Edited. with an Introduction, by the MARQUESS of LORNE, K.T. Cr 8vo, cl. ex. **6s.**

LAMB'S (CHARLES) COMPLETE WORKS, in Prose and Verse,
including "Poetry for Children" and "Prince Dorus." Edited, with Notes and
Introduction, by R. H. SHEPHERD. With Two Portraits and Facsimile of a page
of the "Essay on Roast Pig." Crown 8vo, half-bound, **7s. 6d.**
THE ESSAYS OF ELIA. Post 8vo, printed on laid paper and half-bound, **2s.**
LITTLE ESSAYS: Sketches and Characters by CHARLES LAMB, selected from his
Letters by PERCY FITZGERALD. Post 8vo, cloth limp, **2s. 6d.**
THE DRAMATIC ESSAYS OF CHARLES LAMB. With Introduction and Notes
by BRANDER MATTHEWS, and Steel-plate Portrait. Fcap. 8vo, hf.-bd., **2s. 6d.**

LANDOR.—CITATION AND EXAMINATION OF WILLIAM SHAKS-
PEARE, &c., before Sir THOMAS LUCY, touching Deer-stealing, 19th September, 1582.
To which is added, A CONFERENCE OF MASTER EDMUND SPENSER with the
Earl of Essex, touching the State of Ireland, 1595. By WALTER SAVAGE LANDOR.
Fcap. 8vo, half-Roxburghe, **2s. 6d.**

LANE.—THE THOUSAND AND ONE NIGHTS, commonly called in
England THE ARABIAN NIGHTS' ENTERTAINMENTS. Translated from the
Arabic, with Notes, by EDWARD WILLIAM LANE. Illustrated by many hundred
Engravings from Designs by HARVEY. Edited by EDWARD STANLEY POOLE. With a
Preface by STANLEY LANE-POOLE. Three Vols., demy 8vo, cloth extra, **7s. 6d.** each.

LARWOOD (JACOB), WORKS BY.
THE STORY OF THE LONDON PARKS. With Illusts. Cr. 8vo, cl. extra, **3s. 6d.**
ANECDOTES OF THE CLERGY. Post 8vo, laid paper, half-bound, **2s.**
Post 8vo, cloth limp, **2s. 6d.** each.
FORENSIC ANECDOTES, | THEATRICAL ANECDOTES.

LEHMANN (R. C.) WORKS BY. Post 8vo, pict. cover, **1s.** ea.; cloth, **1s. 6d.** ea.
HARRY FLUDYER AT CAMBRIDGE.
CONVERSATIONAL HINTS FOR YOUNG SHOOTERS: A Guide to Polite Talk.

LEIGH (HENRY S.), WORKS BY.
CAROLS OF COCKAYNE. Printed on hand-made paper, bound in buckram, **5s.**
JEUX D'ESPRIT. Edited by HENRY S. LEIGH. Post 8vo, cloth limp, **2s. 6d.**

LEYS (JOHN).—THE LINDSAYS : A Romance. Post 8vo, illust. bds., **2s.**

LINTON (E. LYNN), WORKS BY. Post 8vo, cloth limp, **2s. 6d.** each.
WITCH STORIES. | OURSELVES: ESSAYS ON WOMEN.
Crown 8vo, cloth extra, **3s. 6d.** each; post 8vo, illustrated boards, **2s.** each.
PATRICIA KEMBALL. | IONE.   UNDER WHICH LORD?
ATONEMENT OF LEAM DUNDAS.   "MY LOVE!" | SOWING THE WIND.
THE WORLD WELL LOST.   PASTON CAREW, Millionaire & Miser.
Post 8vo, illustrated boards, **2s.** each.
THE REBEL OF THE FAMILY. | WITH A SILKEN THREAD.
THE ONE TOO MANY. Crown 8vo, cloth, **3s. 6d.**   [Shortly.
FREESHOOTING : Extracts from Works of Mrs. LINTON. Post 8vo, cloth, **2s. 6d.**

LONGFELLOW'S POETICAL WORKS. With numerous Illustrations
on Steel and Wood. Crown 8vo, cloth extra, **7s. 6d.**

LUCY.—GIDEON FLEYCE : A Novel. By HENRY W. LUCY. Crown
8vo, cloth extra, **3s. 6d.**; post 8vo, illustrated boards, **2s.**

MACALPINE (AVERY), NOVELS BY.
TERESA ITASCA. Crown 8vo, cloth extra, **1s.**
BROKEN WINGS. With 6 Illusts. by W. J. HENNESSY. Crown 8vo, cloth extra, **6s.**

MACCOLL (HUGH), NOVELS BY.
MR. STRANGER'S SEALED PACKET. Post 8vo, illustrated boards, **2s.**
EDNOR WHITLOCK. Crown 8vo, cloth extra, **6s.**

McCARTHY (JUSTIN, M.P.), WORKS BY.

A HISTORY OF OUR OWN TIMES, from the Accession of Queen Victoria to the
General Election of 1880. Four Vols. demy 8vo, cloth extra, **12s.** each.—Also
a POPULAR EDITION, in Four Vols., crown 8vo, cloth extra, **6s.** each.—And a
JUBILEE EDITION, with an Appendix of Events to the end of 1886, in Two Vols.,
large crown 8vo, cloth extra, **7s. 6d.** each.

A SHORT HISTORY OF OUR OWN TIMES. One Vol., crown 8vo, cloth extra, **6s.**
—Also a CHEAP POPULAR EDITION, post 8vo, cloth limp, **2s. 6d.**

A HISTORY OF THE FOUR GEORGES. Four Vols. demy 8vo, cloth extra,
12s. each. [Vols. I. & II. ready.

Cr. 8vo, cl. extra, **3s. 6d.** each; post 8vo, illust. bds., **2s.** each; cl. limp, **2s. 6d.** each.

THE WATERDALE NEIGHBOURS.	MISS MISANTHROPE.
MY ENEMY'S DAUGHTER.	DONNA QUIXOTE.
A FAIR SAXON.	THE COMET OF A SEASON.
LINLEY ROCHFORD.	MAID OF ATHENS.
DEAR LADY DISDAIN.	CAMIOLA: A Girl with a Fortune.

Crown 8vo, cloth extra, **3s. 6d.** each.

THE DICTATOR.	RED DIAMONDS.

"THE RIGHT HONOURABLE." By JUSTIN McCARTHY, M.P., and Mrs. CAMPBELL-
PRAED. Fourth Edition. Crown 8vo, cloth extra, **6s.**

McCARTHY (JUSTIN H.), WORKS BY.

THE FRENCH REVOLUTION. Four Vols., 8vo, **12s.** each. [Vols. I. & II. ready.

AN OUTLINE OF THE HISTORY OF IRELAND. Crown 8vo, **1s.**; cloth, **1s. 6d.**

IRELAND SINCE THE UNION: Irish History, 1798-1886. Crown 8vo, cloth, **6s.**

HAFIZ IN LONDON: Poems. Small 8vo, gold cloth, **3s. 6d.**

HARLEQUINADE: Poems. Small 4to, Japanese vellum, **8s.**

OUR SENSATION NOVEL. Crown 8vo, picture cover, **1s.**; cloth limp, **1s. 6d.**

DOOM! An Atlantic Episode. Crown 8vo, picture cover, **1s.**

DOLLY: A Sketch. Crown 8vo, picture cover, **1s.**; cloth limp, **1s. 6d.**

LILY LASS: A Romance. Crown 8vo, picture cover, **1s.**; cloth limp, **1s. 6d.**

THE THOUSAND AND ONE DAYS: Persian Tales. With 2 Photogravures by
STANLEY L. WOOD. Two Vols., crown 8vo, half-bound, **12s.**

MACDONALD (GEORGE, LL.D.), WORKS BY.

WORKS OF FANCY AND IMAGINATION. Ten Vols., cl. extra, gilt edges, in cloth
case, **21s.** Or the Vols. may be had separately, in grolier cl., at **2s. 6d.** each.

Vol. I. WITHIN AND WITHOUT.—THE HIDDEN LIFE.

„ II. THE DISCIPLE.—THE GOSPEL WOMEN.—BOOK OF SONNETS.—ORGAN SONGS.

„ III. VIOLIN SONGS.—SONGS OF THE DAYS AND NIGHTS.—A BOOK OF DREAMS.—
ROADSIDE POEMS.—POEMS FOR CHILDREN.

„ IV. PARABLES.—BALLADS.—SCOTCH SONGS.

„ V. & VI. PHANTASTES: A Faerie Romance. | Vol. VII. THE PORTENT.

„ VIII. THE LIGHT PRINCESS.—THE GIANT'S HEART.—SHADOWS.

„ IX. CROSS PURPOSES.—THE GOLDEN KEY.—THE CARASOYN.—LITTLE DAYLIGHT

„ X. THE CRUEL PAINTER.—THE WOW o' RIVVEN.—THE CASTLE.—THE BROKEN
SWORDS.—THE GRAY WOLF.—UNCLE CORNELIUS.

POETICAL WORKS OF GEORGE MACDONALD. Collected and arranged by the
Author. 2 vols., crown 8vo, buckram, **12s.**

A THREEFOLD CORD. Edited by GEORGE MACDONALD. Post 8vo, cloth, **5s.**

HEATHER AND SNOW: A Novel. Crown 8vo, cloth extra, **3s. 6d.**

PHANTASTES: A Faerie Romance. A New Edition. With 25 Illustrations by J.
BELL. Crown 8vo, cloth extra, **3s. 6d.** [Shortly.

MACLISE PORTRAIT GALLERY (THE) OF ILLUSTRIOUS LITER-

MAGNA CHARTA. An Exact Facsimile of the Original in the British
Museum, 3 feet by 2 feet, with Arms and Seals emblazoned in Gold and Colours, **5s.**

MALLOCK (W. H.), WORKS BY.
THE NEW REPUBLIC. Post 8vo, picture cover, **2s.**; cloth limp, **2s. 6d.**
THE NEW PAUL & VIRGINIA: Positivism on an Island. Post 8vo, cloth, **2s. 6d.**
POEMS. Small 4to, parchment, **8s.**
IS LIFE WORTH LIVING? Crown 8vo, cloth extra, **6s.**
A ROMANCE OF THE NINETEENTH CENTURY. Crown 8vo, cloth, **6s.**; post 8vo,
illustrated boards, **2s.**

MALLORY'S (SIR THOMAS) MORT D'ARTHUR: The Stories of
King Arthur and of the Knights of the Round Table. (A Selection.) Edited by B.
MONTGOMERIE RANKING. Post 8vo, cloth limp, **2s.**

MARK TWAIN, WORKS BY. Crown 8vo, cloth extra, **7s. 6d.** each.
THE CHOICE WORKS OF MARK TWAIN. Revised and Corrected throughout
by the Author. With Life, Portrait, and numerous Illustrations.
ROUGHING IT, and INNOCENTS AT HOME. With 200 Illusts. by F. A. FRASER.
MARK TWAIN'S LIBRARY OF HUMOUR. With 197 Illustrations.
Crown 8vo, cloth extra (illustrated), **7s. 6d.** each; post 8vo, illust. boards, **2s.** each.
THE INNOCENTS ABROAD; or, New Pilgrim's Progress. With 234 Illustrations.
(The Two-Shilling Edition is entitled MARK TWAIN'S PLEASURE TRIP.)
THE GILDED AGE. By MARK TWAIN and C. D. WARNER. With 212 Illustrations.
THE ADVENTURES OF TOM SAWYER. With 111 Illustrations.
A TRAMP ABROAD. With 314 Illustrations.
THE PRINCE AND THE PAUPER. With 190 Illustrations.
LIFE ON THE MISSISSIPPI. With 300 Illustrations.
ADVENTURES OF HUCKLEBERRY FINN. With 174 Illusts. by E. W. KEMBLE.
A YANKEE AT THE COURT OF KING ARTHUR With 220 Illusts. by BEARD.
Post 8vo, illustrated boards, **2s.** each.
THE STOLEN WHITE ELEPHANT. | MARK TWAIN'S SKETCHES.
Crown 8vo, cloth extra, **3s. 6d.** each.
THE AMERICAN CLAIMANT. With 81 Illustrations by HAL HURST, &c.
THE £1,000,000 BANK-NOTE, and other New Stories.
TOM SAWYER ABROAD. Illustrated by DAN BEARD.
PUDD'NHEAD WILSON.

MARKS (H. S., R.A.), PEN AND PENCIL SKETCHES BY. With 4
Photogravures and 126 Illustrations. Two Vols., demy 8vo, cloth, **32s.**   [*Shortly.*

MARLOWE'S WORKS. Including his Translations. Edited, with Notes
and Introductions, by Col. CUNNINGHAM. Crown 8vo, cloth extra, **6s.**

MARRYAT (FLORENCE), NOVELS BY. Post 8vo, illust. boards, **2s.** each.
A HARVEST OF WILD OATS. | FIGHTING THE AIR.
OPEN! SESAME! | WRITTEN IN FIRE.

MASSINGER'S PLAYS. From the Text of WILLIAM GIFFORD. Edited
by Col. CUNNINGHAM. Crown 8vo, cloth extra, **6s.**

MASTERMAN.—HALF-A-DOZEN DAUGHTERS: A Novel. By J.
MASTERMAN. Post 8vo, illustrated boards, **2s.**

MILTON (J. L.), WORKS BY. Post 8vo, 1s. each; cloth, 1s. 6d. each.
THE HYGIENE OF THE SKIN. With Directions for Diet, Soaps, Baths, &c.
THE BATH IN DISEASES OF THE SKIN.
THE LAWS OF LIFE, AND THEIR RELATION TO DISEASES OF THE SKIN.
THE SUCCESSFUL TREATMENT OF LEPROSY. Demy 8vo, 1s.

MINTO (WM.)—WAS SHE GOOD OR BAD? Cr. 8vo, 1s. ; cloth, 1s. 6d.

MITFORD (BERTRAM), NOVELS BY. Crown 8vo, cloth extra, 3s. 6d. each.
THE GUN-RUNNER: A Romance of Zululand. With Frontispiece by S. L. WOOD.
THE LUCK OF GERARD RIDGELEY. With a Frontispiece by STANLEY L. WOOD.
THE KING'S ASSEGAI. With Six full-page Illustrations.
RENSHAW FANNING'S QUEST. With Frontispiece by S. L. WOOD. [Shortly.

MOLESWORTH (MRS.), NOVELS BY.
HATHERCOURT RECTORY. Post 8vo, illustrated boards, 2s.
THAT GIRL IN BLACK. Crown 8vo, cloth, 1s. 6d.

MOORE (THOMAS), WORKS BY.
THE EPICUREAN; and ALCIPHRON. Post 8vo, half-bound, 2s.
PROSE AND VERSE. With Suppressed Passages from the MEMOIRS OF LORD
BYRON. Edited by R. H. SHEPHERD. With Portrait. Cr. 8vo, cl. ex., 7s. 6d.

MUDDOCK (J. E.), STORIES BY.
STORIES WEIRD AND WONDERFUL. Post 8vo, illust. boards, 2s.; cloth, 2s. 6d.
THE DEAD MAN'S SECRET; or, The Valley of Gold. With Frontispiece by
F. BARNARD. Crown 8vo, cloth extra, 5s.; post 8vo, illustrated boards, 2s.
FROM THE BOSOM OF THE DEEP. Post 8vo, illustrated boards, 2s.
MAID MARIAN AND ROBIN HOOD: A Romance of Old Sherwood Forest. With
12 Illustrations by STANLEY L. WOOD. Crown 8vo, cloth extra, 3s. 6d.

MURRAY (D. CHRISTIE), NOVELS BY.
Crown 8vo, cloth extra, 3s. 6d. each: post 8vo, illustrated boards, 2s. each.

A LIFE'S ATONEMENT.	WAY OF THE WORLD	BY THE GATE OF THE SEA.
JOSEPH'S COAT.	A MODEL FATHER.	A BIT OF HUMAN NATURE.
COALS OF FIRE.	OLD BLAZER'S HERO.	FIRST PERSON SINGULAR.
VAL STRANGE.	HEARTS.	CYNIC FORTUNE.	BOB MARTIN'S LITTLE
		[GIRL.

Crown 8vo, cloth extra, 3s. 6d. each.
TIME'S REVENGES. | A WASTED CRIME. | IN DIREST PERIL. [Shortly.
THE MAKING OF A NOVELIST: An Experiment in Autobiography. With a
Collotype Portrait and Vignette. Crown 8vo, Irish linen, 6s.

MURRAY (D. CHRISTIE) & HENRY HERMAN, WORKS BY.
Crown 8vo, cloth extra, 3s. 6d. each; post 8vo, illustrated boards, 2s. each.
ONE TRAVELLER RETURNS. | PAUL JONES'S ALIAS. | THE BISHOPS' BIBLE.

MURRAY (HENRY), NOVELS BY. Post 8vo, illust. bds., 2s. ea.; cl., 2s. 6d. ea.
A GAME OF BLUFF. | A SONG OF SIXPENCE.

NEWBOLT.—TAKEN FROM THE ENEMY. By HENRY NEWBOLT.
Fcap. 8vo, cloth boards, 1s. 6d.

NISBET (HUME), BOOKS BY.
"BAIL UP!" Crown 8vo, cloth extra, 3s. 6d.; post 8vo, illustrated boards, 2s.
DR. BERNARD ST. VINCENT. Post 8vo, illustrated boards, 2s.
LESSONS IN ART. With 21 Illustrations. Crown 8vo, cloth extra, 2s. 6d.
WHERE ART BEGINS. With 27 Illusts. Square 8vo, cloth extra, 7s. 6d.

NORRIS.—ST. ANN'S: A Novel. By W. E. NORRIS. Cr. 8vo, 3s. 6d. [Shortly.

O'HANLON (ALICE) NOVELS BY. Post 8vo, illustrated boards, 2s. each

OUIDA, NOVELS BY. Cr. 8vo, cl., 3s. 6d. each; post 8vo. illust. bds., 2s. each.

HELD IN BONDAGE.	FOLLE-FARINE.	MOTHS. | PIPISTRELLO.
TRICOTRIN.	A DOG OF FLANDERS.	A VILLAGE COMMUNE.
STRATHMORE.	PASCAREL. | SIGNA.	IN MAREMMA.
CHANDOS.	TWO LITTLE WOODEN	BIMBI | SYRLIN.
CECIL CASTLEMAINE'S	SHOES.	WANDA.
GAGE.	IN A WINTER CITY.	FRESCOES. | OTHMAR.
UNDER TWO FLAGS.	ARIADNE.	PRINCESS NAPRAXINE.
PUCK. | IDALIA.	FRIENDSHIP.	GUILDEROY. | RUFFINO.

Square 8vo, cloth extra, 5s. each.

BIMBI. With Nine Illustrations by EDMUND H. GARRETT.
A DOG OF FLANDERS, &c. With Six Illustrations by EDMUND H. GARRETT.
SANTA BARBARA, &c. Square 8vo, cloth, 6s.; crown 8vo, cloth, 3s. 6d.; post 8vo, illustrated boards, 2s.
TWO OFFENDERS. Square 8vo, cloth extra, 6s.; crown 8vo, cloth extra, 3s. 6d.
WISDOM, WIT, AND PATHOS, selected from the Works of OUIDA by F. SYDNEY MORRIS. Post 8vo, cloth extra, 5s. CHEAP EDITION, illustrated boards, 2s.

PAGE (H. A.), WORKS BY.
THOREAU: His Life and Aims. With Portrait. Post 8vo, cloth limp, 2s. 6d.
ANIMAL ANECDOTES. Arranged on a New Principle. Crown 8vo, cloth extra, 5s.

PASCAL'S PROVINCIAL LETTERS. A New Translation, with Historical Introduction and Notes by T. M'CRIE, D.D. Post 8vo, cloth limp, 2s.

PAUL.—GENTLE AND SIMPLE. By MARGARET A. PAUL. With Frontispiece by HELEN PATERSON Crown 8vo, cloth, 3s. 6d.; post 8vo, illust. boards, 2s.

PAYN (JAMES), NOVELS BY.
Crown 8vo, cloth extra, 3s. 6d. each; post 8vo, illustrated boards, 2s. each.

LOST SIR MASSINGBERD.	A GRAPE FROM A THORN.
WALTER'S WORD.	FROM EXILE. | HOLIDAY TASKS.
LESS BLACK THAN WE'RE	THE CANON'S WARD.
PAINTED.	THE TALK OF THE TOWN.
BY PROXY. | FOR CASH ONLY.	GLOW-WORM TALES.
HIGH SPIRITS.	THE MYSTERY OF MIRBRIDGE.
UNDER ONE ROOF.	THE WORD AND THE WILL.
A CONFIDENTIAL AGENT.	THE BURNT MILLION.

Post 8vo, illustrated boards, 2s. each.

HUMOROUS STORIES.	FOUND DEAD.
THE FOSTER-BROTHERS.	GWENDOLINE'S HARVEST.
THE FAMILY SCAPEGRACE.	A MARINE RESIDENCE.
MARRIED BENEATH HIM.	MIRK ABBEY.|SOME PRIVATE VIEWS.
BENTINCK'S TUTOR.	NOT WOOED, BUT WON.
A PERFECT TREASURE.	TWO HUNDRED POUNDS REWARD.
A COUNTY FAMILY.	THE BEST OF HUSBANDS.
LIKE FATHER, LIKE SON.	HALVES.
A WOMAN'S VENGEANCE.	FALLEN FORTUNES.
CARLYON'S YEAR.|CECIL'S TRYST.	WHAT HE COST HER.
MURPHY'S MASTER.	KIT: A MEMORY.
AT HER MERCY.	A PRINCE OF THE BLOOD.
THE CLYFFARDS OF CLYFFE.	SUNNY STORIES.

Crown 8vo, cloth extra, 3s. 6d. each.
A TRYING PATIENT, &c. With a Frontispiece by STANLEY L. WOOD.
IN PERIL AND PRIVATION: Stories of MARINE ADVENTURE. With 17 Illusts.
NOTES FROM THE "NEWS." Crown 8vo, portrait cover, 1s.; cloth, 1s. 6d.

PENNELL (H. CHOLMONDELEY), WORKS BY. Post 8vo, cl., 2s. 6d. each.
PUCK ON PEGASUS. With Illustrations.
PEGASUS RE-SADDLED. With Ten full-page Illustrations by G. DU MAURIER.
THE MUSES OF MAYFAIR. Vers de Société, Selected by H. C. PENNELL.

PHELPS (E. STUART), WORKS BY. Post 8vo 1s. each; cloth 1s. 6d. each.

PLUTARCH'S LIVES OF ILLUSTRIOUS MEN. With Notes and Life of Plutarch by J. and WM. LANGHORNE. Portraits. Two Vols., demy 8vo, **10s. 6d.**

POE'S (EDGAR ALLAN) CHOICE WORKS, in Prose and Poetry. Introduction by CHAS. BAUDELAIRE, Portrait, and Facsimiles. Cr. 8vo, cloth, **7s. 6d.**
    THE MYSTERY OF MARIE ROGET, &c. Post 8vo, illustrated boards, **2s.**

POPE'S POETICAL WORKS. Post 8vo, cloth limp, **2s.**

PRAED (MRS. CAMPBELL), NOVELS BY. Post 8vo, illust. bds., **2s.** ea.
    THE ROMANCE OF A STATION. | THE SOUL OF COUNTESS ADRIAN.
             Crown 8vo, cloth, **3s. 6d.** each.
    OUTLAW AND LAWMAKER. | CHRISTINA CHARD. [*Shortly.*

PRICE (E. C.), NOVELS BY.
    Crown 8vo, cloth extra, **3s. 6d.** each; post 8vo, Illustrated boards, **2s.** each.
    VALENTINA. | THE FOREIGNERS. | MRS. LANCASTER'S RIVAL.
    GERALD. Post 8vo, illustrated boards, **2s.**

PRINCESS OLGA.—RADNA. By Princess OLGA. Crown 8vo, cloth extra, **6s.**

PROCTOR (RICHARD A., B.A.), WORKS BY.
    FLOWERS OF THE SKY. With 55 Illusts. Small crown 8vo, cloth extra, **3s. 6d.**
    EASY STAR LESSONS. With Star Maps for Every Night in the Year. Cr. 8vo, **6s.**
    FAMILIAR SCIENCE STUDIES. Crown 8vo, cloth extra, **6s.**
    SATURN AND ITS SYSTEM. With 13 Steel Plates. Demy 8vo, cloth ex., **10s. 6d.**
    MYSTERIES OF TIME AND SPACE. With Illustrations. Cr. 8vo, cloth extra, **6s.**
    THE UNIVERSE OF SUNS. With numerous Illustrations. Cr. 8vo, cloth ex., **6s.**
    WAGES AND WANTS OF SCIENCE WORKERS. Crown 8vo, **1s. 6d.**

PRYCE.—MISS MAXWELL'S AFFECTIONS. By RICHARD PRYCE. Frontispiece by HAL LUDLOW. Cr. 8vo, cl., **3s. 6d.**; post 8vo, illust. boards., **2s.**

RAMBOSSON.—POPULAR ASTRONOMY. By J. RAMBOSSON, Laureate of the Institute of France. With numerous Illusts. Crown 8vo, cloth extra, **7s. 6d.**

RANDOLPH.—AUNT ABIGAIL DYKES : A Novel. By Lt.-Colonel GEORGE RANDOLPH, U.S.A. Crown 8vo, cloth extra, **7s. 6d.**

READE (CHARLES), NOVELS BY.
    Crown 8vo, cloth extra, illustrated, **3s. 6d.** each; post 8vo, illust. bds., **2s.** each.
    PEG WOFFINGTON. Illustrated by S. L. FILDES, R.A.—Also a POCKET EDITION, set in New Type, in Elzevir style, fcap. 8vo, half-leather, **2s. 6d.**—And a Cheap POPULAR EDITION of PEG WOFFINGTON and CHRISTIE JOHNSTONE, the two Stories in One Volume, medium 8vo. **6d.**; cloth, **1s.**
    CHRISTIE JOHNSTONE. Illustrated by WILLIAM SMALL.—Also a POCKET EDITION, set in New Type, in Elzevir style, fcap. 8vo, half-leather, **2s. 6d.**
    IT IS NEVER TOO LATE TO MEND. Illustrated by G. J. PINWELL.—Also a Cheap POPULAR EDITION, medium 8vo, portrait cover. **6d.**; cloth, **1s.**
    COURSE OF TRUE LOVE NEVER DID RUN SMOOTH. Illust. HELEN PATERSON.
    THE AUTOBIOGRAPHY OF A THIEF, &c. Illustrated by MATT STRETCH.
    LOVE ME LITTLE, LOVE ME LONG. Illustrated by M. ELLEN EDWARDS.
    THE DOUBLE MARRIAGE. Illusts. by Sir JOHN GILBERT, R.A., and C. KEENE.
    THE CLOISTER AND THE HEARTH. Illustrated by CHARLES KEENE.—Also a CHEAP POPULAR EDITION, medium 8vo, **6d.**; cloth, **1s.**
    HARD CASH. Illustrated by F. W. LAWSON.
    GRIFFITH GAUNT. Illustrated by S. L. FILDES, R.A., and WILLIAM SMALL.
    FOUL PLAY. Illustrated by GEORGE DU MAURIER.
    PUT YOURSELF IN HIS PLACE. Illustrated by ROBERT BARNES.
    A TERRIBLE TEMPTATION. Illustrated by EDWARD HUGHES and A. W. COOPER.
    A SIMPLETON. Illustrated by KATE CRAUFURD.
    THE WANDERING HEIR. Illust. by H. PATERSON, S. L. FILDES, C. GREEN, &c.
    A WOMAN-HATER. Illustrated by THOMAS COULDERY.
    SINGLEHEART AND DOUBLEFACE. Illustrated by P. MACNAB.
    GOOD STORIES OF MEN AND OTHER ANIMALS. Illust. by E. A. ABBEY, &c.
    THE JILT, and other Stories. Illustrated by JOSEPH NASH.
    A PERILOUS SECRET. Illustrated by FRED. BARNARD.
    READIANA. With a Steel-plate Portrait of CHARLES READE.

RIDDELL (MRS. J. H.), NOVELS BY.
Crown 8vo, cloth extra, 3s. 6d. each; post 8vo, illustrated boards, 2s. each.
THE PRINCE OF WALES'S GARDEN PARTY. | WEIRD STORIES.

Post 8vo, illustrated boards, 2s. each.
THE UNINHABITED HOUSE. | HER MOTHER'S DARLING.
MYSTERY IN PALACE GARDENS. | THE NUN'S CURSE.
FAIRY WATER. | IDLE TALES.

RIMMER (ALFRED), WORKS BY. Square 8vo, cloth gilt, 7s. 6d. each.
OUR OLD COUNTRY TOWNS. With 55 Illustrations.
RAMBLES ROUND ETON AND HARROW. With 50 Illustrations.
ABOUT ENGLAND WITH DICKENS. With 58 Illusts. by C. A. VANDERHOOF, &c.

ROBINSON CRUSOE. By DANIEL DEFOE. (MAJOR'S EDITION.) With
37 Illustrations by GEORGE CRUIKSHANK. Post 8vo, half-bound, 2s.

ROBINSON (F. W.), NOVELS BY.
WOMEN ARE STRANGE. Post 8vo, illustrated boards, 2s.
THE HANDS OF JUSTICE. Cr. 8vo, cloth ex., 3s. 6d.; post 8vo, illust. bds., 2s.

ROBINSON (PHIL), WORKS BY. Crown 8vo, cloth extra, 6s. each.
THE POETS' BIRDS. | THE POETS' BEASTS.
THE POETS AND NATURE: REPTILES, FISHES, AND INSECTS.

ROCHEFOUCAULD'S MAXIMS AND MORAL REFLECTIONS. With
Notes, and an Introductory Essay by SAINTE-BEUVE. Post 8vo, cloth limp, 2s.

ROLL OF BATTLE ABBEY, THE : A List of the Principal Warriors
who came from Normandy with William the Conqueror. Handsomely printed, 5s.

ROWLEY (HON. HUGH), WORKS BY. Post 8vo, cloth, 2s. 6d. each.
PUNIANA: RIDDLES AND JOKES. With numerous Illustrations.
MORE PUNIANA. Profusely Illustrated.

RUNCIMAN (JAMES), STORIES BY. Post 8vo, bds., 2s. ea.; cl., 2s. 6d. ea.
SKIPPERS AND SHELLBACKS. | GRACE BALMAIGN'S SWEETHEART.
SCHOOLS AND SCHOLARS.

RUSSELL (W. CLARK), BOOKS AND NOVELS BY:
Cr. 8vo, cloth extra, 6s. each; post 8vo, illust. boards, 2s. each; cloth limp, 2s. 6d. ea.
ROUND THE GALLEY-FIRE. | A BOOK FOR THE HAMMOCK.
IN THE MIDDLE WATCH. | MYSTERY OF THE "OCEAN STAR."
A VOYAGE TO THE CAPE. | THE ROMANCE OF JENNY HARLOWE.

Cr. 8vo, cl. extra, 3s. 6d. ea.; post 8vo, illust. boards, 2s. ea.; cloth limp, 2s. 6d. ea.
AN OCEAN TRAGEDY. | MY SHIPMATE LOUISE.
ALONE ON A WIDE WIDE SEA.

ON THE FO'K'SLE HEAD. Post 8vo, illust. boards, 2s.; cloth limp, 2s. 6d.
THE GOOD SHIP "MOHOCK." Two Vols., cr. 8vo, cloth, 10s. net. [Shortly.

RUSSELL (DORA).—A COUNTRY SWEETHEART. Three Vols.,
crown 8vo, 15s. net.

SAINT AUBYN (ALAN), NOVELS BY.
Crown 8vo, cloth extra, 3s. 6d. each; post 8vo, illust. boards, 2s. each.
A FELLOW OF TRINITY. Note by OLIVER WENDELL HOLMES and Frontispiece.
THE JUNIOR DEAN, | THE MASTER OF ST. BENEDICT'S.

Fcap. 8vo, cloth boards, 1s. 6d. each.
THE OLD MAID'S SWEETHEART. | MODEST LITTLE SARA.

Crown 8vo, cloth extra, 3s. 6d. each.
TO HIS OWN MASTER. | IN THE FACE OF THE WORLD. [Shortly.

SALA (G. A.).—GASLIGHT AND DAYLIGHT. Post 8vo, boards, 2s.

SCOTLAND YARD, Past and Present: Experiences of 37 Years. By Ex-Chief-Inspector CAVANAGH. Post 8vo, illustrated boards, 2s.; cloth, 2s. 6d.

SECRET OUT, THE: One Thousand Tricks with Cards; with Entertaining Experiments in Drawing-room or "White Magic." By W. H. CREMER. With 300 Illustrations. Crown 8vo, cloth extra, 4s. 6d.

SEGUIN (L. G.), WORKS BY.
THE COUNTRY OF THE PASSION PLAY (OBERAMMERGAU) and the Highlands of Bavaria. With Map and 37 Illustrations. Crown 8vo, cloth extra, 3s. 6d.
WALKS IN ALGIERS. With 2 Maps and 16 Illusts. Crown 8vo, cloth extra, 6s.

SENIOR (WM.).—BY STREAM AND SEA. Post 8vo, cloth, 2s. 6d.

SERGEANT (A.).—DR. ENDICOTT'S EXPERIMENT. 2 vols., 10s. net.

SHAKESPEARE FOR CHILDREN: LAMB'S TALES FROM SHAKE-SPEARE. With Illusts., coloured and plain, by J. MOYR SMITH. Cr. 4to, 3s. 6d.

SHARP.—CHILDREN OF TO-MORROW: A Novel. By WILLIAM SHARP. Crown 8vo, cloth extra, 6s.

SHELLEY.—THE COMPLETE WORKS IN VERSE AND PROSE OF PERCY BYSSHE SHELLEY. Edited, Prefaced, and Annotated by R. HERNE SHEPHERD. Five Vols., crown 8vo, cloth boards, 3s. 6d. each.
POETICAL WORKS, in Three Vols.:
Vol. I. Introduction by the Editor; Posthumous Fragments of Margaret Nicholson; Shelley's Correspondence with Stockdale; The Wandering Jew; Queen Mab, with the Notes; Alastor, and other Poems; Rosalind and Helen; Prometheus Unbound; Adonais, &c.
Vol. II. Laon and Cythna; The Cenci; Julian and Maddalo; Swellfoot the Tyrant; The Witch of Atlas; Epipsychidion; Hellas.
Vol. III. Posthumous Poems; The Masque of Anarchy; and other Pieces.
PROSE WORKS, in Two Vols.:
Vol. I. The Two Romances of Zastrozzi and St. Irvyne; the Dublin and Marlow Pamphlets; A Refutation of Deism; Letters to Leigh Hunt, and some Minor Writings and Fragments.
Vol. II. The Essays; Letters from Abroad; Translations and Fragments, Edited by Mrs. SHELLEY. With a Bibliography of Shelley, and an Index of the Prose Works.

SHERARD (R. H.).—ROGUES: A Novel. Crown 8vo, 1s.; cloth, 1s. 6d.

SHERIDAN (GENERAL). — PERSONAL MEMOIRS OF GENERAL P. H. SHERIDAN. With Portraits and Facsimiles. Two Vols., demy 8vo, cloth, 24s.

SHERIDAN'S (RICHARD BRINSLEY) COMPLETE WORKS. With Life and Anecdotes. Including his Dramatic Writings, his Works in Prose and Poetry, Translations, Speeches and Jokes. 10 Illusts. Cr. 8vo, hf.-bound, 7s. 6d.
THE RIVALS, THE SCHOOL FOR SCANDAL, and other Plays. Post 8vo, printed on laid paper and half-bound, 2s.
SHERIDAN'S COMEDIES: THE RIVALS and THE SCHOOL FOR SCANDAL. Edited, with an Introduction and Notes to each Play, and a Biographical Sketch, by BRANDER MATTHEWS. With Illustrations. Demy 8vo, half-parchment, 12s. 6d.

SIDNEY'S (SIR PHILIP) COMPLETE POETICAL WORKS, including all those in "Arcadia." With Portrait, Memorial-Introduction, Notes, &c. by the Rev. A. B. GROSART, D.D. Three Vols., crown 8vo, cloth boards, 18s.

SIGNBOARDS: Their History. With Anecdotes of Famous Taverns and Remarkable Characters. By JACOB LARWOOD and JOHN CAMDEN HOTTEN. With Coloured Frontispiece and 94 Illustrations. Crown 8vo, cloth extra, 7s. 6d.

SIMS (GEO. R.), WORKS BY. Post 8vo, illust. bds., 2s. ea.; cl. limp, 2s. 6d. ea.

ROGUES AND VAGABONDS.	MARY JANE MARRIED.
THE RING O' BELLS.	TALES OF TO-DAY.
MARY JANE'S MEMOIRS.	DRAMAS OF LIFE. With 60 Illustrations.
TINKLETOP'S CRIME. With a Frontispiece by MAURICE GREIFFENHAGEN.	
ZEPH: A Circus Story, &c.	MY TWO WIVES.
MEMOIRS OF A LANDLADY.	SCENES FROM THE SHOW. [Shortly.

Crown 8vo, picture cover, 1s. each; cloth, 1s. 6d. each.
HOW THE POOR LIVE; and HORRIBLE LONDON.
THE DAGONET RECITER AND READER: being Readings and Recitations in Prose and Verse, selected from his own Works by GEORGE R. SIMS.

SLANG DICTIONARY (THE): Etymological, Historical, and Anecdotal. Crown 8vo, cloth extra, 6s. 6d.

SMITH (J. MOYR), WORKS BY.
THE PRINCE OF ARGOLIS. With 130 Illusts. Post 8vo, cloth extra, 3s. 6d.
THE WOOING OF THE WATER WITCH. Illustrated. Post 8vo, cloth, 6s.

SOCIETY IN LONDON. Crown 8vo, 1s. ; cloth, 1s. 6d.

SOCIETY IN PARIS: The Upper Ten Thousand. A Series of Letters from Count PAUL VASILI to a Young French Diplomat. Crown 8vo, cloth, 6s.

SOMERSET.—SONGS OF ADIEU. By Lord HENRY SOMERSET. Small 4to, Japanese vellum, 6s.

SPALDING.—ELIZABETHAN DEMONOLOGY: An Essay on the Belief in the Existence of Devils. By T. A. SPALDING, LL.B. Crown 8vo, cloth extra, 5s.

SPEIGHT (T. W.), NOVELS BY.
Post 8vo, illustrated boards, 2s. each,

THE MYSTERIES OF HERON DYKE.	THE GOLDEN HOOP.
BY DEVIOUS WAYS, &c.	BACK TO LIFE.
HOODWINKED; and THE SANDY-	THE LOUDWATER TRAGEDY.
CROFT MYSTERY.	BURGO'S ROMANCE.

Post 8vo, cloth limp, 1s. 6d. each.

A BARREN TITLE.	WIFE OR NO WIFE?

THE SANDYCROFT MYSTERY. Crown 8vo, picture cover, 1s.
A SECRET OF THE SEA. Crown 8vo, cloth extra, 3s. 6d.

SPENSER FOR CHILDREN. By M. H. TOWRY. With Illustrations by WALTER J. MORGAN. Crown 4to, cloth extra, 3s. 6d.

STARRY HEAVENS (THE): A POETICAL BIRTHDAY BOOK. Royal 16mo, cloth extra, 2s. 6d.

STAUNTON.—THE LAWS AND PRACTICE OF CHESS. With an Analysis of the Openings. By HOWARD STAUNTON. Edited by ROBERT B. WORMALD. Crown 8vo, cloth extra, 5s.

STEDMAN (E. C.), WORKS BY. Crown 8vo, cloth extra, 9s. each.
VICTORIAN POETS.   THE POETS OF AMERICA.

STERNDALE.—THE AFGHAN KNIFE: A Novel. By ROBERT ARMITAGE STERNDALE. Cr. 8vo, cloth extra, 3s. 6d.; post 8vo, illust. boards, 2s.

STEVENSON (R. LOUIS), WORKS BY. Post 8vo, cl. limp, 2s. 6d. each.
TRAVELS WITH A DONKEY. Seventh Edit. With a Frontis. by WALTER CRANE.
AN INLAND VOYAGE. Fourth Edition. With a Frontispiece by WALTER CRANE.
Crown 8vo, buckram, gilt top, 6s. each.
FAMILIAR STUDIES OF MEN AND BOOKS. Sixth Edition.
THE MERRY MEN. Third Edition. | UNDERWOODS: Poems. Fifth Edition.
MEMORIES AND PORTRAITS. Third Edition.
VIRGINIBUS PUERISQUE, and other Papers. Seventh Edition. | BALLADS.
ACROSS THE PLAINS, with other Memories and Essays.
NEW ARABIAN NIGHTS. Eleventh Edition. Crown 8vo, buckram, gilt top, 6s.; post 8vo, illustrated boards, 2s.
THE SUICIDE CLUB; and THE RAJAH'S DIAMOND. (From NEW ARABIAN NIGHTS.) With 8 Illustrations by W. J. HENNESSY. Crown 8vo, cloth, 5s.
PRINCE OTTO. Sixth Edition. Post 8vo, illustrated boards, 2s.
FATHER DAMIEN: An Open Letter to the Rev. Dr. Hyde. Second Edition. Crown 8vo, hand-made and brown paper, 1s.

STRUTT'S SPORTS AND PASTIMES OF THE PEOPLE OF ENGLAND; including the Rural and Domestic Recreations, May Games, Mummeries, Shows, &c., from the Earliest Period to the Present Time. Edited by WILLIAM HONE. With 140 Illustrations. Crown 8vo, cloth extra, **7s. 6d.**

SWIFT'S (DEAN) CHOICE WORKS, in Prose and Verse. With Memoir, Portrait, and Facsimiles of the Maps in "Gulliver's Travels." Cr. 8vo, cl., **7s. 6d.**
GULLIVER'S TRAVELS, and A TALE OF A TUB. Post 8vo, half-bound, **2s.**
JONATHAN SWIFT: A Study. By J. CHURTON COLLINS. Crown 8vo, cloth extra, **8s.**

SWINBURNE (ALGERNON C.), WORKS BY.

SELECTIONS FROM POETICAL WORKS OF A. C. SWINBURNE. Fcap. 8vo, 6s.
ATALANTA IN CALYDON. Crown 8vo, 6s.
CHASTELARD: A Tragedy. Crown 8vo, 7s.
POEMS AND BALLADS. FIRST SERIES. Crown 8vo or fcap. 8vo, 9s.
POEMS AND BALLADS. SECOND SERIES. Crown 8vo or fcap. 8vo, 9s.
POEMS & BALLADS. THIRD SERIES. Cr. 8vo, 7s.
SONGS BEFORE SUNRISE. Crown 8vo, 10s. 6d.
BOTHWELL: A Tragedy. Crown 8vo, 12s. 6d.
SONGS OF TWO NATIONS. Crown 8vo, 6s.
GEORGE CHAPMAN. (See Vol. II. of G. CHAPMAN's Works.) Crown 8vo, 6s.
ESSAYS AND STUDIES. Crown 8vo, 12s.
ERECHTHEUS: A Tragedy. Crown 8vo, 6s.

A NOTE ON CHARLOTTE BRONTE. Cr. 8vo, 6s.
SONGS OF THE SPRINGTIDES. Crown 8vo, 6s.
STUDIES IN SONG. Crown 8vo, 7s.
MARY STUART. A Tragedy. Crown 8vo, 8s.
TRISTRAM OF LYONESSE. Crown 8vo, 9s.
A CENTURY OF ROUNDELS. Small 4to, 8s.
A MIDSUMMER HOLIDAY. Crown 8vo, 7s.
MARINO FALIERO. A Tragedy. Crown 8vo, 6s.
A STUDY OF VICTOR HUGO. Crown 8vo, 6s.
MISCELLANIES. Crown 8vo, 12s.
LOCRINE. A Tragedy. Crown 8vo, 6s.
A STUDY OF BEN JONSON. Crown 8vo, 7s.
THE SISTERS: A Tragedy. Crown 8vo, 6s.
ASTROPHEL, &c. Crown 8vo, 7s.
STUDIES IN PROSE AND POETRY. Crown 8vo, 9s.

SYNTAX'S (DR.) THREE TOURS: In Search of the Picturesque, in Search of Consolation, and in Search of a Wife. With ROWLANDSON's Coloured Illustrations, and Life of the Author by J. C. HOTTEN. Crown 8vo, cloth extra, **7s. 6d.**

TAINE'S HISTORY OF ENGLISH LITERATURE. Translated by HENRY VAN LAUN. Four Vols., small demy 8vo, cl. bds., **30s.**—POPULAR EDITION, Two Vols., large crown 8vo, cloth extra, **15s.**

TAYLOR'S (BAYARD) DIVERSIONS OF THE ECHO CLUB: Burlesques of Modern Writers. Post 8vo, cloth limp, **2s.**

TAYLOR (DR. J. E., F.L.S.), WORKS BY. Crown 8vo, cloth, **5s.** each.
THE SAGACITY AND MORALITY OF PLANTS: A Sketch of the Life and Conduct of the Vegetable Kingdom. With a Coloured Frontispiece and 100 Illustrations.
OUR COMMON BRITISH FOSSILS, and Where to Find Them. 331 Illustrations.
THE PLAYTIME NATURALIST. With 366 Illustrations.

TAYLOR'S (TOM) HISTORICAL DRAMAS. Containing "Clancarty," "Jeanne Darc," "'Twixt Axe and Crown," "The Fool's Revenge," "Arkwright's Wife," "Anne Boleyn," "Plot and Passion." Crown 8vo, cloth extra, **7s. 6d.**
. The Plays may also be had separately, at **1s.** each.

TENNYSON (LORD): A Biographical Sketch. By H. J. JENNINGS. With a Photograph-Portrait. Crown 8vo, cloth extra, **6s.**—Cheap Edition, post 8vo, portrait cover, **1s.;** cloth, **1s. 6d.**

THACKERAYANA: Notes and Anecdotes. Illustrated by Hundreds of Sketches by WILLIAM MAKEPEACE THACKERAY. Crown 8vo, cloth extra, **7s. 6d.**

THAMES.—A NEW PICTORIAL HISTORY OF THE THAMES. By A. S. KRAUSSE. With 340 Illustrations. Post 8vo, **1s.;** cloth, **1s. 6d.**

THIERS.—HISTORY OF THE CONSULATE & EMPIRE OF FRANCE UNDER NAPOLEON. By A. THIERS. Translated by D. FORBES CAMPBELL and JOHN STEBBING. With 36 Steel Plates. 12 vols., demy 8vo, cloth extra, **12s.** each.

THOMAS (BERTHA), NOVELS BY. Cr. 8vo, cl., **3s. 6d.** ea.; post 8vo, **2s.** ea.

TIMBS (JOHN), WORKS BY. Crown 8vo, cloth extra, 7s. 6d. each.
THE HISTORY OF CLUBS AND CLUB LIFE IN LONDON: Anecdotes of its Famous Coffee-houses, Hostelries, and Taverns. With 42 Illustrations.
ENGLISH ECCENTRICS AND ECCENTRICITIES: Stories of Delusions, Impostures, Sporting Scenes, Eccentric Artists, Theatrical Folk, &c. 48 Illustrations.

TROLLOPE (ANTHONY), NOVELS BY.
Crown 8vo, cloth extra, 3s. 6d. each; post 8vo, illustrated boards, 2s. each.
THE WAY WE LIVE NOW. | MR. SCARBOROUGH'S FAMILY.
FRAU FROHMANN. | MARION FAY. | THE LAND-LEAGUERS.
Post 8vo, Illustrated boards, 2s. each.
KEPT IN THE DARK. | AMERICAN SENATOR.
GOLDEN LION OF GRANPERE. | JOHN CALDIGATE.

TROLLOPE (FRANCES E.), NOVELS BY.
Crown 8vo, cloth extra, 3s. 6d. each; post 8vo, illustrated boards, 2s. each.
LIKE SHIPS UPON THE SEA. | MABEL'S PROGRESS. | ANNE FURNESS.

TROLLOPE (T. A.).—DIAMOND CUT DIAMOND. Post 8vo, illust. bds., 2s.

TROWBRIDGE.—FARNELL'S FOLLY: A Novel. By J. T. TROWBRIDGE. Post 8vo, illustrated boards, 2s.

TYTLER (C. C. FRASER-).—MISTRESS JUDITH: A Novel. By C. C. FRASER-TYTLER. Crown 8vo, cloth extra, 3s. 6d.; post 8vo, illust. boards, 2s.

TYTLER (SARAH), NOVELS BY.
Crown 8vo, cloth extra, 3s. 6d. each; post 8vo, illustrated boards, 2s. each.
THE BRIDE'S PASS. | BURIED DIAMONDS.
LADY BELL. | THE BLACKHALL GHOSTS.
Post 8vo, illustrated boards, 2s. each.
WHAT SHE CAME THROUGH. | BEAUTY AND THE BEAST.
CITOYENNE JACQUELINE | DISAPPEARED. | NOBLESSE OBLIGE.
SAINT MUNGO'S CITY. | THE HUGUENOT FAMILY.

UNDERHILL.—WALTER BESANT: A Study. By JOHN UNDERHILL. With Portraits. Crown 8vo, Irish linen, 6s. [Shortly.

UPWARD.—THE QUEEN AGAINST OWEN. By ALLEN UPWARD. With Frontispiece by J. S. CROMPTON. Crown 8vo, cloth extra, 3s. 6d.

VASHTI AND ESTHER. By the Writer of "Belle's" Letters in The World. Crown 8vo, cloth extra, 3s. 6d.

VILLARI.—A DOUBLE BOND. By LINDA VILLARI. Fcap. 8vo, 1s.

VIZETELLY (E. A.).—THE SCORPION: A Romance of Spain. With a Frontispiece. Crown 8vo, cloth extra, 3s. 6d.

WALFORD (EDWARD, M.A.), WORKS BY.
WALFORD'S COUNTY FAMILIES OF THE UNITED KINGDOM (1895). Containing the Descent, Birth, Marriage, Education, &c., of 12,000 Heads of Families, their Heirs, Offices, Addresses, Clubs, &c. Royal 8vo, cloth gilt, 50s.
WALFORD'S SHILLING PEERAGE (1895). Containing a List of the House of Lords, Scotch and Irish Peers, &c. 32mo, cloth, 1s.
WALFORD'S SHILLING BARONETAGE (1895). Containing a List of the Baronets of the United Kingdom, Biographical Notices, Addresses, &c. 32mo, cloth, 1s.
WALFORD'S SHILLING KNIGHTAGE (1895). Containing a List of the Knights of the United Kingdom, Biographical Notices, Addresses, &c. 32mo, cloth, 1s.
WALFORD'S SHILLING HOUSE OF COMMONS (1895). Containing a List of all the Members of the New Parliament, their Addresses, Clubs, &c. 32mo, cloth, 1s.
WALFORD'S COMPLETE PEERAGE, BARONETAGE, KNIGHTAGE, AND HOUSE OF COMMONS (1895). Royal 32mo, cloth, gilt edges, 5s. [Shortly.
TALES OF OUR GREAT FAMILIES. Crown 8vo, cloth extra, 3s. 6d.

WALT WHITMAN, POEMS BY. Edited, with Introduct

WARNER.—A ROUNDABOUT JOURNEY. By CHARLES DUDLEY WARNER. Crown 8vo, cloth extra, **6s.**

WARRANT TO EXECUTE CHARLES I. A Facsimile, with the 59 Signatures and Seals. Printed on paper 22 in. by 14 in. **2s.**
WARRANT TO EXECUTE MARY QUEEN OF SCOTS. A Facsimile, including Queen Elizabeth's Signature and the Great Seal. **2s.**

WASSERMANN (LILLIAS), NOVELS BY.
THE DAFFODILS. Crown 8vo, **1s.**; cloth, **1s. 6d.**
THE MARQUIS OF CARABAS. By AARON WATSON and LILLIAS WASSERMANN. Post 8vo, illustrated boards, **2s.**

WEATHER, HOW TO FORETELL THE, WITH POCKET SPEC-TROSCOPE. By F. W. CORY. With 10 Illustrations. Cr. 8vo, **1s.**; cloth, **1s. 6d.**

WESTALL (William).—TRUST-MONEY. Post 8vo, illust. bds., **2s.**

WHIST.—HOW TO PLAY SOLO WHIST. By ABRAHAM S. WILKS and CHARLES F. PARDON. New Edition. Post 8vo, cloth limp, **2s.**

WHITE.—THE NATURAL HISTORY OF SELBORNE. By GILBERT WHITE, M.A. Post 8vo, printed on laid paper and half-bound, **2s.**

WILLIAMS (W. MATTIEU, F.R.A.S.), WORKS BY.
SCIENCE IN SHORT CHAPTERS. Crown 8vo, cloth extra, **7s. 6d.**
A SIMPLE TREATISE ON HEAT. With Illusts. Cr. 8vo, cloth limp, **2s. 6d.**
THE CHEMISTRY OF COOKERY. Crown 8vo, cloth extra, **6s.**
THE CHEMISTRY OF IRON AND STEEL MAKING. Crown 8vo, cloth extra, **9s.**
A VINDICATION OF PHRENOLOGY. With Portrait and over 40 Illustrations. Demy 8vo, cloth extra, **12s. 6d.**

WILLIAMSON (MRS. F. H.).—A CHILD WIDOW. Post 8vo, bds., **2s.**

WILSON (DR. ANDREW, F.R.S.E.), WORKS BY.
CHAPTERS ON EVOLUTION. With 259 Illustrations. Cr. 8vo, cloth extra, **7s. 6d.**
LEAVES FROM A NATURALIST'S NOTE-BOOK. Post 8vo, cloth limp, **2s. 6d.**
LEISURE-TIME STUDIES. With Illustrations. Crown 8vo, cloth extra, **6s.**
STUDIES IN LIFE AND SENSE. With numerous Illusts. Cr. 8vo, cl. ex., **6s.**
COMMON ACCIDENTS: HOW TO TREAT THEM. Illusts. Cr. 8vo, **1s.**; cl., **1s. 6d.**
GLIMPSES OF NATURE. With 35 Illustrations. Crown 8vo, cloth extra, **3s. 6d.**

WINTER (J. S.), STORIES BY. Post 8vo, illustrated boards, **2s.** each; cloth limp, **2s. 6d.** each.
CAVALRY LIFE. | REGIMENTAL LEGENDS.
A SOLDIER'S CHILDREN. With 34 Illustrations by E. G. THOMSON and E. STUART HARDY. Crown 8vo, cloth extra, **3s. 6d.**

WISSMANN.—MY SECOND JOURNEY THROUGH EQUATORIAL AFRICA. By HERMANN VON WISSMANN. With 92 Illusts. Demy 8vo, **16s.**

WOOD.—SABINA: A Novel. By Lady WOOD. Post 8vo, boards, **2s.**

WOOD (H. F.), DETECTIVE STORIES BY. Post 8vo, boards, **2s.** each.
PASSENGER FROM SCOTLAND YARD. | ENGLISHMAN OF THE RUE CAIN.

WOOLLEY.—RACHEL ARMSTRONG; or, Love and Theology. By CELIA PARKER WOOLLEY. Post 8vo, illustrated boards, **2s.**; cloth, **2s. 6d.**

WRIGHT (THOMAS), WORKS BY. Crown 8vo, cloth extra, **7s. 6d.** each.
CARICATURE HISTORY OF THE GEORGES. With 400 Caricatures, Squibs, &c.
HISTORY OF CARICATURE AND OF THE GROTESQUE IN ART, LITERA-TURE, SCULPTURE, AND PAINTING. Illustrated by F. W. FAIRHOLT, F.S.A.

WYNMAN.—MY FLIRTATIONS. By MARGARET WYNMAN. With 13 Illustrations by J. BERNARD PARTRIDGE. Crown 8vo, cloth extra, **3s. 6d.**

YATES (EDMUND), NOVELS BY. Post 8vo, illustrated boards, **2s.** each.

LISTS OF BOOKS CLASSIFIED IN SERIES.

. *For fuller cataloguing, see alphabetical arrangement, pp. 1-25.*

THE MAYFAIR LIBRARY. Post 8vo, cloth limp, 2s. 6d. per Volume.

A Journey Round My Room. By XAVIER DE MAISTRE.
Quips and Quiddities. By W. D. ADAMS.
The Agony Column of "The Times."
Melancholy Anatomised: Abridgment of "Burton's Anatomy of Melancholy."
Poetical Ingenuities. By W. T. DOBSON.
The Cupboard Papers. By FIN-BEC.
W. S. Gilbert's Plays. FIRST SERIES.
W. S. Gilbert's Plays. SECOND SERIES.
Songs of Irish Wit and Humour.
Animals and Masters. By Sir A. HELPS.
Social Pressure. By Sir A. HELPS.
Curiosities of Criticism. H. J. JENNINGS.
Holmes's Autocrat of the Breakfast-Table.
Pencil and Palette. By R. KEMPT.
Little Essays: from LAMB'S Letters.

Forensic Anecdotes. By JACOB LARWOOD.
Theatrical Anecdotes. JACOB LARWOOD.
Jeux d'Esprit. Edited by HENRY S. LEIGH.
Witch Stories. By E. LYNN LINTON.
Ourselves. By E. LYNN LINTON.
Pastimes & Players. By R. MACGREGOR.
New Paul and Virginia. W. H. MALLOCK.
New Republic. By W. H. MALLOCK.
Puck on Pegasus. By H. C. PENNELL.
Pegasus Re-Saddled. By H. C. PENNELL.
Muses of Mayfair. Ed. H. C. PENNELL.
Thoreau: His Life & Aims. By H. A. PAGE.
Puniana. By Hon. HUGH ROWLEY.
More Puniana. By Hon. HUGH ROWLEY.
The Philosophy of Handwriting.
By Stream and Sea. By WM. SENIOR.
Leaves from a Naturalist's Note-Book. By Dr. ANDREW WILSON.

THE GOLDEN LIBRARY. Post 8vo, cloth limp, 2s. per Volume.

Bayard Taylor's Diversions of the Echo Club.
Bennett's Ballad History of England.
Bennett's Songs for Sailors.
Godwin's Lives of the Necromancers.
Pope's Poetical Works.
Holmes's Autocrat of Breakfast Table.

Jesse's Scenes of Country Life.
Leigh Hunt's Tale for a Chimney Corner.
Mallory's Mort d'Arthur: Selections.
Pascal's Provincial Letters.
Rochefoucauld's Maxims & Reflections.

THE WANDERER'S LIBRARY. Crown 8vo, cloth extra, 3s. 6d. each.

Wanderings in Patagonia. By JULIUS BEERBOHM. Illustrated.
Camp Notes. By FREDERICK BOYLE.
Savage Life. By FREDERICK BOYLE.
Merrie England in the Olden Time. By G. DANIEL. Illustrated by CRUIKSHANK.
Circus Life. By THOMAS FROST.
Lives of the Conjurers. THOMAS FROST.
The Old Showmen and the Old London Fairs. By THOMAS FROST.
Low-Life Deeps. By JAMES GREENWOOD.

Wilds of London. JAMES GREENWOOD.
Tunis. Chev. HESSE-WARTEGG. 22 Illusts.
Life and Adventures of a Cheap Jack.
World Behind the Scenes. P. FITZGERALD.
Tavern Anecdotes and Sayings.
The Genial Showman. By E. P. HINGSTON.
Story of London Parks. JACOB LARWOOD.
London Characters. By HENRY MAYHEW.
Seven Generations of Executioners.
Summer Cruising in the South Seas. By C. WARREN STODDARD. Illustrated.

POPULAR SHILLING BOOKS.

Harry Fludyer at Cambridge.
Jeff Briggs's Love Story. BRET HARTE.
Twins of Table Mountain. BRET HARTE.

Lily Lass. JUSTIN H. McCARTHY.
Was She Good or Bad? By W. MINTO.
Notes from the "News." By JAS. PAYN.

MY LIBRARY. Printed on laid paper, post 8vo, half-Roxburghe, **2s. 6d.** each.

Four Frenchwomen. By AUSTIN DOBSON.
Citation and Examination of William Shakspeare. By W. S. LANDOR.
The Journal of Maurice de Guerin.

Christie Johnstone. By CHARLES READE. With a Photogravure Frontispiece.
Peg Woffington. By CHARLES READE.
The Dramatic Essays of Charles Lamb.

THE POCKET LIBRARY. Post 8vo, printed on laid paper and hf.-bd., **2s.** each.

The Essays of Elia. By CHARLES LAMB.
Robinson Crusoe. Illust. G. CRUIKSHANK.
Whims and Oddities. By THOMAS HOOD. With 85 Illustrations.
The Barber's Chair, &c. By D. JERROLD.
Gastronomy. By BRILLAT-SAVARIN.
The Epicurean, &c. By THOMAS MOORE.
Leigh Hunt's Essays. Ed. E. OLLIER.

White's Natural History of Selborne.
Gulliver's Travels, &c. By Dean SWIFT.
Plays. By RICHARD BRINSLEY SHERIDAN.
Anecdotes of the Clergy. J. LARWOOD.
Thomson's Seasons. Illustrated.
The Autocrat of the Breakfast-Table and The Professor at the Breakfast-Table. By OLIVER WENDELL HOLMES.

THE PICCADILLY NOVELS.

LIBRARY EDITIONS OF NOVELS, many Illustrated, crown 8vo, cloth extra, **3s. 6d.** each.

By F. M. ALLEN.
Green as Grass.

By GRANT ALLEN.
Philistia.
Babylon.
Strange Stories.
Beckoning Hand.
In all Shades.
The Tents of Shem.
For Maimie's Sake.
The Devil's Die.

This Mortal Coil.
The Great Taboo.
Dumaresq's Daughter.
Blood Royal.
Duchess of Powysland.
Ivan Greet's Masterpiece.
The Scallywag.

By EDWIN L. ARNOLD.
Phra the Phœnician.
The Constable of St. Nicholas.

By ALAN ST. AUBYN.
A Fellow of Trinity.
The Junior Dean.
Master of St. Benedict's.

To his Own Master.
In the Face of the World.

By Rev. S. BARING GOULD.
Red Spider. | Eve.

By ROBERT BARR.
In a Steamer Chair. | From Whose Bourne.

By FRANK BARRETT.
The Woman of the Iron Bracelets.

By "BELLE."
Vashti and Esther.

By W. BESANT & J. RICE.
My Little Girl.
Case of Mr. Lucraft.
This Son of Vulcan.
The Golden Butterfly.
By Celia's Arbour.
The Monks of Thelema.
The Seamy Side.

The Ten Years' Tenant.
Ready-Money Mortiboy.
With Harp and Crown.
'Twas in Trafalgar's Bay.
The Chaplain of the Fleet.

By WALTER BESANT.
All Sorts and Conditions of Men.
The Captains' Room.
All in a Garden Fair.
Herr Paulus.
The Ivory Gate.
The World Went Very Well Then.

Uncle Jack.
Children of Gibeon.
Bell of St. Paul's.
To Call Her Mine.
The Holy Rose.
Armorel of Lyonesse.
St. Katherine's by the Tower.

By HALL CAINE.
The Shadow of a Crime.
A Son of Hagar.

The Deemster.

By MACLAREN COBBAN.
The Red Sultan. | The Burden of Isabel.

ROBT. & FRANCES COLLINS.
Transmigration.
Blacksmith & Scholar.
The Village Comedy.

From Midnight to Midnight.
You Play me False.

By WILKIE COLLINS.
Armadale.
After Dark.
No Name.
Antonina.
Basil.
Hide and Seek.
The Dead Secret.
Queen of Hearts.
My Miscellanies.
The Woman in White.
The Moonstone.
Man and Wife.
Poor Miss Finch.
Miss or Mrs. ?
The New Magdalen.

The Frozen Deep.
The Two Destinies.
The Law and the Lady.
The Haunted Hotel.
The Fallen Leaves.
Jezebel's Daughter.
The Black Robe.
Heart and Science.
"I Say No."
Little Novels.
The Evil Genius.
The Legacy of Cain.
A Rogue's Life.
Blind Love.

By DUTTON COOK.
Paul Foster's Daughter.

By E. H. COOPER.
Geoffory Hamilton.

By V. CECIL COTES.
Two Girls on a Barge.

By C. EGBERT CRADDOCK.
His Vanished Star.

By MATT CRIM.
Adventures of a Fair Rebel.

By B. M. CROKER.
Diana Barrington.
Proper Pride.
A Family Likeness.

Pretty Miss Neville.
A Bird of Passage.
"To Let."

By WILLIAM CYPLES.
Hearts of Gold.

By ALPHONSE DAUDET.

THE PICCADILLY (3/6) NOVELS—*continued.*

By DICK DONOVAN.

Tracked to Doom. | Man from Manchester.

By A. CONAN DOYLE.

The Firm of Girdlestone.

By Mrs. ANNIE EDWARDES.

Archie Lovell.

By G. MANVILLE FENN.

The New Mistress. | Witness to the Deed.
The Tiger Lily. | The White Virgin.

By PERCY FITZGERALD.

Fatal Zero.

By R. E. FRANCILLON.

Queen Cophetua. | King or Knave?
One by One. | Ropes of Sand.
A Dog and his Shadow. | Jack Doyle's Daughter.
A Real Queen. |

Pref. by Sir BARTLE FRERE.

Pandurang Hari.

By EDWARD GARRETT.

The Capel Girls.

By PAUL GAULOT.

The Red Shirts.

By CHARLES GIBBON.

Robin Gray. | Of High Degree.
Loving a Dream. | The Flower of the
The Golden Shaft. | Forest.

By E. GLANVILLE.

The Lost Heiress. | The Fossicker.
A Fair Colonist. |

By E. J. GOODMAN.

The Fate of Herbert Wayne.

By CECIL GRIFFITH.

Corinthia Marazion.

By SYDNEY GRUNDY.

The Days of his Vanity.

By THOMAS HARDY.

Under the Greenwood Tree.

By BRET HARTE.

A Waif of the Plains. | Colonel Starbottle's
Sally Dows. | Client.
A Ward of the Golden | Susy.
  Gate. | A Protégée of Jack
A Sappho of Green | Hamlin's.
  Springs. | Bell-Ringer of Angel's.

By JULIAN HAWTHORNE.

Garth. | Beatrix Randolph.
Ellice Quentin. | David Poindexter's Dis-
Sebastian Strome. | appearance.
Dust. | The Spectre of the
Fortune's Fool. | Camera

By Sir A. HELPS.

Ivan de Biron.

By I. HENDERSON.

Agatha Page.

By G. A. HENTY.

Rujub the Juggler. | Dorothy's Double.

By JOHN HILL.

The Common Ancestor.

THE PICCADILLY (3/6) NOVELS—*continued.*

By E. LYNN LINTON.

Patricia Kemball. | Sowing the Wind.
Under which Lord? | The Atonement of Leam
'My Love!" | Dundas.
Ione. | The World Well Lost.
Paston Carew. | The One Too Many.

By H. W. LUCY.

Gideon Fleyce.

By JUSTIN McCARTHY.

A Fair Saxon. | Waterdale Neighbours.
Linley Rochford. | My Enemy's Daughter.
Miss Misanthrope. | Red Diamonds.
Donna Quixota. | Dear Lady Disdain.
Maid of Athens. | The Dictator.
Camiola. | The Comet of a Season.

By GEORGE MACDONALD.

Heather and Snow.

By AGNES MACDONELL.

Quaker Cousins.

By L. T. MEADE.

A Soldier of Fortune.

By BERTRAM MITFORD.

The Gun-Runner. | The King's Assegai.
The Luck of Gerard | Renshaw Fanning's
  Ridgeley. | Quest.

By J. E. MUDDOCK.

Maid Marian and Robin Hood.

By D. CHRISTIE MURRAY.

A Life's Atonement. | By the Gate of the Sea.
Joseph's Coat. | A Bit of Human Nature.
Coals of Fire. | First Person Singular.
Old Blazer's Hero. | Cynic Fortune.
Val Strange. | The Way of the World.
Hearts. | Bob Martin's Little Girl.
A Model Father. | A Wasted Crime.
Time's Revenges. | In Direst Peril.

By MURRAY & HERMAN.

The Bishops' Bible. | Paul Jones's Alias.
One Traveller Returns. |

By HUME NISBET.

" Bail Up !"

By W. E. NORRIS.

Saint Ann's.

By G. OHNET.

A Weird Gift.

By OUIDA.

Held in Bondage. | Two Little Wooden
Strathmore. | Shoes.
Chandos. | In a Winter City.
Under Two Flags. | Friendship.
Idalia. | Moths.
Cecil Castlemaine's | Ruffino.
  Gage. | Pipistrello.
Tricotrin. | A Village Commune.
Puck. | Bimbi.
Folle Farine. | Wanda.
A Dog of Flanders. | Frescoes.
Pascarel. | Othmar.
Signa. | In Maremma.
Princess Napraxine. | Syrlin. | Guilderoy.
Ariadne. | Santa Barbara.

By MARGARET A. PAUL.

Gentle and Simple.

By JAMES PAYN.

Two-Shilling Novels—*continued.*

By AMBROSE BIERCE.
In the Midst of Life.

By FREDERICK BOYLE.
Camp Notes.
Savage Life.
Chronicles of No-man's Land.

By BRET HARTE.
Californian Stories.
Gabriel Conroy.
The Luck of Roaring Camp.
An Heiress of Red Dog.
Flip.
Maruja.
A Phyllis of the Sierras.

By HAROLD BRYDGES.
Uncle Sam at Home.

By ROBERT BUCHANAN.
Shadow of the Sword.
A Child of Nature.
God and the Man.
Love Me for Ever.
Foxglove Manor.
The Master of the Mine.
The Martyrdom of Madeline.
Annan Water.
The New Abelard.
Matt.
The Heir of Linne.

By HALL CAINE.
The Shadow of a Crime.
A Son of Hagar.
The Deemster.

By Commander CAMERON.
The Cruise of the "Black Prince."

By Mrs. LOVETT CAMERON.
Deceivers Ever.
Juliet's Guardian.

By AUSTIN CLARE.
For the Love of a Lass.

By Mrs. ARCHER CLIVE.
Paul Ferroll.
Why Paul Ferroll Killed his Wife.

By MACLAREN COBBAN.
The Cure of Souls.

By C. ALLSTON COLLINS.
The Bar Sinister.

MORT. & FRANCES COLLINS.
Sweet Anne Page.
Transmigration.
From Midnight to Midnight.
A Fight with Fortune.
Sweet and Twenty.
The Village Comedy.
You Play me False.
Blacksmith and Scholar.
Frances.

By WILKIE COLLINS.
Armadale.
After Dark.
No Name.
Antonina.
Basil.
Hide and Seek.
The Dead Secret.
Queen of Hearts.
Miss or Mrs.?
The New Magdalen.
The Frozen Deep.
The Law and the Lady.
The Two Destinies.
The Haunted Hotel.
A Rogue's Life.
My Miscellanies.
The Woman in White.
The Moonstone.
Man and Wife.
Poor Miss Finch.
The Fallen Leaves.
Jezebel's Daughter.
The Black Robe.
Heart and Science.
"I Say No:"
The Evil Genius.
Little Novels.
Legacy of Cain.
Blind Love.

By M. J. COLQUHOUN.
Every Inch a Soldier.

Two-Shilling Novels—*continued.*

By JAMES DE MILLE.
A Castle in Spain.

By J. LEITH DERWENT.
Our Lady of Tears.
Circe's Lovers.

By CHARLES DICKENS.
Sketches by Boz.
Pickwick Papers.
Oliver Twist.
Nicholas Nickleby.

By DICK DONOVAN.
The Man-Hunter.
Tracked and Taken.
Caught at Last!
Wanted!
Who Poisoned Hetty Duncan?
Man from Manchester.
A Detective's Triumphs
In the Grip of the Law.
From Information Received.
Tracked to Doom.
Link by Link
Suspicion Aroused.

By Mrs. ANNIE EDWARDES.
A Point of Honour.
Archie Lovell.

By M. BETHAM-EDWARDS.
Felicia.
Kitty.

By EDW. EGGLESTON.
Roxy.

By G. MANVILLE FENN.
The New Mistress.

By PERCY FITZGERALD.
Bella Donna.
Never Forgotten.
Polly.
Fatal Zero.
Second Mrs. Tillotson.
Seventy-five Brooke Street.
The Lady of Brantome.

By P. FITZGERALD and others.
Strange Secrets.

ALBANY DE FONBLANQUE.
Filthy Lucre.

By R. E. FRANCILLON.
Olympia.
One by One.
A Real Queen.
Queen Cophetua.
King or Knave?
Romances of the Law.

By HAROLD FREDERIC.
Seth's Brother's Wife.
The Lawton Girl.

Pref. by Sir BARTLE FRERE.
Pandurang Hari.

By HAIN FRISWELL.
One of Two.

By EDWARD GARRETT.
The Capel Girls.

By GILBERT GAUL.
A Strange Manuscript.

By CHARLES GIBBON.
Robin Gray.
Fancy Free.
For Lack of Gold.
What will the World Say?
In Love and War.
For the King.
In Pastures Green.
Queen of the Meadow.
A Heart's Problem
In Honour Bound.
Flower of the Forest.
The Braes of Yarrow.
The Golden Shaft.
Of High Degree.
By Mead and Stream.
Loving a Dream.
A Hard Knot.
Heart's Delight.
Blood-Money

By THOMAS HARDY.
Under the Greenwood Tree.

By J. BERWICK HARWOOD.
The Tenth Earl.

By JULIAN HAWTHORNE.
Garth.
Ellice Quentin.
Fortune's Fool.
Miss Cadogna.
Sebastian Strome.
Dust.

Beatrix Randolph.
Love—or a Name.
David Poindexter's Disappearance.
The Spectre of the Camera.

By Sir ARTHUR HELPS.
Ivan de Biron.

By HENRY HERMAN.
A Leading Lady.

By HEADON HILL.
Zambra the Detective.

By JOHN HILL.
Treason Felony.

By Mrs. CASHEL HOEY.
The Lover's Creed.

By Mrs. GEORGE HOOPER.
The House of Raby.

By TIGHE HOPKINS.
Twixt Love and Duty.

By Mrs. HUNGERFORD.
A Maiden all Forlorn.
In Durance Vile.
Marvel.
A Mental Struggle.
A Modern Circe.

By Mrs. ALFRED HUNT.
Thornicroft's Model.
That Other Person.
Self-Condemned.
The Leaden Casket.

By JEAN INGELOW.
Fated to be Free.

By WM. JAMESON.
My Dead Self.

By HARRIETT JAY.
The Dark Colleen.
Queen of Connaught.

By MARK KERSHAW.
Colonial Facts and Fictions.

By R. ASHE KING.
A Drawn Game.
"The Wearing of the Green."
Passion's Slave.
Bell Barry.

By JOHN LEYS.
The Lindsays.

By E. LYNN LINTON.
Patricia Kemball.
The World Well Lost.
Under which Lord?
Paston Carew.
"My Love!"
Ione.
The Atonement of Leam Dundas.
With a Silken Thread.
The Rebel of the Family.
Sowing the Wind.

By HENRY W. LUCY.
Gideon Fleyce.

By JUSTIN McCARTHY.
A Fair Saxon.
Linley Rochford.
Miss Misanthrope.
Donna Quixote.
Maid of Athens.
Camiola.
Dear Lady Disdain.
Waterdale Neighbours.
My Enemy's Daughter.
The Comet of a Season.

By HUGH MACCOLL.
Mr. Stranger's Sealed Packet.

Two-Shilling Novels—*continued.*

By FLORENCE MARRYAT.
Open! Sesame!
Fighting the Air.
A Harvest of Wild Oats.
Written in Fire.

By J. MASTERMAN.
Half-a-dozen Daughters.

By BRANDER MATTHEWS.
A Secret of the Sea.

By LEONARD MERRICK.
The Man who was Good.

By JEAN MIDDLEMASS.
Touch and Go.
Mr. Dorillion.

By Mrs. MOLESWORTH.
Hathercourt Rectory.

By J. E. MUDDOCK.
Stories Weird and Wonderful.
The Dead Man's Secret.
From the Bosom of the Deep.

By MURRAY and HERMAN.
One Traveller Returns.
Paul Jones's Alias.
The Bishops' Bible.

By D. CHRISTIE MURRAY.
A Model Father.
Joseph's Coat.
Coals of Fire.
Val Strange.
Old Blazer's Hero.
Hearts.
The Way of the World.
Cynic Fortune.
A Life's Atonement.
By the Gate of the Sea.
A Bit of Human Nature.
First Person Singular.
Bob Martin's Little Girl.

By HENRY MURRAY.
A Game of Bluff.
A Song of Sixpence.

By HUME NISBET.
"Bail Up!"
Dr. Bernard St. Vincent.

By ALICE O'HANLON.
The Unforeseen.
Chance? or Fate?

By GEORGES OHNET.
Dr. Rameau.
A Last Love.
A Weird Gift.

By Mrs. OLIPHANT.
Whiteladies.
The Primrose Path.
The Greatest Heiress in England.

By Mrs. ROBERT O'REILLY.
Phœbe's Fortunes.

By OUIDA.
Held in Bondage.
Strathmore.
Chandos.
Idalia.
Under Two Flags.
Cecil Castlemaine's Gage.
Tricotrin.
Puck.
Folle Farine.
A Dog of Flanders.
Pascarel.
Signa.
Princess Napraxine.
In a Winter City.
Ariadne.
Friendship.
Two Little Wooden Shoes.
Moths.
Bimbi.
Pipistrello.
A Village Commune.
Wanda.
Othmar.
Frescoes.
In Maremma.
Guilderoy.
Ruffino.
Syrlin.
Santa Barbara.
Ouida's Wisdom, Wit, and Pathos.

MARGARET AGNES PAUL.
Gentle and Simple.

By C. L. PIRKIS.
Lady Lovelace.

By EDGAR A. POE.
The Mystery of Marie Roget.

By Mrs. CAMPBELL PRAED.

Lightning Source UK Ltd.
Milton Keynes UK
UKOW07f0607290817

308156UK00007B/550/P